MUNICH
PLAYGROUND

BY ERNEST R. POPE

1941

Contents

PUBLISHER'S NOTES 6

PREFACE...8

DER FÜHRER AT PLAY..10

MY FRIENDS THE GESTAPO 20

HITLER DABBLES IN ART 48

THE ONE-LEGGED BOSS OF BAVARIA.....................................62

CATHOLICISM IN THE NAZI CAPITAL.....................................73

LUNCH WITH JULIUS STREICHER..82

NON-ARYANS 94

THE BROWN-SHIRT PRESS..104

TEA FOR TWO..130

DEATH TAKES A HOLIDAY...138

BRASS HATS IN BAVARIA...151

"FRÄULEIN, GIVE ME LONDON..." 174

NAZI NIGHT LIFE 207

NAZI MORALS 221

HITLER BREAKS HIS TOYS 235

CONCLUSION 249

PUBLISHER'S NOTES

There isn't much information available today about Ernest R. Pope, American correspondent for Reuters in Munich from 1936-1941. *Foreign Affairs* gave this book a one line review when it was first published in 1941. It must have sold somewhat well, as it was republished in the early 1950s. However, the copyright was allowed to lapse. As far as I can determine through the WorldCat library catalog, this is the only book that Pope ever wrote and published.

That's a shame because he lived in Munich during a crucial time, met and observed all of the important Nazis, and had a concise, ironic, and often hilarious style of writing. He also worked with William L. Shirer (author of *The Rise and Fall of the Third Reich*) at CBS radio in Berlin before the United States entered the war. I doubt that there is another book like this about the period.

We do have *this* book, however, and this is the first time it's been made available in a fully edited edition with new footnotes and introduction.

It's important to remember that at the time Pope wrote, Hitler had smashed his way across western Europe, defeated France, seriously threatened Britain, and attacked Russia. Many saw the German war machine as invincible and viewed the Nazis as, in Pope's words, "an awe-inspiring group of ascetic, fanatic, and inhuman supermen." Pope tells us that this could not be more illusory.

In the past 70 years, entire forests have been sacrificed to print books about Hitler, the Nazis, and WWII. But when Pope was in Munich, few knew the Germany that he saw and fewer were writing about it. Even today, his book reads like a fresh assessment of the corruption, graft, and debauchery of the Nazi hierarchy.

There were plenty of people warning about the Nazis at the time. Pope's closest friend, Captain Christopher J. Phillips (British Consul-General in Munich) had been warning his government for years but felt ignored.

Pope himself was walking a tightrope in Munich. He needed access to Nazis to continue gathering information and reporting, but his sense of ire and frustration at them meant he could not entirely constrain his reporting, however cloaked, in the dispatches he sent to London. It also meant he could not resist poking fun at Nazi officials to their faces at times, since they seldom caught on. And yet his Nazi hosts told him they felt he was one of the fair foreign correspondents (the ones who could say the words "foreign correspondent" without gagging on their bratwurst).

As noted in this volume, when European correspondents were canvassed in August, 1939 for their opinions on the likelihood of war that year, ten out of twelve said no. Pope, referred to in the article as "...the most reserved of the reporters in Germany" on the subject, stated "Barring accidents, I do not believe there will be a European war this year, but I would not bet more than a week's salary to back up my belief." Less than one month later, the war began.

Back in the United States, Pope was free to say all that he had not said as a correspondent. He writes of his beloved Munich friends and others who hated and even defied the Nazis before the war. He tells of a German editor friend, so despondent at the outbreak of war, he decides to join the *Luftwaffe* as a tail gunner to go out in a blaze of thrilling glory, instead of living a life that was no life in Nazi Germany.

Pope holds back little from his readers. Hilarious, scathing, and ultimately sad about the outcome, he takes us into the world of Nazi spectacles, beer halls, nightclubs, and warfare that he knew in Munich. We see the mundane, the ugly, and the hopeful side of the *Deutche volk*. Along the way, he provides a stream of anecdotes and stories that will entertain you from cover to cover.

BRIAN V. HUNT

2013

***

PREFACE

An unshaken confidence in the American way of life has encouraged the author of this book on the Nazi way of life to present his picture of the Third Reich in a manner somewhat different from previous treatments of the same subject. It is founded in the belief that one of the inexhaustible sources of Anglo-Saxon democratic strength is the ability—unlike the grim Teutons of Germany—to "keep smiling."

We Americans, I trust, will never lose our sense of humor. We can appreciate Shakespeare's reasons for invariably including buffoonery in his great tragedies. The drama of the present European tragedy likewise would be incomplete if the roles of certain Nazi clowns were to be censored or deleted.

Competent foreign correspondents have returned to this country to publish accurate documents on the brutal blitzkrieg machine and the men who set this machine in motion. These colleagues of mine have done an excellent job of presenting the American public with a true picture of Nazi Germany. Yet some elements in this picture have been neglected. Consequently, it is the purpose of this book to supply these elements.

A full knowledge of the world's Brown Plague, I am convinced, should include the exposure of the myth that Hitler and his disciples are an awe-inspiring group of ascetic, fanatic, and inhuman supermen. Indeed, their human failings are far greater than those of other national leaders. They represent a *reductio ad absurdum* of mortal weaknesses.

As the only American journalist to be stationed at the Nazi party capital, Munich, throughout the momentous years from 1936 to 1940, I have enjoyed the unique advantage of observing the Nazi clowns in many of their informal moments. I have witnessed the clumsiness, self-indulgence, and ridiculousness of Ringmaster Hitler and his party leaders in the privacy of their Bavarian haunts.

The following chapters are intended to provide the reader with an intimate insight into some phases of Nazi life as experienced by a foreign correspondent, who has left it to his fellow journalists to record in more erudite form the macabre history of the Third Reich.

The portrayal of Bavaria under Nazi rule is informal and somewhat discursive—because that is the spirit of southern Germany, as contrasted with Prussianism. I have drawn not only upon my experiences as a journalist in the birthplace of National Socialism, but also from an uninterrupted stay of six years in the Third Reich and previous visits to Bavaria in the days when an Austrian post-card peddler was planning his first beer-hall putsch. At that time I was "interned" in a Munich boarding school on— shades of coming events—the *Hess Strasse*. A thorough knowledge of the Bavarians, and subsequently of their Nazi masters, has been the background against which this book has been written. Its kaleidoscopic treatment has been chosen as the best method of reflecting the impressions gained by a foreign correspondent assigned to that fateful European city, Munich.

Munich Playground presents itself to the reader in the hope that it may contribute to a better understanding of history's strange nightmare, the Third Reich, by recording some hitherto unpublished aspects of the scene, without excluding the burlesque elements of the tragedy.

ERNEST R. POPE

Ithaca, N. Y.

***

DER FÜHRER AT PLAY

Slowly, to the syncopated rhythm of the leading Nazi jazz orchestra, the supple, nude figure of the German Beauty Dancer ascends in the dazzling spotlight from a trap door on the stage of the Theater am Gärtnerplatz in Munich—the capital of the National-Socialist movement. As her body becomes completely visible to the enthusiastic audience, the Supreme Commander of the German Armed Forces focuses his powerful binoculars on her youthful nakedness. No detail of Dorothy van Bruck's blitz-tease escapes the penetrating gaze of Adolf Hitler, as he follows every movement of this completely undressed girl. It is a scene from his favorite comic opera, the *Merry Widow*.

Munich is Hitler's playground. Der Führer is on his best behavior in Berlin, which he likes about as much as the average boy likes the little red schoolhouse. The Chancellery on the Wilhelmstrasse is more luxurious, to be sure, but Adolf only sits at his desk inside its bomb-proof marble walls when affairs of state make his attendance at the Reich's capital imperative. Whenever possible, Hitler plays hookey, romping around in his favorite Bavarian haunts, far from the prying eyes of ambassadors and Berlin correspondents. In Munich the Nazi Chancellor relaxes, indulging his pet appetites and hobbies. South Germany is his native habitat. It is in this natural environment that one can best study the prototype of the *Homo Naziertsis*.

If I had a dollar for every time I have seen Hitler in Munich and his other Bavarian hideouts, I would probably buy myself a supercharged, twelve-cylinder auto, something like his own big black Mercedes which, convoyed by three other cars filled with armed SS Guards, has passed my little roadster countless times on the *Reichsautobahn* from Munich to Salzburg—the route to Berchtesgaden and Hitler's glamorized chalet on the Obersalzberg. Often I have paused over my *Leberkraidel* at the Osteria Bavaria restaurant in Munich's artist colony, Schwabing, to watch him munch a vegetable in the midst of his beef-eating staff.

He and I have sniffed the same air on Oberwiesenfeld, while his private 'plane was taxying up the landing field for one of his frequent flying trips. I could have touched him—but didn't—as he inspected the various exhibitions and country fairs on the Theresienwiese. He and I have spent delightful hours under the same roof, admiring the Nordic nudes in the House of German art, which the thoughtful Adolf had built at a cost of many millions on the same street as his Munich apartment, the Prinzregenten Strasse.

I have held up dispatches to London an extra hour to get some more views of Adolf in ecstasy at Wagnerian operas, or frowning at Shaw's plays in Munich theaters. And last, but by no means least, I have reluctantly turned my eyes from the stage of the Theater am Gärtnerplatz to watch the Führer, resplendent in a white jacket and black trousers, whip out his high-powered opera glasses when Dorothy, his pet nude "Beauty Dancer," made her erotic appearances at the Nazi theater in Lehar's *Merry Widow,* Künnecke's *Happy Journey,* Strauss's *Fledermaus,* and other operettas. The Theater am Gürtnerplatz is a "must" in the schedule of entertainment for the honored guests of the Reich from the Axis and elsewhere, before they sign on the dotted line.

Let me take you to a performance of the *Merry Widow.* As streamlined by Herr Fritz Fischer, the manager of the Theater am Gärtnerplatz and incidentally the adjutant of Hitler's Bavarian Gauleiter, Adolf Wagner, the show is worth seeing.

Of course we have no idea that the Führer will slip into his royal box when the curtain rises. Oh no! But then why did the cast have to go through an extra rehearsal without pay yesterday afternoon? Why are there new flowers and other decorations in the theater? Why are there so many hatchet-faced young men in plain dark suits distributed generously through-out the audience? Why don't the girls in their dressing rooms throw something at other hatchet-faced strangers who pop into their sanctuary as they are about to slip into their scanty costumes (which still could conceal some weapon under a bust pad, if nowhere else)? You guessed it, and will have to see the show again some other night to enjoy Dorothy, the Can Can Ballet, the American dancers and acrobats, and the rest of the lumbers, since tonight you will be watching Adolf as he thrills to these sights from his private box in the middle of the First Balcony.

The lights go out, the curtain goes up, and Adolf comes in, with his adjutant, Wilhelm Bruckner, on his left and his favorite Gauleiter, Boss Adolf Wagner, on his right. The gold-embroidered Swastika Führer Standard appears like magic over the balustrade of the royal box. A murmur runs through the "Strength-through-Joy" audience. The hatchet-faces grow tenser and more vigilant.

The Nazi "swing champion," Peter Kreuder, directs his special adaptation of Lehar's music as the *Merry Widow* starts off in a blaze of glory that would make even Billy Rose envious. Next to his *Wehrmacht,* Hitler has lavished more money on his comic operas than on any other single piece of Nazi showmanship. And as in the army, most of his money is spent on equipment and the generals, rather than on the privates.

Taking orders from his chief, Fritz Fischer packed the stage with a cast of two hundred actors and extras. He was empowered to pay the male lead, Danilo, the Dutch film star Johanes Heesters, five hundred dollars per night. He imported other foreign stars for special numbers in the show. And Hitler has always boasted that German citizens receive first consideration in the Third Reich, where "materialistic matters come last" as smacking too much of the despised pluto-democracies! But he spent over one thousand dollars on the costumes of each extra. The poor girls who were obliged to change these costumes ten times during each performance earned one dime per hour for their work in front of the Führer.

Even a scrubwoman gets better pay than Hitler's comic-opera extras, without risking broken legs on intricate props, pneumonia in the chilly rooms backstage, or getting critical infections from the ersatz make-up. In one year alone, several *Merry Widow* actresses died of pneumonia, while more than a dozen spent over a month in Munich hospitals—footing their own bills after hoofing for Hitler. Many more extras lost their jobs because they refused to "Heil" the assistant stage managers or visit them after the performances. But they look very lovely with or without their one thousand dollar costumes.

When the lights go on after the first act, the two Adolfs, Hitler and Wagner, are all smiles as the audience quickly follows the example set by the plainclothes men rising and about-facing to point their outstretched right arms to the Führer's box to "Heil" his "unexpected" presence. At the intermission, uniformed SS Black Guards block off part of the First Balcony and the red-carpeted path to Hitler's private refreshment room, while the audience repairs to the theater restaurant to guzzle beer and chortle how wonderfully lucky they are tonight to have their beloved Führer with them in the theater.

Hitler waits until the bells have rung and the lights have dimmed again before he slides into his box. His adjutant has polished up the lenses of his opera glasses, for Dorothy, the Can Can Chorus, and the American dancers don't perform until the second half. (For this reason Adolf sometimes does not arrive at the theater until after the intermission.)

Dorothy begins her blitz-tease number. Sometimes her costume is a pair of transparent butterfly wings, more often she is completely nude. I have seen Hitler nudge his Gauleiter and smirk when Dorothy does her famous back-bending number in the spotlight. Watching Adolf ogle Germany's naked "Beauty Dancer" is just one more reason why I discredit the stories to the effect that the Führer does not nurture a carnal interest in the female of the species.

A few years ago Dorothy was an unknown Munich film extra named Ilse Stange. Fritz Fischer made her a chorus girl, changed her name, then took off her clothes and sent her around the circuit of German vaudevilles and night clubs. When Hitler saw her weaving her glamorous body around a bubble in the Wintergarten at Berlin, he was so fascinated that he ordered Fischer to bring Dorothy back to Munich and work her into the *Merry Widow*. Now she has become a permanent fixture at the Theater am Gärtnerplatz. Recently Fraulein van Bruck hired one of the best German plastic surgeons to lift her figure so that Adolf would keep on nudging his neighbor.

Fischer certainly can put on a good show. His arrangements of comic operas are excellent. That is why Hitler gave him the job of managing his state operetta theater at Munich—after Fritz had successfully stage-managed two shows in London. Fritz always gave me the best seat (next to Hitler's) at his performances, and in return I gave him the clippings of my stories on the shows in the leading London newspapers. He confessed to me that he hoped to move to London again for bigger and better stage-managing, but then came the war, so Fritz remained a loyal Nazi subject and London lost a good producer.

At Berlin, the Führer orders his Propaganda Minister Goebbels to beat the drum for pure German culture, German clothing, German art, German music, and German acting. For his own pleasure in Munich, however, Hitler sent his private 'plane to France to pick up American dancers for the *Merry Widow*, which in addition to these has paraded English chorus girls, Czech and Yugoslav Widows, Danish acrobatic dancers, Dutch movie heroes, and Russian balalaika orchestras across its stage in lavish costumes made of expensive foreign materials so that he might be assured the best performance of a comic opera composed by an Austro-Hungarian.

Where his tastes for actresses and the stage are involved, Hitler drops his mask of Germanic Knight and becomes an internationalist. That is why he again glues his eyes to the binoculars when the French Can Can Chorus "Heils" the Führer with elevated right legs instead of outstretched arms in the closing scene of the Maxim Bar. And that is why the stars, at the end of the performances, get huge bouquets and expensive presents with the Führer's name. At one showing of the *Merry Widow*, Hitler himself applauded for twelve curtain calls before he left his box amid the "Heils" of the audience.

No wonder that the Führer officially named Munich the "Home of the National Socialist Party," for when the Nazis have a party they throw it in the Bavarian capital, where Hitlerism was born and where it spent its adolescent days carousing in beer halls and other amusement centers. Like successful businessmen returning to their alma mater at reunion time, Hitler and his Brown-Shirt bigwigs come back to Munich from their administrative desks in the Wilhelmstrasse to play. Munich is the alma mater of the Nazis. It was here that they received their training to go forth and conquer the world, beginning with the German government at Berlin. Here the Hitler-endowed halls of the garish National Socialist party buildings form the Nazi campus, from which the Brown Shirts graduate to enter the business of running the Third Reich and its subsidiaries according to the teachings of Hitler. It is to this campus that they return to take graduate courses in National Socialism at Haushofer's geopolitical institute, or to forget the cares and intrigues of state by whooping it up as they did in the old days before Hitlerism had come of age.

Munich is the home of the Nazi party. Berlin is its business address. In Munich, Adolf is the leader of his gang. In Berlin, he is the Chancellor of the Reich. In Berlin, Hitler receives and "entertains" diplomats. In Munich, he receives and is entertained by glamour girls.

After the *Merry Widow,* Fritz Fischer, in full dress, accompanies Hitler down the theater steps to his bullet-proof Mercedes limousine, where he is joined by his adjutant and his Gauleiter. Around the corner, by the stage entrance, several busses chartered by the theater begin filling up with the cast in their costumes and makeup. Both the limousine and the busses have the same destination—another of Hitler's pet Munich projects, the Künstlerhaus (Artists' House). Adolf wishes to treat the cast and the girl extras (and himself, of course) to a private after-the-theater party in this very special Nazi building.

Hitler's extravagant theater parties within the jealously guarded walls of this Nazi club are famous in Munich theatrical circles. Almost invariably when the Führer attends a performance at the Theater am Gärtnerplatz, he invites the most attractive members of the cast to the Künstlerhaus. Somehow the male extras fail to be asked. Hitler likes to be surrounded with beautiful women in his leisure moments.

The Artists' House on the Lenbach Platz was rebuilt by order of the Führer shortly after he had remodeled the Gärtnerplatz theater in the autumn of 1937 to make it the official Nazi stronghold of comic opera. Hitler proclaimed that the Künstlerhaus was to be the

15

club of Munich film and stage artists, Nazi painters, sculptors, authors, and journalists, where the Bavarian world of art and letters could dine, drink, and dance in luxurious halls away from the envious eyes of the ordinary German public. In the years before Hitler tore it apart and pounded it together again with a Swastika, the historic building had been the dearly beloved home of internationally famous artistic geniuses. In a few months, however, the Künstlerhaus developed into a hotbed of Nazi intrigue, orgies, and artistic turpitude. Nonparty artists, especially the young women who refused to gain fame by gratifying the "artistic interest" of Nazi brass hats, shun the club like the plague. They do their drinking and dancing where there are not so many party bosses whose word is law. They know that the Artists' House is teeming with Gestapo, and that the word "No" is taboo in this Nazi club.

A special suite in the Künstlerhaus is reserved for Adolf. While the house was under construction, he inspected this suite. His view from one window was blocked by a large brick building fifty yards away. *"Verdammt!"* the Führer exclaimed to his following. "That is the Munich Synagogue. Tear it down, at once!" They did, in exactly six days. Now the site where it stood is an all-night parking space for the cars of the Nazis visiting the Künstlerhaus.

The Reich Chancellor's theater parties are held in an ornate hall decorated with oriental rugs, furnished in the height of style and comfort. At one end of this hall the actresses and chorus of the Gärtnerplatz theater give intimate command performances for Adolf and his retinue in return for his champagne and company. The vaulted ceiling is covered with astrological figures of gold on a lapis lazuli background.

Before these parties, Hitler's adjutant informs the Gestapo manager of the Künstlerhaus that the Führer is again "in the mood." The manager promptly orders an abundance of champagne and other drinks, expensive food, and decorations for the evening. He does even more. Knowing that Adolf wants beautiful girls, he regiments them as living decorations for the entire house.

The Nazi Artists' Guild in Munich has a complete file of several hundred Munich extras and models, with their physical

16

characteristics painstakingly described and photographed. The Künstlerhaus management has access to these files for just such occasions.

A telephone call goes out to the hundred prettiest girls on the afternoon before Hitler's party. The girls are ordered to wear their best evening gowns and to prepare to spend the night at the Artists' House. They are told that the Führer is coming, and that it is their National Socialistic honor and duty to be in evidence at the bars, dance halls, and lounges, so that Adolf will beam happily at all the pulchritude and the glorious success of his pet art scheme. The girls are warned to keep the Führer's presence in Munich a strict secret.

Four hours after the Munich extras had been told to show up at the Nazi club, I called the management in my capacity as Munich Reuters correspondent and asked, "Is the rumor true that Der Führer will visit the Künstlerhaus tonight?"

"We know nothing about any such visit," the Gestapo manager snapped. He had just finished making the arrangements for Adolf's entertainment. He had directed the best-looking girls to stand "informally" at strategic points on the long flight of stairs leading to the Astrological Hall, and had pressed huge bouquets of flowers into the arms of two tall blondes, rehearsing their curtsies for Adolf's triumphal entry.

In the luxurious seclusion of Hitler's banquet hall, the ballet and solo dancers of the Theater am Gärtnerplatz go through their paces. As champagne bottles pop, Dorothy van Bruck contributes an extra blitz-tease number so close to him that Adolf no longer needs his binoculars. He tells the Merry Widow to sing encores of his favorite songs. These private performances in the Künstlerhaus are the climax of the Führer's indulgence in his passion for bright lights and colors, reductive music, and gorgeous women. Billy Rose[1] is a blushing amateur compared to the streamlined Nazi efficiency in getting the most out of beautiful girls.

[1]*Billy Rose was an American theatrical showman and songwriter. He was once married to Fanny Brice, whose life was later depicted by Barbra Streisand in* Funny Girl.

Hitler's theater parties last from midnight until ten o'clock the next morning, or later. The Great Man himself leaves for his Munich apartment between three and four A.M., while his retinue, Boss Wagner, Fritz Fischer, local party and Gestapo chiefs, and the female cast of the *Merry Widow* remain to make the most of Hitler's champagne, food, and comfortable furniture. The favorite actress or dancer of the evening has a way of leaving the party shortly after Adolf. A closed Horch, Maybach, or Mercedes provided either by Fritz or the Führer's adjutant calls for her at the Künstlerhaus. I have trailed these cars several times along the Prinzregenten Strasse *past* the House of German Art to Hitler's apartment. Perhaps I was guilty of *lese-majeste*. But, parked at a discreet distance in the dark Possart Strasse, I watched the young lady being escorted into the Führer's house. After somewhat less than an hour, she returned to the waiting Mercedes with her uniformed chauffeur and was driven away. Adolf Hitler is a great protagonist of the blitz technique!

The war did not put a stop to Nazi theater life in the Reich. Hitler hardly dared risk billing the *Merry Widow* at the Gärtnerplatz after creating tens of thousands of sad German widows. So he ordered Fischer to substitute Strauss's *Fledermaus—with* the same beauty dancers, actresses, and underpaid extras.

Comic opera and blitz-teasing were regimented to make the dissatisfied German people forget the privations of rationed, blitzkrieging Germany. The exhausted munitions and armament workers were given cheap "Strength-through-Joy" tickets to the Theater am Gärtnerplatz to keep them from grumbling—which they ceased for a while when they saw Dorothy.

Theatrical Adolf Hitler believes with Shakespeare that "all the world's a stage, and all the men and women merely players." As the all-powerful stage manager of the Third Reich, Adolf made his male actors put over his blitzkrieg show. And he made the women give him his blitz-tease inside the Reich. Hitler directed the ghastly tragedy of his war after intoxicating himself in 1938-1939 with sexy, glamorous comic operas. The destitute, bitter war widows who today mourn for the dead actors and extras of the Continental blitzkrieg do not realize how closely their own widowhood is connected with

Franz Lehar's *Merry Widow* as performed in the Theater am Gärtnerplatz at Munich

***

MY FRIENDS THE GESTAPO

The ubiquitous Gestapo were a great help in brightening my life as a foreign correspondent assigned to the birthplace of National Socialism. It is always more fun kidding an officer of the law than one of your self-selected friends, especially if he is an officer of Nazi law, or whatever you wish to call the organized miscarriage of justice in the Third Reich.

I left Germany with the benign feeling that I had at least taught several of Heinrich Himmler's henchmen better English. In return, they had improved my command of Nazi German. In the Bavarian Alps, the Gestapo developed my skiing technique. They put money into my pocket by unwittingly giving me stories for the British press. They helped me keep my waistline down below the average for Munich beer addicts by making me fast every so often. They developed my sense of hearing and tact in the use of the telephone, as well as my memory for faces.

Naturally I was annoyed when the Gestapo listened to my telephone conversations with my girl, and it exasperated me to be held up by the *Geheime Staatspolizei* when I had an important story to rush to London. I regretted forcibly having to push some of Himmler's SS Black Guards out of my way when they refused to let me cross a street along which the Führer was due to pass any time within the next half day. I hated to miss my dinner because a Gestapo commissar insisted on asking a thousand foolish questions. And I was both incensed and sad when four of them carted off my Jewish landlady. But with credentials from a powerful press, a passport from a still more powerful nation, and a good working knowledge of Deutsch and its Bavarian dialect, you can enjoy a bit of comedy furnished by the somber executors of Hitler's will—provided you know where to draw the line in dealing with them.

Two months after the beginning of the war, a bomb explosion in the Bürgerbräu Beer Hall killed six Nazis and one waitress, injured scores of other Brown Shirts, but was timed to miss Adolf by eleven minutes. I happened to be the only American correspondent in Munich when the bomb went off. The Führer had been addressing his Old Guard in the beer hall, commemorating the anniversary of the night when, sixteen years previously, he had started the unsuccessful Nazi Putsch by firing a pistol into the same ceiling that crashed down too late to bury him in 1939.

Since journalists were barred from the Bürgerbräu meeting, I listened to Hitler's speech by radio. The only way to obtain further information on these annual celebrations was to corner one of the Old Guard Nazis in the Gestapo-managed Vier Jahreszeiten Hotel, where the higher-up Nazis always stay when in Munich. The beer-hall was as unapproachable on these nights as the Siegfried Line or Hitler's bedroom.

When the broadcast ended with a description of Hitler leaving the hall for the station, I drove to the hotel. But the Nazis were too busy to stop and chat. "We must hurry back to Berlin; this is wartime, you know," was all they contributed to this frustrated journalist, except to add that the Bürgerbräu jamboree "was the same as last year." So I comforted myself at a nearby bar and left my Berlin colleagues to worry about translating and dispatching the Führer's speech. The customary blackout shrouded Munich in complete darkness.

Suddenly the waiters began clearing the tables. I was requested to pay and leave. Since Munich had no curfew hours and it was only about 1:30 A.M., I asked, "Why all the rush?"

"Because of the police curfew," answered the waiter, pocketing my tip.

"Why is there a curfew tonight?"

"On account of the explosion."

"What explosion?"

"In the Bürgerbräu Beer Hall," the waiter finally confessed, but knew no more. He didn't need to urge me to leave!

Outside, the city lights glared brightly, while the nighthawks cheered and celebrated drunkenly. The bright lights which the police had switched on after the ambulances had removed the victims from the wrecked beer hall across the Isar River, had started a wild rumor that the war was over.

I raced to my Munich office after a police cordon had turned me back from the Bürgerbräu to file "blitz" calls to Berlin. (Blitz calls cost ten times as much as the ordinary long-distance rate. They are the only calls which assure you of an immediate connection with your party.)

While Berlin offices were relaying my first messages to America, I returned to the Bürgerbräu to resume my efforts at entering the building. The police always turned me back. But I could see the army engineers and Nazi labor service clearing away the wreckage, and noticed that the roof of the hall was gone. I left once more to send Berlin a follow-up description of the beer hall from the outside.

At ten A.M. Jack Raleigh and Percy Knauth of the Chicago *Tribune* and the New York *Times* knocked at my door, frozen and hungry from a marathon dash on the Hitler Highway from Berlin to Munich in Percy's car.

Knauth left us for another November Nazi ceremony, while Jack followed me back again to the Bürgerbräu. My six years in Germany against Jack's three months naturally gave me the responsibility for doing most of the talking. But all my eloquence did not procure even a glimpse of the shattered hall, so Jack and I started for my car to get permission from Gestapo Headquarters. Just as we were driving off to the Lions' Den, a regular policeman and a diminutive plainclothesman stopped us and asked "What did the gentlemen wish?" I told them, whereupon the little fellow said, "Come along and I'll see what I can do."

In good faith we followed him through the courtyard of the Bürgerbräu and just outside the main hall where the explosion had brought down the roof, but our captor took us to a corner where we could see nothing but the entrance to the building. "Wait a minute," he said, placing us between two burly Gestapo colleagues. We cooled our heels for an hour, but at least could watch Adolf Wagner, Ritter von Epp, Julius Streicher, Reich Labor Service Leader Hierl, and other Nazi big shots enter the mysterious door to the hall while the

Munich Police Chief, Herr von Eberstein, stomped around barking out arrest orders as liberally as a politician shouting promises in a campaign. Finally our Gestapo midget, an Austrian, returned. With a disarming smile he asked for our passports "for identification." He implied that this was the last step in getting permission for us to see what we wanted. Our two Gestapo book ends remained impassive as our SS Mickey Mouse popped back into a huddle somewhere among the sepulchral beer vaults.

Our heels had dropped almost to the freezing point before Mickey Gestapo returned, simulating deep chagrin. "Sorry, *Meine Herren,* but I'll have to take you to Headquarters"—all in the name of "Identification."

"Well, let's get a move on," I suggested impatiently. "It's past lunchtime, and I'm hungry," Jack's displeasure, as registered in his expressive face, made up for any failings in his mastery of south German dialects.

"You must wait; the car has not been sent yet from H.Q.," replied Mickey.

"We can get there quicker in my car," volunteered your correspondent.

"Yah, but how will I get back? I'm on duty here at the beer hall, you know," queried our half-pint guardian.

"I'll drive you back, my friend, since I promise you that we will get out of Gestapo Headquarters just as quickly as you will. Shall we go now?" I argued, this time with results, for Mickey led the way to my car.

"You can get in between us, since you're shorter. We won't bite you," I kidded, emboldened by hunger pangs.

"Aw, I ain't scared," retorted our plucky little dick.

For the first and last time in my life I was allowed to park my car in the awe-inspiring courtyard of grim Wittelsbacher Palace, which Gestapo Headquarters had "inherited" from Bavarian royalty shortly after Hitler had moved into his Brown House one block to the west.

As we passed the armed SS sentry, Mickey Mouse waved his Gestapo pass and snapped, "These two men belong to me!"

We ascended the broad stairs past a large hall in which Bavarian kings had entertained many courtiers in happier days. Now the hall was filled with hundreds of frightened Germans herded into line.

"Who are these people?" I asked.

"Oh, just some Munichers who wish to contribute their knowledge about the explosion," our guide answered sheepishly, hurrying us into another room where the plainclothes boss was waiting for us. He had evidently had at least a high-school education, moreover was excessively polite and solicitous of our welfare.

In the course of three hours, we told the chief all about where we lived in Munich, in Berlin, in the United States; our sex; the color of our eyes and hair; why it could be plausible that a foreign correspondent might want to see the blasted remains of what just escaped being the tomb of the greatest dictator in the world; that we still wanted to see the hall; etc., etc.; and that we at least hoped he would release us in time for the *Kaffeestunde,* even if the ersatz coffee and cake wasn't as good as it is in America. Fortunately we were not searched. Jack had a hot story burning a hole in his pocket on its devious way out of the Reich. I had certain documents which would have required more explaining than I cared to tackle before supper.

At last, with an eloquent gesture, the SS Master Mind handed us back our passports, but no permission to see the junk pile. "The detectives are still at work in the debris," he explained apologetically, "but of course you, as members of the foreign press, will receive the first permission to view the interior of the Bürgerbräu." We never were given the permit, and while he was stalling us off, the *Volkischer Beobachter* already was going to press with a picture of the wreckage and a description of the scene by a trusted Nazi journalist.

Amid reciprocal compliments, we left the Lions' Den in tow of our patient mouse, whose turn it had been to cool his own little heels. As he passed the SS sentry—a new one by this time—he repeated his pass waving and the legend that "these men belong to me."

"Oh no!" I corrected him. "You belong to us now, for I promised to drive you back to the Bürgerbräu." He actually grinned! I drove very slowly, pumping our man on how things looked inside, what he thought had caused the explosion, and other details of the affair. Mickey was so glad that he had not created an international incident by arresting us that he volunteered enough information to make a fine story —the kind that begins "according to an official source..."— the moment we reached our telephones. First, however, we dropped him in front of the bombed beer hall.

"Please don't take all this amiss;" "Okay, forget it," ended the conversation and a quaint friendship which cost us precious hours, our lunches, and an insight into the historic scene of shattered walls and hopes.

The rest of the news about the Munich bombing was sifted out of official German newspaper and radio accounts. But what none of the foreign correspondents in Naziland dared tell the world via censored channels was the reaction of the German people, as typified by the remark a Munich *Hausfrau* made to me after reading the Nazi newspaper explanations, which placed the blame on Chamberlain and his "Secret Service agents."

"Of course it was the Secret Service that planted the bomb in the Bürgerbräu," she jeered, "for the abbreviation of Secret Service is 'SS'—and SS is the insignia of Himmler's *Schutz Staffel*."

Nor did I risk telephoning my Berlin colleagues what I discovered two days after the explosion: Printed slips had been placed on the desk of each pupil in some Munich schools the morning after the crash. These slips told the schoolchildren: "That Satanic British Prime Minister Chamberlain tried to kill your beloved Führer last night. But The Dear God has saved him for Germany." Pretty quick work for school printers!

There were many other telltale indications that the Munich explosion was an inside Nazi job. Once more Goebbels' propaganda machine tripped over itself by asserting that Gestapo investigations revealed that "the preparations for the attempt on the Führer's life have been traced back to the month of August." If Goebbels had been up on his toes, instead of limping mentally as well as physically, he never would have credited England's secret service with the ability to work inside the Reich and Adolf's beer hall for almost four months without being discovered by the super-efficient Gestapo.

The immediate scapegoat accused of planting the bomb, Georg Elser,[2] had never been heard of in Munich. If he had really been a British agent, determined to assassinate Hitler, he never would have been so foolish as to return to Munich from the German frontier, just to make sure that the bomb was still ticking. Yet the lurid Nazi version of his capture claimed that he had done this very thing.

[2]*Some researchers believe today that Elser did plan and execute the bombing. He was caught trying to cross into Switzerland. He was shot in Dauchau in 1945. Germany has issued a commemorative stamp with his image.*

I had returned to Munich from Berlin expecting fireworks of some sort at Adolf's November Eight Reunion. Listening to his speech with some friends that evening, I had remarked, "I wonder when we'll hear the 'Bang'." I had thought it very possible that some irreconcilable anti-Soviet member of Hitler's Old Guard would shoot him on this occasion for concluding a pact with the arch-enemy Stalin since their last get-together in the Bürgerbräu. Lucky for me that my Gestapo hosts at Himmler's Munich headquarters were ignorant of my remark the next day, otherwise they might have spared themselves the trouble of digging up a Georg Elser!

My own opinion is that the Bürgerbrau explosion was a job inspired by Goebbels and executed by Himmler in order to make the Germans hate the British. The jubilation over the Polish conquest had expired, there was a dismal stalemate on the western front, and the disgruntled Germans were beginning to grumble more audibly about the blackout, the rationed food, and the freezing temperatures in their homes. They were still angry at Hitler for plunging their country into war, and had not yet been seriously bombed or attacked by the Allies, so had no reason to hate England. The Munichers especially remembered Chamberlain vividly as their angel of peace. Goebbels thought that six dead, petty Brown Shirts and one Munich waitress was a bargain price to pay for getting obstinate Germans to curse the British Prime Minister. But his project backfired, much to the embarrassment of his foreign-press contact men in the Wilhelmstrasse.

My theory about the propagandistic nature of the explosion was seconded by a prominent Municher, who expressed his own belief to me as somberly as this:

"After this explosion," he whispered, "we can expect anything. The next surprise will be British 'planes dropping poison gas bombs over Munich. They will be our own 'planes in disguise, with RAF markings. This will be Goebbels' method of switching the recalcitrant Bavarians' hate from the Führer to the British, and simultaneously will provide Hitler with an excuse to launch a gas attack against the Allies."

The wheels of the Gestapo do not always mesh as they should in order to live up to the fantastic reputation this nefarious organization has acquired abroad. I had been occupying my office and apartment in the same little private house in Munich for more than two years when the Gestapo called one morning to search the room of an Austrian Jew living in the same building. I was up on the roof at the time, taking a sunbath, when the maid stuck her frightened face through the skylight and whispered, "Please come down, Herr Pope. The Gestapo are here; you know more about them than I do."

I wrapped my bathrobe around me, descended, and without knocking entered the room in which two Nazis—one young and bespectacled, the other gray-haired and weatherbeaten—were busily ransacking the absent boarder's bureau drawers.

"You gents are doubtless of the Gestapo," I ventured in my friendliest manner.

"That's none of your business. Who in hell are you, anyway?" snarled the elder State Snooper.

"Oh, just one of those foreign correspondents. Got a story for me, fellows?" I kidded them.

"I'd advise you not to print anything," growled the Bavarian Sherlock, turning back to the papers to conceal his embarrassment. I closed the door and went to my room, returning with my press card.

"This proves who I am, but I'm not so sure you really are of the Gestapo," I said, handing them the card. "May I see your badges?" Obediently, both men dug into their pockets and produced their tin shields. Then they pawed over my press card, finally copying every word of it in their notebooks. Although I had not moved for two years, and my telephone had been tapped regularly for the same period, the particular Gestapo commissar in charge of Jewish matters at Munich was not even aware that he was sending his two flunkeys to the home of one of those annoying foreign correspondents. If he had known what a boner he was making, he might have thought twice before exposing his men to the scrutiny of the foreign press merely to obtain evidence of Jewish "race-shaming."

The Telephone Tappers are a separate unit in the Munich Gestapo organization. They even occupy a different building from the general H.Q. The latter is on the Brienner Strasse near Hitler's Brown House and the Königlicher Platz. Every good Munich citizen passes it with an inconspicuous shudder. But he passes the Gestapo listening post without even knowing that this harmless-looking building in the 30 block of Franz Joseph Strasse, with a front like an ordinary apartment house, contains the intricate complex of switchboards and recording apparatus that make life interesting for the foreign correspondent and miserable for the careless German who expresses his pent-up feelings over the telephone. It is in this building that the Gestapo learn good English and better Yankee slang. I have never been aware of seeing any of my bright, black-uniformed pupils, but they have heard my voice countless times; and, when the Gestapo machinery slips a cog, as it does quite often, I have heard theirs.

Once I picked up the receiver to make a call from my office. Before I could dial, I heard the familiar rasping sound made by a Teutonic superior giving orders to his subordinate. This was shortly after the infamous Jewish pogrom, which started on November 10, 1938,[3] with the wholesale arrests of Jews and the smashing of their shops after the murder of Herr von Rath in the German Embassy at Paris. The Nazi boss of Bavaria, Gauleiter Wagner, had announced a rally of "public indignation" against Jews and Communists in the Munich circus building (Circus Krone). The German newspapers had been given orders to splash stories about the record crowds attending the rally.

[3]*Kristallnacht, or "Night of Broken Glass."*

As I listened to the grating voice in my receiver, I knew that I had a story for London. For what I heard was the commander of the Munich SS Black Guards giving orders for all the men in the huge SS barracks around Munich to appear at the "Spontaneous Rally of Indignant Munich Citizens" in civilian clothing. No right-thinking Municher approved of the pogrom or went to the circus unless he were very curious about the kind of show boss Wagner was to stage. Therefore I knew in advance that the record crowd would owe its size to the obedient SS men—all because their own wires had got twisted somewhere on Franz Joseph Strasse.

Another time a Danish colleague of mine called a fellow countryman on my 'phone. In their native language they were referring to so many Nazi institutions during their conversation that after a few minutes they found it simpler to continue in German. "Jesus, they also speak German!" was the unexpected but clearly audible exclamation both Danes heard in the receivers as they switched languages. Someone at the listening post had been careless in commenting to another Gestapo telephonist!

It seemed advisable to improve my invisible, wire-tapping audience's command of my mother tongue, so I lost no opportunity to give them gratuitous English lessons. I did not wish to create any misunderstanding! Take the following instance:

The London *Daily Express* 'phoned me for a description of the Führer Building on the Küniglicher Platz the night before it was to become the scene of the fateful Munich Conference, in which

Chamberlain, Daladier, and Mussolini persuaded Hitler to postpone the war for a year. Part of my message to London via long distance ran like this:

"Every Nazi minister at Berlin, like Hitler, has a spare office in this building, complete in every detail, so that if Berlin is threatened, the entire government can be shot down to Munich in a flash. Pardon me a moment while I explain this last phrase to my inseparable friends at this end of the line." I then proceeded in careful German to point out that "shot down in a flash" does not necessarily mean "suddenly assassinated," but in this particular connotation was intended to convey the idea of rapid transfer from one point to another, to wit from the Reich capital to the "capital of the Nazi movement." I added that it would never, never occur to me to put malicious ideas into the heads of potential enemies of the Reich.

You could usually hear the click and the subsequent fading of the other party's voice as the Ears of State began recording your conversation. Sometimes I heard much more, getting request numbers from the boys in black. While talking to a friend, I would hear victrola music, as the listening posts killed time at their exchange rooms on uninteresting days. "Play that record again, please," I would say jocularly, and sure enough, the same piece would be repeated without a word from that rare phenomenon, a Gestapo lad with a sense of humor. Other times, however, my telephone would ring, a gruff voice would say "Who is there?" then hang up again. The boys in this case were checking up to find out if I were at home, or if their wires were still tapped correctly.

The most annoying part of this business was the incessant cutting-off resorted to by the Gestapo censors whenever I was 'phoning a precarious story to London. News unfavorable to the Reich, but both true and important, went over the trunk lines a drop at a time. The Gestapo, misjudging Anglo-Saxon perseverance, thought that they could wear the foreign correspondent down and make him cancel his call if they kept interrupting him and making him repeat often enough. These tactics sometimes made me so angry that I would shout into the 'phone:

"Get the hell off that line, you mugs; I don't interfere with your work, so why are you sabotaging mine?" Surprisingly enough, this often proved effective, and I could finish dictating my story to London without being cut off again. Other times it made no difference, but at least gave me some satisfaction and never, so far as I could ascertain, did me any harm.

A friend of mine called me up one day and wanted to borrow ten marks. I was rather low myself (the cost of living is high in the Reich), so I hesitated.

"Listen, pal," he pleaded, "if you loan me ten marks tonight, pay you back twelve tomorrow."

"Okay," I agreed, "but don't forget I have witnesses." One always does on telephones in Germany.

It is difficult to keep from meeting Himmler's staunch minions no matter what you are doing or where you are. I was skiing down a narrow trail in the wooded mountains above Garmisch one fine winter morning, and had succeeded in forgetting that there ever was a man called Adolf Hitler. Suddenly someone behind me shouted to clear the track. Since I was proceeding at a good clip, this seemed an unreasonable demand, so I shouted back the Bavarian equivalent of "Nuts to you!" without turning my head. The next moment my pursuer crashed into me. We both went down.

"What the hell d'you think you're doing?" I complained, then looked. "Why, *guten Morgen,* Dr. Christmann, so you're following me around even in the pure white snow of the Bavarian Alps," I added more politely, for the skier who had knocked me down was none other than the Munich Gestapo Press Chief. He apologized, and even proceeded to show me some new tricks on skis, for this particularly tough Nazi was a national SS skiing champion.

When Stanley Simpson of the London *Times* and I got a hunch that the Germans were planning to march into Austria one day, we hopped into the car and drove down the *Reichsautobahn* to Kiefersfelden, a little town just across the border from Austria's Kufstein. We passed hundreds of army trucks, tanks, pontoon trucks, and other blitzkrieg equipment which confirmed our hunch.

When we arrived at Kiefersfelden, freight trains were dumping several thousand soldiers from their cars. Every few feet along the highway to Kufstein, artillery and antitank guns were pointing toward Austria and a possible counterattack. And yet the same morning the local press chief had told me, "Go home, Herr Pope, there isn't a thing doing today, so you might as well make up some sleep."

Stan and I relayed some calls on what we had seen so far, then started for the customhouse on the frontier to have a look at the Austrian side. Before we could get to the toll gate, two plainclothes SS stopped us, and the following conversation in German ensued:

"Heil Hitler! What are you doing here?"

"Just enjoying the scenery."

"Why did you come to Kiefersfelden today?"

"Well, I'll tell you. It's like this. I'm an American student, and I came to Munich when I read the fascinating travel prospectuses which invited me to 'Visit the beautiful Alps.' My friend and I have already seen the Alps at Garmisch, so we thought we might look at them today around Kufstein. They really are pretty, in spite of all the uniforms we didn't expect to find here. But I do think it is odd of you to ask me why I am here. For if I were walking in Central Park in New York, I would not expect a policeman to ask me why I wasn't feeding the pigeons in front of the Public Library."

"Careful, don't get his goat," Stan cautioned me in English.

One of the Gestapo men wheeled around. "Aha, but you after all speaking English!" he blurted triumphantly.

"We never claimed that we couldn't. You did not even ask us if we could. When you addressed us in German, we answered you in the same idiom. I'm sure we can understand your language better than you can ours," I explained very politely.

The conversation was therefore continued in German, as the Gestapo linguist escorted us into the customhouse. His partner disappeared to do a bit of telephoning back to Munich H.Q. Our man, now thoroughly distrustful since he had discovered two foreigners who could speak English, gloated as he thumbed Stan's passport. "Aha, you are a British military agent!" he proclaimed. "See, you don't think I know English." Here he pointed significantly to the large letters which stated Stanley S. Simpson's (former) profession to be "General Merchant." I gave another free English lesson.

My own passport was safely locked up at home. My driver's license was a useful substitute for identification purposes. The Gestapo have a way of sequestering your passport and taking their time about returning it.

"What's the idea of keeping us here? We want to enjoy the scenery."

"That's none of your business. What's your name?"

"You have it in front of you on my license. What's yours?"

"None of your business."

"Come, come, that isn't what we Anglo-Saxons call fair play. You ask my name. I tell you. You should tell me yours."

"I'm on duty, so I don't have to tell you my name," he said truculantly.

"Very well, but this is a hell of a way to enjoy the Bavarian Alps after spending so much money to get to Germany. The prospectuses didn't say anything about getting locked up in customhouses. We wouldn't do anything like that to you in America. That isn't fair. I shall complain about your robbing us of our freedom to Dr. Christmann (here our burly friend gave a start), to my friend Adolf Wagner (he twitched again), to the President of Munich University (this did not seem to bother him in the least), and I shall lodge a protest with the Consuls-General of Great Britain and the United States of America." Our captor obviously was getting worried, wondering just what kind of strange birds he had snared. After more tiffs and waiting, the other agent entered. *"Meine Herren,"* he bowed, "you may go now."

"What do you mean, *may* go? What assurance can you give us that we won't be annoyed by people like you any more today?"

"*Meine Herren*, I promise you. I have telephoned down the line to all the policemen between here and Munich not to stop you or your car. *Aufwiedersehen*. Heil Hitler!"

"Go to hell," Stan and I mumbled under our breath, for we had lost three hours at the hands of these two SS clowns. But we were not molested any more all day, and gave our papers good coverage on that historic day of the Anschluss.

One bleak, wintry morning in March, 1939, I arose and attempted to 'phone my colleague, Stan. The telephone was dead. I went downstairs to try the house 'phone. Before I could pick up the receiver, four plainclothesmen jumped out of an adjoining room and stopped me. "Don't you dare use that 'phone!"

Somewhat startled, I still managed not to lose face. "Look here. I'm a foreign correspondent. I must make a professional call. You cut off my own line, but you have no right to interfere with my business."

"Don't use that 'phone. Where is your landlady?"

"I haven't the foggiest idea." I thought I knew where I could reach her, since she was a Jewish doctor with a large clientele of suffering Jewish patients whom no Aryan physician was permitted to touch. (She had rented the house from my first landlady, who had moved out after the suicide, there, of my first—non-Aryan—landlord.) But I had no intention of telling these men. They questioned me some more, but finally gave it up and retired to their room to lie in wait for their prey. I got my hat and coat. As I opened the front door, one of the professional Jew-catchers popped out and warned me:

"Do not attempt to cross us. Use telephones for professional purposes only."

"You mind your business and I'll mind mine," I growled, making tracks for the nearest public 'phone booth, which is never very near in the Third Reich. I managed to pass on a warning to my landlady about the "reception committee." This gave her all day to say good-

34

by to her friends and wind up her affairs, or the most important at least, since permanent escape would have been impossible even if the Gestapo do grind their gears occasionally. My landlady came home late in the evening. The next morning they took her away. After a half year's imprisonment she was acquitted by the regular German courts of the usual charge, "Race-shaming." (She had been seen skiing on the same slope with an Aryan.) The moment she was released, the Gestapo took my landlady into their hands. The regular German courts have no jurisdiction over the acts of Heinrich Himmler's organization. I never saw her again, so paid my rent to her faithful old Aryan maid instead.

To be on the safe side, I always had a few anti-Communist pamphlets lying around my rooms and office in prominent places. They proved quite handy on one occasion. The Gestapo took it into their heads to raid me because someone had tried to improve his standing in the Nazi party by reporting that I was a suspicious-looking foreigner, probably a Soviet agent. While I was sipping my coffee, three sour-looking individuals knocked, came in, and stated that they were going to examine my room. "Go ahead," I said. It did not take long for them to discover the pamphlets. Eagerly they read the word "Communist" out loud to each other several times before they stumbled into the "Anti-." Hereupon the Soviet exterminators stopped, apologized profusely for the intrusion, and beat a hasty retreat, chagrin written all over their faces. After the signing of the Berlin-Moscow Pact, I burned the same pamphlets so that future SS ferrets would not find them during that odd, peaceful interlude between Hitler and his "undying enemy," Soviet Russia.

***

PORTRAIT OF A NAZI GRAFTER

Munichers delight in relating the story of Christian Weber's[4] sole visit to an art gallery, one in which the portraits of Nazi leaders were exhibited. After gazing at Hitler, Hess, Himmler, Hierl, and the other H's, as well as the rest of the alphabet soup of Third-Reich brass hats, Christian peered intently and with ever-increasing anger at one particular frame. His huge jowls hoisted themselves ponderously into a frown; his little red eyes glared through their fleshy sockets.

[4]*Weber was an SS General and one of Hitler's early followers. He was despised in Munich and was killed by Bavarians just after the regime fell.*

"That portrait of me is terrible. Remove it at once. It makes me look like a pig," Christian grunted to his adjutant.

"Very well," replied the subordinate obediently, calling an attendant. "Heil Hitler, Attendant; Herr Weber orders you to remove this mirror immediately."

His name is the only Christian part of these 350 pounds of degenerate fat. Christian has been squatting on the head chair of the Munich Town Council ever since Hitler came to power. He is too heavy to remove and boil down to soap or oil, in which form he could do even the Third Reich more good than waddling clumsily around beer halls in his uniform of an Himmler SS Regiment Commander. Christian Weber is a classic example of the bevy of Nazi racketeer-grafters who helped themselves to the gravy after helping Adolf Hitler to the head of the German table.

Starting as a Munich stable boy, Christian's career and girth have developed into a well-rounded fulfillment, culminating in the impressive offices of: Chairman of the Munich Town Council, President ofthe Munich "Kreigstag" (the subdivision of the Bavarian political province called "Gau," which is administered by Gauleiter Adolf Wagner), President of the International Congress for Thoroughbreeding and Racing, President of the Brown Ribbon of Germany, Director-in-Chief of the Nazi bacchanalia, "The Night of the Amazons," and, as a profitable sideline, President of Christian Weber's Trucking Company, with offices in the *Residenz*—the City

Palace of Bavarian Kings. It was in the historic royal bed of this erstwhile palace that Weber often chose to sleep with his mistresses after closing his trucking office for the day.

A wide variety of interests keeps our Nazi Falstaff happy from one Brown Ribbon sweepstakes to the next annual races. In order of importance, Christian's spiritual stimuli are: 1. Horses; 2. Money and Women, both of which he chases with equal enthusiasm and perseverance; 3. Eating and Drinking. National Socialism means as much to him as Cupid to the madame of one of those houses which Christian visited on his trip to Paris—it symbolizes nothing more than a meal ticket. Christian Weber is the boss of Munich's Tammany Hall.

Christian has his own manner of consorting with royalty. He holds the unique record of being the only dignitary ever to have insulted the Duke and Duchess of Kent. This royal couple paid frequent visits to Munich, where the sister of the Duchess lives with her husband, Count Törring-Jettenbach. Driving back to the city from an inspection tour of his studs, Christian was greatly annoyed when a car ahead seemed in the way of his fast-moving Mercedes. He ordered his chauffeur to pass this car and crowd it off the road. The maneuver succeeded. Both cars stopped.

"Where the hell d'you think you're going. Get that manure wagon off the road," Christian Weber bellowed apoplectically at the passengers in the other car—the brother of His Majesty the King of England and his Duchess. Nor did fearless Christian apologize after soberer members of the Nazi party called his attention to his *faux pas*.

It is difficult to associate thoroughbred horses with their Munich sponsor, who looks more at home against a background of pork than at the head of his studs of high-strung mares and relatives of Man o' War. But we must follow him around the stables to gain an insight into the character of this Nazi grafter. It was in a Munich stable that Christian got his start, toting oats and their products (he still speaks fondly of those days to his cronies who followed him from the stables to his offices in the Royal Palace), and currying horses.

When Hitler came along, Christian backed the right horse with unerring instinct. He curried Adolf, finding this more profitable than patting the backs of his brown four-legged friends. By joining the 1923 Beer-Hall Putsch and helping to run the Nazi machine in Munich's pre-Third-Reich days, the smart horse trader assured himself of a lasting sinecure and a position from which he could engage in local racketeering and racing to his heart's content.

Weber sold the Führer the idea of the Brown Ribbon of Germany, which was intended to show the world that the Third Reich was not only the stronghold of everything fine in culture, but also in the way of deluxe racing and thoroughbreds. The Reich Chancellor gave Christian free rein to organize the Brown Ribbon, as an international race for the Grand Prix of the Führer and also 100,000 Reichsmarks, which the winner could collect in foreign exchange at the artificial rate of 21/2, or $40,000.

Christian Weber lost no time in organizing the race and his own profits. With admirable foresight, he had previously acquired extensive farmland on the outskirts of Munich at rock-bottom prices. On a section of this territory he erected the new Riem racecourse, complete with betting machines, grandstands, restaurants, and beer gardens. He sold this valuable property to the Municipality of Munich with the approval of the Chairman of the Town Council, which was not difficult to obtain. The transaction netted him an enormous profit. Incidentally, when Munich's airport at Oberwiesenfeld became too small for Third Reich commercial aviation and blitzkrieg pilot training, Christian persuaded Hitler to order a new and much larger airport to be constructed on the remainder of his Riem farmland. This property he sold to the Third Reich for a paltry few millions more in 1937.

Originally designed to attract foreign tourists and racing enthusiasts to the Brown Ribbon Derby every July, thus contributing to Munich's reputation as an international amusement center, and swelling the coffers of the party capital, the Riem racecourse became a profitable enterprise for the Number One Nazi Horseman. Whenever the turf permitted, Christian staged local races, entering his champion horses and pocketing the prize money, bets, and admissions collected from the thousands of Munichers who hoped desperately to compensate for the Reich's crushing taxes by betting on a winner at Riem. It worried him little to see two French owners romp away with the Brown Ribbon of Germany in 1938 and 1939, even if Adolf grimaced when his prize plus $80,000 went abroad. (Probably the Führer consoled himself with thp thought that he would get it back, as well as the horses, in 1940.) For the racecourse provided one more inexhaustible source of revenue for Christian's pockets, which have an appetite as ravenous as his own digestive system.

Having succeeded in attracting foreign competition to Munich races, including the Aga Kahn's son, Prince Aly, with several fine horses ridden by English jockeys, as well as French, Italian, Hungarian, and other owners, riders and horses, Christian launched his next scheme, the "International Congress for Thoroughbreeding and Racing." This organization, with Weber in the saddle, likewise moved into the dignified halls of the Royal Munich Palace. Large sums were appropriated by the Town Fathers to promote the good work, which was Christian's little idea of a world peace conference. He reasoned that stable talk would be the most efficient method of achieving international understanding. He initiated the publication of a four-language journal on racing and breeding horses. I know how much money was lavished on this organ, for, as a special favor to Christian, I translated articles on pregnancy in mares, operations for roaring, minutes of the Congress's meetings, and other hippological matters for the journal. One typewritten page netted me enough marks to buy nine quarts of *Lowenbrau,* i.e. about one swallow per translated word. If a mere foreigner could obtain such a fee, imagine what editor-in-chief Christian pocketed in the name of international horseyness. I also made a tidy sum interpreting for Christian when Britishers visited Weber's studs and attended the Munich meetings of the International Congress while I was gathering the news stories I sent to racing-minded England about them. These meetings were held in the Munich Town Hall, interrupted by lavish banquets unsurpassed in luxury even in the despised "pluto-democracies." I am indebted to Herr Weber's dabblings as an international host for some of the best dinners it has ever been my pleasure to wash down with their customary sequence of two kinds of beer, three different wines, excellent champagne, genuine coffee, and French cognac.

Weber's congresses met several times annually: once or twice at Munich, then in other cities on the Continent. In 1939 a session was celebrated at Budapest. This time Christian's car got the worst of an encounter on the highways: instead of crowding royalty off the road, Christian was bounced into a ditch by the bona fide manure wagon of an Hungarian farmer. Our hero lay there, spluttering and cursing like Major Hoople of the comics, and with a slight limp as the total physical damage. Christian soon forgot his grief in the taverns of gay Budapest as well as in other houses catering to his life interests. The convention was therefore pronounced a complete success. Of course Fatty was compelled to purchase a new Mercedes, but this trifle was relegated to the expense account of international hippology.

One of Christian's thoroughbreds broke a leg at a local steeplechase on the Riem racecourse. In front of 10,000 spectators, Weber's adjutant in his black SS uniform stepped out on the course, whipped his ever-ready automatic from his side, and fired at the agonized animal. It kicked, struggled, and attempted piteously to rise, but five minutes and six bullets were required from the SS supermarksman to put the horse out of its misery. (Probably the Gestapo henchman had a legitimate excuse for this clumsy torture— he had had much less experience in dispensing sudden death to *animals.)* I believe it is conventional procedure to inject a large hypodermic of painkiller into horses that break their legs, then remove them from the eyes of the public before consigning their souls to happier pastures. Christian, however, prefers to be different, original, and, whenever possible, dramatic. At the Riem incident, the Munich crowd booed and hissed his method roundly. Thereupon the 350 pounds of irate fat slapped the face of the nearest spectator in a top hat, then stepped to the microphone of the public address system and threatened to arrest the entire audience if they didn't "behave." And indeed it was in Christian Weber's Hitler-entrusted power to carry our his threat, so silence and order were quickly restored. Brave Christian!

But let us leave the stables and the turf for the finer things of life. Let us observe our Nazi rhinoceros as he sponsors feminine beauty, *joie de vivre,* and gaiety in the artistic ronghold of the Third Reich. He devotes his efforts unstintingly to this lofty ideal both winter and summer.

In the summer of 1937, the Nazi pilgrim's progress took him to the World's Fair at Paris, a city he had been itching to visit all his life. Christian did the town in a manner befitting a person of his rank and station in Munich life. When he returned, he declared to fellow members of the Town Council:

"We can capture the international tourist trade that has been swamping Paris in pursuit of unveiled feminine puchrinide! Judging from what I saw in the French capital, our naked German girls are better looking than the French women. All we have to do is take off the clothes of the girls right here at home, put them in the spotlight, and men with money to spend will forsake Paris for Munich. *Jawohl! Heil Hitler!*"

No time was lost in putting his tourist-decoy theory into practice. Christian put his jowls by the cheeks of his favorite town councillors to plan the coming winter Carnival according to a stable boy's dream of the Body Beautiful. With Teutonic efficiency and technique, Herr Weber huffed and he puffed and he blew the Munich maidens' clothes off.

After several secret sessions with his sycophantic municipal officials, Christian was seized with a brain wave that provided a brilliant solution to his Carnival problem. Why not combine all his life interests in one magnificent show? No sooner said than "Heiled." The result was Christian Weber's gargantuan *Aufgalopp*— a concoction of horsy themes, extravagant decorations, and still more expensive admission prices, naked women, champagne, and *Weisswurst* (Munich sausage), stirred together from eight P.M. to eight A.M. in Munich's largest vaudeville theater, the Deutsches Theater, near the railway station.

In the long, romantic history of Munich's six-week winter Carnival, made famous by the inspired spontaneity of participants

41

such as Bavarian royalty, Lenbach, Kaulbach, Stuck, Schwind, Corinth, and other internationally known painters and artists, a carnival program like Christian's *Aufgalopp* had never been dreamed of as an actuality, featured for the benefit of flesh-and-blood Munichers. Such an orgy was thought possible only in the days of decadent Rome, or in imaginative paintings. But nothing daunts our Christian. After months of careful preparation, equaled solely by blitzkrieg strategy, the *Aufgalopp* (which is Third Reich German for the turf-cutting parade of horses and jockeys past the grandstands before the first race) invaded the party capital and swept even the seasoned Munichers off their feet.

Imagine the Metropolitan Opera House in New York with the orchestra seats removed to make way for a dance floor. Picture to yourself the cellar of the Metropolitan as a maze of beer halls, *chambres-separees* and necking laboratories, where beer, champagne, kisses, hot dogs, re- and pro-creation mingle in gay abandon, according to the individual's needs and tastes. Imagine further a succession of horses and nude women parading across the stage of this theater, while bottles pop and curtains are drawn in the box seats and balconies. Visualize an inebriated, radiant 350-pound ex-stable boy in billowing starched shirt and tails as the patron saint of the night's festivities. Add a buxom contralto from the legitimate Munich State Opera, a nude ballet of clumsy former milkmaids and shopgirls (unshaven), a Turkish striptease artiste that Christian himself salvaged specially for the occasion from Paris, rococo waltzes danced to the music of an SS Black Guard orchestra, a poor, naked girl trying very hard to look like Diana as she straddles a rather ripe deer shot in the Bavarian forests last week, and hundreds of "Strength-through-Joy" workers, Riem stable fans, local Nazi brass hats, reckless Munich students, and all kinds of women from Christian's mistresses to blond Hitler Girl Leaders—and this may give you an approximate description of the *Aufgalopp,* Christian Weber's artistic triumph, the crowning glory of countless decades in the history of Munich carnivals.

If you bear in mind that your correspondent unearthed the interesting fact that the Gestapo themselves confiscated all photographs taken at Christian's Carnal Carnival—and this in a country where one of their main Himmler-assigned tasks is to stimulate "healthy eroticism"—it may help you to form an impression of the lengths to which Stable Boy went in order to assure the success of his nights of beauty and romance.

Several Munich artists submitted their sketches to Christian for billboard announcements of the *Aufgalopp*. The main figure on all sketches naturally was a young, scantily dressed woman. Fatty, wedged in the time-honored chair of the Munich fathers, turned them all down.

"They ain't naked enough. Give 'em nipples. They gotta have tits an' big breasts *(sic)*," thundered our art critic in his inimitable Bavarian vernacular. The starving artists reluctantly altered their drawings. The final, Weber-approved placards proved so effective that those not torn down by eager Hitler Youths were eradicated from the billboards by the Gestapo. At the risk of disappointing some readers, I must testify that there are limits to bad taste strictly enforced even by Heinrich Himmler's Guards in the capital of the Nazi party.

Christian's Carnival feature was a tremendous financial feather in his hat. I need hardly add that he also enjoyed the evening thoroughly. For after the official part of the program was over, I saw no more of the jovial sponsor. He disappeared behind the heavy red curtains of his private box, one of his self-selected chorus girls in each beefy paw. Christian has many children in Munich. If they only knew it.

During the intervals between Christian's winter bacchanalia and the summer highlights of his Munich regime, we can leave him to his hippological conventions and the quiet pursuit of his trucking and bus-transport monopolies, directed from the former town home of Bavarian kings. But it would be unfair not to render homage to Christian's efforts for the promotion of the happiness and artistic stimulation of mankind, which reach their climax in his "Night of the Amazons." This outdoor undress function is Christian's annual pageant-prelude to the apple of his eye, the rich fruit of his life work: the Race for the Brown Ribbon of Germany. I summarized the two events as follows for Lord Beaverbrook's *Daily Express* of July 31, 1939: "Hitler disappointed thousands of visitors to Munich this week end, who expected him to attend last night the famous Nazi glamour show, the Night of the Amazons, and to watch today the horse race for the Führer's Brown Ribbon of Germany. Instead, Hitler remained at Bayreuth to listen to operas by Richard Wagner. This is what he missed, and what 20,000 eager spectators saw, at the Night of the Amazons.

"For two and a half hours scene followed scene in the magnificent park behind Nymphenburg Palace, home of the former Bavarian kings.

"More than a hundred practically naked girls took part, with 700 horses, and 2,000 actors and supers—many of them S. S. Guards disguised in the romantic costumes of the seventeenth century.

"The girls and actors danced, or formed tableaux to show the splendor of gay court life in ancient days. Some of the girls, dressed in the scantiest of tights, waved spears as Amazons while riding barebacked horses. Others, in tights and with butterfly wings attached to their arms, danced on the grass in the glare of powerful searchlights.

"Girls, with no covering but silver paint, posed round horse-drawn pedestals on which stood naked goddesses: Diana, goddess of the hunt; the Amazon queen, wearing a huge plumed helmet; Venus, goddess of love, standing silver-painted in front of a sea shell; and a Chinese temple goddess.

"The police at times could not control the crowds outside the palace gates.

"It is thought that Hitler stayed away from today's race to avoid the disappointment of seeing a foreign victory.

"The Brown Ribbon went to a Frenchman for the second year in succession. M. Boussac's Goya ü, ridden by the English jockey, E. C. Elliott, won by half a length from last year's winner, Antonym.

"Goya ü, which has run many times in England, paid its backers at the rate of 13-2. There was little cheering by the 30,000 German racing fans when it passed the post."

Even the official program of Weber's brown bacchanalia in Nymphenburg Park contained the following clear-cut words: "The pageant-host for the 1939 Night of the Amazons is Max Emanuel, who helped to free Vienna from the Turks, and conquered Belgrade, a daredevil soldier who—as his contemporaries assure us—was a 'connoisseur of female beauty and skylarking'....

"That which was formerly guarded carefully and offered to a select few behind high walls, today comes to life for all of us—in the nocturnal magic of Nymphenburg Park...in the scanty clothing of the Muses, in the undressed freedom of beautiful figures...Those who shout exultantly, filled with the joyful enthusiasm of action and gazing, are the German Youth of 1939....

"In the familiar statuettes of Old Nymphenburg Porcelain, we live the spirit of playful heroicism in the adorned and yet unhampered image of the beautiful nakedness of those times. The porcelain art of Nymphenburg comes to life in this group, 'Diana with her Huntresses.' The playful, graceful woman of rococo times, woman as a keen huntress, as a joyful comrade of man in the noble chase, was celebrated in the previous scene; the Grand Finale of the gallant frolic is dedicated to triumphant Venus, the mistress of man, and the Amazon, the godlike and yet so human rider, who surrenders herself to man only after a hard struggle. Venus, born of foam, appears on the high float of Tritons, surrounded by her maids. Then comes the grand float of the Queen of the Amazons, followed by the battling horsewomen and—as a symbol of the festival—the decorative Amazons ride on unsaddled horses with their spears held aloft."

There is one scene in the pageant in which these nude Amazons wage a sham battle with bare-chested men on horseback. It is described as follows: "Swords and shields ring out, figures on foot and on horseback charge at each other; some flee and again take the offensive; sometimes it looks as if one side, and then the other is winning. The Battle of the Amazons rages in a hot struggle."

45

I must confess that the Battle of the Amazons gave me an insight into what the war of the sexes must have been like before clothing had been invented. Some of the poor girls fell off their horses in the fray, and stood disconsolately in the floodlights, instinctively attempting to readjust clothing that simply wasn't there.

A footnote to the program announced that the girls were supplied by various dancing schools and extras from the casts of German vaudevilles and theaters, and that some of the Centaurs were members of Heinrich Himmler's No. 1 crack regiment, the SS Instant-Duty "Deutschland" Troops.

I throttled my journalistic conscience to the extent of putting some covering on a few of the girls for the sake of Britishers who might otherwise spill their morning coffee or rather the editors assumed the censoring themselves, since I 'phoned them "off the record" that a score of the girls on horseback actually wore nothing at all as they rode Godiva-like (but more slowly) between the grandstands, hoping, perhaps, to keep warm and acquire a coat of tan from the super-powerful searchlights requisitioned for the occasion from the Munich antiaircraft batteries. I have often wondered whether the young RAF pilots, flying over Munich at night, realize that the same death-luring beams which they try desperately to avoid, were shining just as relentlessly on blushing young Dianas, Junos, Venuses, and Amazon Queens one month before World War Two erupted.

Nor could I entrust to the Gestapo-tapped wires the aftermath of the Night of the Amazons. How many moldering Bavarian monarchs turned over in their graves I cannot say, but I do know this: When the 20,000 thrilled spectators had been herded out of Nymphenburg Palace grounds by the police, and while a trusted flunkey was counting Weber's box-office receipts for the performance, Christian and his cronies were staging their own private little orgy with command performances by the Amazons in one of the wings of Nymphenburg Palace.

The bare-breasted Amazons were paid $2.50 for the evening, the September-Morn riders $5.00, and the nudes on pedestals $12.50. The male horsemen, of course, performed gratis, by order of their SS and army commanders, for the glory of the Third Reich, and to the (bank) credit of Herr Christian Weber.

"Loyal" Adolf Hitler tries hard not to interfere with the private careers of those men who stood by him through the thick and thin of early beer-hall days, when his new party was struggling for its existence. Christian Weber is no exception. With a few modifications caused by the wartime blackout, he can still hang out his sign, "Business as usual."

***

HITLER DABBLES IN ART

"Art is a noble mission, demanding fanatic devotion."—ADOLF HITLER

Little children look forward to Christmas as the happiest day of their year. Turkey breeders consider Thanksgiving the supreme reward for 364 days of travail. Christian Weber's heyday is the twenty-four hours starting with the Night of the Amazons and ending with the Brown Ribbon Race on the last week end in July. Every dictator also has his day.

Adolf's big moment is "The Day of German Art"—a $5,000,000 Munich festival devoted to the Reich Chancellor's pet hobby, the Nazification of German culture. During three July days and nights, the entire Reich pays tribute at Munich to "The World's Greatest Artist," an appellation which the Führer never tires of hearing from the lips of his sycophantic disciples.

The Foreword to the official program of the 1939 Day of German Art explains the avowed purpose of this Nazi Fantasia. I quote:

"A nation that works, and is strong and healthy, has not only the right, but also the duty to celebrate festivals. For the latter are vital symbols of a spiritual attitude and human culture. The heroic principles of will power, the positive attitude toward fate, and the consciousness of blood, are the three roots from which the National Socialist movement has drawn its strength. They could not live merely in the political and social struggle; they were bound to become effective in the spiritual and cultural struggle. Out of this knowledge grew the 'Day of German Art,' the Festival of Life for all Germans. This National Socialist festival, about which the entire year centers, is dedicated to the Goddess of Art.... Thus, on the 'Day of German Art,' the concentrated force of our political will is formed into a living picture of joy and sorrow, in order to lead us to future heights in the life of the nation."

All year long, statesman Adolf Hitler is busy regimenting phase after phase of German life. But none of his political ventures affords him greater pleasure than the regimentation of German art. The annual party congresses at Nuremberg during the first week of September represent the Führer's supreme moment of political ecstasy. The Munich Days of German Art provide the same form of emotional release for Adolf's artistic libido. Hitler's seventy-two-hour cultural spree is summarized as follows in the program of the first Day, in 1937:

"And now, a newly arisen Reich, still echoing from the marching of political battalions, suddenly convoked a Reichstag of the Arts in the capital of its movement, at the cradle of its birth, and over the coffins of its first victims! And through the mouth of its Führer, it bound the artists in oath and duty, as if they had been lords of provinces! And assembled the people to be witnesses on the streets and squares! And embroidered the earnest hour with a garland of merriment, the ringing of songs, the bobbing of dances, and the nocturnal glare of shooting rockets!"

In other words a good time was had by all, especially by Hitler and his retinue—with plenty of exclamation points.

The temple to the great Nazi god of Art, in which its high priest Adolf officiates on this sacred occasion, is the Führer's first contribution to Third Reich architecture: the marble "House of German Art" on the Prinzregenten Strasse. It is known to inconoclastic Bavarians as "The Greek Railway Station," "The College Gymnasium," and "The House of German Tarts," due to its external appearance and the number of nudes inside. This remarkable edifice, a combination art gallery, restaurant, beer hall, and night club, was built in four years at a tremendous cost on the swampy ground at the southern end of Munich's largest park, the English Garden. Adolf's fanatic definition of Art at the head of this chapter is emblazoned above its portals. Its annual exhibition of paintings, etchings, and sculptures by German artists has been opened every July since 1937 by the Führer as one of the two main ceremonies in the Nazi extravaganza, "The Day of German Art."

Hitler laid the cornerstone to his artistic temple on October 15, 1933. "May this House of German Art be a symbol of the everlasting indestructibility of German creative effort. A new and flourishing era in German art commences with the laying of this cornerstone," the Führer said on that occasion. Then he rapped the stone vigorously with a mason's hammer, while the spectators and guests of honor looked on in awed silence. The hammer broke! Hitler, intensely superstitious, turned pale. He was so upset by the incident that he locked himself in his Munich apartment and would see no one all next day. He has never completely recovered from the inauspicious start which he thus gave to Nazi culture.

Venerable, picturesque Munich undergoes a complete metamorphosis of face-lifting for the seventy-two-hour Day of German Art. This operation is a bane to Bavarian fire-insurance companies. For every hook-and-ladder fire truck within radius of a hundred miles around Munich is commandeered by the Brown-Shirt art committee to help decorate the city. Thousands of telegraph poles are erected in the main streets as supports for sixty-foot flags covered with heraldic symbols, Swastikas, and other color combinations. Banners and brilliant acres of cloth are suspended from every roof top, telephone wire, trolley guy, and window sill to make Munich a sea of drapery. It's just too bad for any house that catches fire in a Bavarian town while the trucks are busy hanging these fostoons in Munich.

One week before the great event, the local party orderlies ring the front doorbells and foist candlesticks, candles, and colored shades on every household at a profitable price. Each window facing the street in Munich must burn brightly with these gay candles during the joyful art ritual. Every house must be decorated and illuminated. Roving squads of Nazis enforced this rule as severely on the peaceful nights of German Art as they later patroled the streets to punish citizens for showing the slightest ray of light in the wartime blackouts. Punishment for no lights on art nights—punishment for lights on blitzkrieg nights. It is all a matter of timing in the Third Reich. There were three million red lights shining on the first "Day" of German Art, or four lights per capita, transforming Munich into the world's greatest red-light city by the special will of the Führer.

Overnight, thousands of pedestals bearing hastily bronzed plaster figures of nudes, gods, goddesses, athletes, horses, eagles, Swastikas, and fireballs spring up like gaudy, giant mushrooms on the sidewalks. Elevated safety zones are removed from the streets with crowbars and pneumatic drills, to clear the tracks for processions. Shopkeepers stifle their curses as the Nazi artists cover their show windows with maroon cloth to render all the ground floors of the city blocks a uniform, dull red. Munichers toss restlessly in their beds as miles of wooden grandstands lining the streets are hammered into place. (Tickets up to $8.00, accommodations literally for over a million spectators from the Reich and abroad. The $5,000,000 People's Festival is an ersatz gold mine to the government.) Again the antiaircraft batteries loan their searchlights to the cause. Throughout the year, in special factories devoted to the project, hundreds of seamstresses have been kept busy, sewing costumes for the myriad figures parading in the six-mile-long procession, "2,000 Years of German Culture," which Hitler reviews from his Imperial Canopy Grandstand as the second of the two main ceremonies.

Nor has Adolf himself been idle in preparing his temple for the Grand Opening. From paper hanger to picture hanger is Hitler's metamorphosis from his first jobs in Vienna to his self-appointed office as High Priest of Nazi Art. A few weeks before his inaugural sermon, Germany's Chancellor climbs down into the cellar of his temple to rummage among the thousands of paintings and sculptures stored there. These works have been sent to Munich from all parts of Germany by hopeful Third Reichers at their own expense, trusting that Adolf's art committee will select their canvas or marble for exhibition among the 1500 works of art which the gallery can accommodate. With this gallery still closed to the prying eyes of visitors, who may take their lunch on the building's back terrace, their beer in another part of the cellar, or their women and liquor in the night club on its northeast corner, Hitler drops in at the gallery frequently to watch the progress in the hanging of the latest harvest of Nazi paintings or the *mise en scéne* of Josef Thorak's newest nude. His constant companion on these inspection tours is Frau Gerdy Troost, widow of the House's architect and a member of the Hitler hanging committee. These people trail the Führer through the incompleted exhibit with greater trepidation than that experienced by the submitting artists. For Adolf is very outspoken about his views on German art.

During one of these trips, Hitler dove into the cellar to select an appropriate picture for one wall of the gallery. After much fussing, he finally found what he wanted and ordered the men to carry up the painting and hang it.

"But, *Mein Führer,* you can't hang *that* painting!" objected Gerdy, who knows a thing or two about art. "It is impossible. The people will laugh at it. Look at the horrible color of the sky. And no grass ever has that tinge. It would never do to show the German people this absurd picture as an example of German art."

(In his 1937 inaugural address at the temple, Hitler had vehemently proclaimed that artists who cannot paint the true colors of sky and grass should either be sterilized for the sake of posterity or be criminally prosecuted to safeguard the artistic character of the nation.)

Adolf turned on Frau Troost, his eyes blazing. "I know what I'm doing," he barked. "How dare you question my judgment? In the world of art as well as politics, I am the supreme judge. *Verstanden* (understand)?"

Hitler scolded the widow of his dearest architect so savagely that she fainted on the spot. SS Guards carried her out into the fresh air blowing from the English Garden. Onlookers thought that this woman probably had overindulged in the *Bierstube.* But I was fortunate enough to obtain the true explanation from someone who had witnessed the Führer's outburst and the fainting. It was this person's overindulgence in another beer hall that unloosed this confidential story. Naturally I could never have abused my privileges as a Munich correspondent to send a report of the incident to London.

Hitler's review of the art gallery with his guests of honor after he officially opens the annual exhibits is a mere matter of form, since no painting, sculpture, or etching has been put in its place without his previous approval or orders. In 1938, however, the Great Dictator overlooked one little detail on his last preview of the exhibit. This oversight cost the Nazi art committee thousands of dollars, and one of its members, I am almost certain, his life.

Every country has its pet numbers. "Behind the eight ball" is a typical American way of expressing things numerically. "A thousand years" is a Russian's manner of wishing you happiness. *"Trente et quarante"* is gambling in any Frenchman's vocabulary. But none of these figures convey such instant and ominous meaning as one particular German number, the mere mention of which is a sure-fire method of provoking either a laugh, sneer, shudder, raised eyebrow, or a term in concentration camp. Just say *"Hundertfünfundsiebzig"* (175) to any German, and it will spare you the embarrassment of pronouncing the horrid word "homosexual."

Paragraph 175 of the German Criminal Code defines the crime of homosexuality. This paragraph was invoked by Hitler when he found it expedient to take his old buddy Ernst Boehm for a ride, and order the killing of several hundred other Nazis in the purge of June 30, 1934. Thousands of Germans who failed to shift their activities from manly comradeship to boosting Third Reich census figures at the signal given by their Führer, today are either above or below the ground in concentration camps. "Why did the Gestapo take Fritz away?" Answer: "One hundred and seventy-five," has been a brief, but frequent form of hushed conversation in the Third Reich since 1934.

By some inadvertent but terrific little slip, a member of the Hitler hanging committee in 1938 assigned to a huge oil painting, depicting a column of Hitler's Storm Troopers marching as one man down the strife-torn streets of pre-Third-Reich Germany, *the fatal catalogue and picture-frame number 175!*

I could hardly believe my eyes when I was conducted through the halls of the House of German Art in a press preview of the 1938 exhibition, stood gaping at this monstrous parody of art, found the number on the frame, and looked into my advance copy of the catalogue to discover that No. 175 was entitled "The Spirit of the Storm Troopers." I whispered my startling discovery to my colleagues. Even the Nazi press boys could not suppress several snickers.

Several hundred thousand catalogues already had been printed for public sale at fifty cents each. I still have mine. But for the sake of some fun and credit, I called the attention of the Munich Gestapo to the number scandal, whereupon all the catalogues were destroyed and new ones hastily printed to replace them. In the expurgated copies, a harmless number was assigned to the Storm Troopers, while the catalogue informed you that No. 175 was entitled "Vase of Flowers." No homosexuality in still life.

My public service as the upholder of artistic decency in Munich came about as a part of my standard policy in dealing with the Gestapo. It was my practice to enter the Lions' Den periodically on some pretext or other, to chat with the "Press Chief." He gave me valuable information only once, but always provided me with an opportunity to persuade my friends in black uniforms (and plainclothes) that I was their pal, that I had nothing to conceal, that I looked up to them as invaluable contacts for a foreign correspondent to enjoy, etc. Knowing that the picture's number would soon be brought to their attention anyway, I dropped over to the Wittelsbacher Palace after the press preview and called on the Gestapo chief.

"You know that I am an upright and serious foreign correspondent," I reminded him. "Reuters does not make a business of scandal stories. Therefore I felt it my duty to consult with you about your attitude toward the following news." I then outlined to the Gestapo Press Chief the homosexual condition of the Storm Troopers in the House of German Art.

"Herr Pope," replied the chief, "I always appreciated your being a decent foreigner, and am glad you came to see me. I think you can guess what our attitude toward such a news story would be." This was a polite way of hinting that I would probably follow my story out of the Third Reich. By improving his stock with the Gestapo through such demonstrations of "good will" as killing a nasty story, the wise correspondent can draw on his credit with the authorities to send unfavorable news of real importance on other occasions.

Every ranking Nazi and government official comes to the three-day Munich art picnic, as well as every German artist who has succeeded in earning a living in the Third Reich. Their host for the three-ring culture circus is Bavaria's Gauleiter, Adolf Wagner, who formally opens the Reichstag of Artists on Friday morning in the Congress Hall of the German Museum. His speech invariably praises Adolf Hitler as "The leader of the National Socialist Revolution of Art, who is not only the patron of German Art, but also its greatest master." Then Goebbels shuffles to the rostrum for his two cents' worth about "Jewish decadence, the triumph of the Nazi brush and chisel," etc., etc. Joseph, who has been given dictatorial powers by Adolf for the regimentation of the finer things of life, issues his orders to the assembled artists for their Teutonic endeavors in the coming year. Finally, the President of the Reich Chamber of Arts, roué Adolf Ziegler, reviews Nazi artistic progress in the previous year. Hitler, the rest of the government, and the Great Nazi Masters applaud at the proper moments. A symphony orchestra intones "Deutschland ber Alles" and the Horst Wessel song to conclude the first event on the program of the Day of German Art.

There is one reason why I like the Horst Wessel anthem: its rasping notes wake me up promptly, so that I won't be late in leaving the Congress for Reich Press Chief Dr. Otto Dietrich's luncheon in the Maximilianeum. This pre-Nazi building is a famous Munich landmark in the best tradition of true German art. Dr. Dietrich entertains the domesticated and the foreign press in its galleries with a meal rivaling Christian Weber's Town Hall banquets. We ascend the long flights of stairs between German maidens wearing gauzy Greek robes and bearing lighted candles, to lunch under the Old Masters while Hitler's Press Chief tells us some more about the New Masters in the Third Reich.

Not being a German actor, painter, sculptor, musician, or author, your Munich correspondent was not invited to the next event: Hitler's tea party for the Nazi geniuses in the restaurant of the House of German Art. This is quite a chummy affair, with the Führer moving from table to table to sit next to as many beautiful stars of stage and screen as is possible in one afternoon for a considerate host. The Chancellor also chats with personalities like Max Schmeling, whose pretty little actress-wife was very popular with Hitler. Dancing, champagne, the best orange pekoe or jasmine tea, cake, and liqueurs reward the German artists at the Führer's tea for obedience to Goebbels' cultural edicts during the preceding twelve months.

The party moves to the Artists' House for dinner the same evening with their supreme host. Then on to Grand Opera, which concludes the first day. My complimentary press ticket to this exclusive spectacle has a face value of $12.00—quite a modest price, considering not only the excellent quality of the opera, but also the additional attractions. During the interval the entire audience swarms to the lobby, where all are treated to champagne as the guests of the Minister of the Interior, Herr Wagner. The lobby is lined with young members of the "League of German Girls." This time they wear delicate tight dresses and crowns of flowers, not the drab, brown jackets with which they are usually identified.

Before exhibiting his works in the House of German Art, a German artist must join Adolf Ziegler's Reich Chamber of Arts. Membership in this organization is imperative for any creative worker in the Third Reich who hopes to live by his talents. Saturday of the three-day jamboree is devoted to meetings of the Chamber's subdivisions. The painters, sculptors, etchers, architects, tapestry weavers, interior decorators, and other members of the guild receive their instructions at closed sessions in Munich on this day, giving the foreign correspondent a welcome opportunity to sleep or go sailing on a Bavarian lake, or both. This recreation puts me into fine shape to enjoy the Saturday night extravaganza, the "Summer Festival of the Reich Government," in which little Joe Goebbels invites his government, the party bigwigs, the Nazi artists, the crack troops of Third Reich art critics, and even the foreign press to a nocturnal outdoor function that can best be described as a glorified Nazi version of Shakespeare's *Midsummer Night's Dream.*

The Propaganda Minister's party is held in a sylvan park above Munich's Fair Grounds. His five thousand guests, in their dressiest uniforms or summer clothing, sit at tables around a clearing in the wooded park. His versatile SS Guards, resplendent for a change in white uniforms, act as butlers, serving five-dollar meals and pouring three kinds beer, four brands of wine, and three different vintages of champagne throughout the evening. In the center of the clearing, a huge wooden platform has been erected in the focus of powerful spotlights. Pretty girls in elfish costumes flit about the tables and among the trees, lending their charms to any of the guests who seek their company. The best German ballets, choruses, solo dancers, and stage shows in the country take turns performing on the platform between intervals during which the guests dance with their partners or the elves to the music of Hitler-approved jazz bands.

The inevitable Teutonic touch climaxes Goebbels' midnight enchantment. After the last dance, when the guests return to their champagne-laden tables, a terrific explosion detonates from the far end of the clearing. Fireworks, mostly of the percussion type, bang away in a deafening barrage for fifteen ear-splitting minutes. No bomb-dropping, antiaircraft-shooting air raid could make more noise than the Propaganda Minister's party send-off. Little wonder that the Germans were conditioned against shell shock even before the war started!

Fortunately the Führer waits until late Sunday morning to deliver his sermon on German Art at its temple, thus enabling his government to sleep off their midsummer night's whoopee. The SS Guards are not so lucky. When they shed their white waiters' uniforms, they must climb back into their everyday brown shirts and black jackets to hold hands along the Munich streets, hours before Adolf and his subordinates open their eyes. The SS Guards form these cordons to insure the unhampered passage of the Nazi bosses from their hotels and villas to their seats of honor in the House of German Art, while the simpler Munich folk jockey for positions behind the cordons to get a good view of their Führer as he makes his triumphal appearance at the eleventh hour of the Sabbath. It is futile to attempt to attend church on this morning, since all streets lead only to the Nazi art temple, and crossing them is *verboten*.

At last smiling Adolf arrives, after a fleet of shining black Mercedes has landed the lesser lights of the Reich at the Greek Railway Station. The usual reviewing of the Nazi guard of honor stationed in front of the building is followed by a few introductory remarks by boss Adolf Wagner, whereupon Hitler enters the temple to launch his stereotyped dissertation on German Art into the battery of microphones installed in the gallery's Hall of Honor. Let us follow Adolf and his retinue through the gallery to examine the type of works which he has hung or approved.

First there are the Hitler busts, at least a half dozen distributed at strategic points throughout the building. Then there are the Mussolini busts, fewer in number, but almost as well placed. In 1939 I noticed a little sign under the Duce's brass head. It bore the simple text: "Twice sold." Whether this meant that two admirers had ordered Duce copies from the sculptor, or whether Benito himself had been auctioned to the highest political bidders was not stated, yet events to come proved that both interpretations of the sign were correct. Next come the busts of the satellites like Goebbels, Ley, Streicher, Wagner, *et al.* But the best and most numerous busts in the House of German Art are the most natural ones, either in marble or oils, well-developed and Nordic, testimonials to Adolf Ziegler's decree, "To give German men the incentive to have many German children, German artists must depict beautiful nude women."

Adolf Ziegler's own paintings occupy prominent positions. The President of the Reich Chamber of Arts was elevated to this key position by Hitler after Ziegler had won the Führer's heart by presenting him with a portrait of Hitler's niece. Ziegler had hand-colored a photograph of this girl, faithfully tracing the outlines of the picture with his paint brushes. He has used this masterful technique ever since, merely substituting photographs of his secretaries for dictators' nieces in contributing his annual nudes to the exhibition. Every detail is faithfully reproduced. Hitler encourages both faithfulness and reproduction in his Reich. Nothing is left to the imagination. As Hitler said in his first speech about Nazi art, "To be German is to be clear and exact." He considers the fig leaf un-German.

Adolf's gallery also specializes in pictures of German soldiers and political warriors exemplifying the Nazi spirit of "conquer or bust." The House of German Art does contain some first-class paintings and sculptures. It would be strange indeed if German genius could not produce fine landscapes, peasant portraits, statues of animals and the human body even under the regimented Nazi regime. But the trend is definitely toward eroticism, heroism in battle, pictures of grandiose German steel mills and other armament factories, military highways and political building projects, and the glory of the German farmer who feeds the nation's warriors.

Characteristic of the transition from foreign cubism to Nazi nudism is the work of the Munich painter, Paul Padua. After years of struggling, artist Padua acquired recognition and a bank account through the efforts of his wife to support him by peddling his pictures from door to door. His specialty was peasant portraits. After his wife had sacrificed her best years to his career, Padua deserted her and his children for an artists' model. As late as 1938, however, his contributions to the annual exhibition were portraits. But, following the trend, Padua's chef-d'oeuvre in 1939 was a huge oil painting of his red-headed model, ecstatically embracing a swan. After staring at this picture, Hitler boys and girls had no more questions to ask regarding the mechanics of the Leda mythology. The intertwined swan and redhead hung in the House of German Art all summer to serve their erotic and instructive purpose. Then Heinrich Hoffman, Hitler's official photographer and the father-in-law of the German Youth Leader, Baldur von Schirach, bought Leda for his home, for a paltry $25,000.

A few weeks after Leda had made her reclining bow to the public, I received a letter from the Paris correspondent of the *Daily Telegraph,* who had been transferred recently from Berlin to the French capital. He requested several photographic copies of Leda for his French friends who could not believe that the art of Hitler's "ascetic Third Reich" out-rivaled in vulgarity their native brand of pictures—the kind that are peddled surreptitiously in plain envelopes on dark street corners to lustful male tourists. I had some extra copies made to show my own incredulous friends back home.

The Führer, of course, has first choice of any of the works of art exhibited. Those he wishes to take back to Berchtesgaden are marked "unsaleable," as are those purchased by the other chief patrons. If any of the influential purchasers are in a hurry to take a nude or fighting soldier home with them, they may. This gives Adolf another chance to spend an afternoon delving into the cellar of his art temple to select a replacement. Next to Hitler, Göring and Goebbels are the main "buyers" of works exhibited here. Yet, in his 1937 inaugural, the Führer solemnly had proclaimed, "This House shall not be a public market for artistic wares, but a Temple of Art."

The procession "2,000 Years of German Culture" concludes Adolf's three-day art orgy. It is a six-mile-long potpourri of floats drawn by army horses and portraying every phase of German culture within this period. Thousands of men and women in the costumes of their times accompany the floats. The men are requisitioned from the army and party formations, the women from any part of Munich where they can be hired for fifty cents for the afternoon's marathon masquerade.

The first float is called "The Germanic Ship." Whether it symbolizes the days of the Vikings or the Teutonic ship of state I have never been able to discover; be that as it may, the designers stupidly put the steering oars at the bow and persistently dragged the ship *backward* at the head of 2,000 years of German culture.

The Nordic scow is followed by knights bearing spears and shields, clearing the path for a twenty-foot gilded Swastika. The procession goes on and on for three solid hours, while a battery of loudspeakers strung along the streets monotonously blares out the first part of "Deutschland fiber Alles" every thirty seconds. Floats symbolizing everything under the Germanic sun from "Walhalla" to "Blood and Soil," pass the Reich Government reviewing stand, where Hitler and every other Nazi figure familiar to newspaper readers sit on chairs under their purple-and-gold canopy, clapping their hands at each garish symbol. The ambassadors and consuls to Germany sit on ordinary grandstand benches, holding their umbrellas if it rains.

Other floats follow. The Nibelungen Hoard, Day, Night, The Sea God Aegir, The Heroic German Song, Gothic Handicraft, Music (which developed a hotbox in 1938 and had to be sidetracked), The World of Richard Wagner, The Sacrifice, Faith and Faithfulness, The Return of the Saar, The Danube (nice nudes), Map of Germany (larger each year), and gigantic models of party buildings (including a sixty-foot House of German Art)—all sandwiched between the different kinds of warriors Germany has produced in 2,000 years, and their womenfolk. A dozen lordly kings and kaisers ride proudly past the stands, Barbarossa saluting Hitler as he passes the canopy.

An alert correspondent could detect the shadow of coming European events in Hitler's annual culture procession by studying the floats, such as this one, entitled "Gates to the East," in July, 1939: two Bohemian lions holding wide open some gates behind which could be seen typical Slavic architecture symbolizing Poland, the Balkans, the Ukraine. The same type of float told me in the summer of 1937 that the Reich would swallow Austria and the Sudetenland the following year.

In fact, the Nazi procession itself is an admission of the Führer's restless plans for future conquests. For immediately behind the series of floats representing recent triumphs and hinting the next move into Austria or Poland, comes the symbol of the Third Reich, the "Sovereign German Eagle." The official program of the parade tells you that this mammoth plaster bird, perched on a Swastika, "...stretches gigantically high, as if to scrutinize the entire procession. With him ends the revelation of our past history. At the same time, however, he stares into eternal perspectives, keen and calm, proud and sure of victory, proclaiming the greatness of our times and our will to action. He is the herald of our work and our plans."

But the climax to 2,000 years of German Culture, the concluding group in the procession, and the feature which brings Hitler, his government, and the German spectators to their feet and to thunderous applause, is the goose-stepping *Wehrmacht,* and last of all, to cap the climax of twenty centuries of Teutonic contributions to civilization—the Führer's and Himmler's SS Instant-Duty "Deutschland" Regiment. The pounding of their heavy boots, tramping in the wake of Richard Wagner, German Science, Bavarian Rococo, Romanticism, and Art, drowns out the memories of earlier Reichs and makes a brutal mockery of Germany's contributions to the world of culture.

***

THE ONE-LEGGED BOSS OF BAVARIA

The supervisor of Hitler's Bavarian playground is hard-drinking, Catholic-baiting, art-loving, one-legged Gauleiter Adolf Wagner, one of the Führer's few intimate friends. Wagner probably knows more about Hitler's private life and thoughts than any other Nazi, not excepting Himmler, Hess, Göring, Goebbels, or Ribbentrop. For Number Two Adolf practically grew up with the Nazi dictator, and has been his most constant playmate and companion throughout the years of Hitler's plotting, dreaming, and play-acting in the city dearest to the Führer's heart—Munich.

Together the two Adolfs marched through the Munich streets in the 1923 Putsch. Together they motored through the Bavarian Alps and dined in Hitler's mountain retreat at Berehtesgaden. Together they planned and executed the revamping of the "City of German Art." Together they rounded up the associates of Ernst Roehm and the Storm Troop Leader on the night of June 30, 1934, and executed them. In adjacent plush-and-gold seats, the boss of Germany and the boss of Bavaria have heard countless Wagnerian operas and have gloated over sensual *Merry Widows*. Big and Little Adolf joined forces as the Machiavellian hosts to Chamberlain, Daldier, Mussolini, and other historic guests of the party captial.

Whenever the Führer returns to Munich from Berlin or other parts foreign to his tastes, Wagner is right there to welcome him home like the perfect housekeeper or devoted mistress. And whenever Hitler has a bad cold, his Bavarian satrap is ready to read his speech for him, since Adolf Wagner is the Nazis' official "Führer Voice"— with the same pitch, intonations, raspings, whispers, and yells of Hitler's very special type of oratory. No other man can imitate Hitler's voice as faithfully as Wagner, nor is any other man permitted to do so. It is Wagner who reads the Führer's annual proclamation at the opening of the Nuremberg Party Rally, to save his master's voice. In short, Adolf Wagner is Adolf Hitler's understudy as well as his most trusted companion.

The machinery of national government in the Third Reich is situated at Berlin, principally along the Wilhelmstrasse. Hitler's ministerial engineers, such as Propaganda Minister Goebbels, Minister of Economics Funk, Minister of Agriculture Darre, etc., tend this administrative apparatus at the Reich capital. But the wheels of the Nazi government would not turn and produce blitzkriegs, four-year plans, wartime rationing, and the other phenomena of a totalitarian state without the supercharging provided by the Führer's party bosses (as distinguished from his state officials) within the framework of a nationwide Nazi hegemony.

Germany is divided into provinces or states familiar to most readers: Saxony, Prussia, Silesia, Swabia, etc. In addition to these national subdivisions, however, the Third Reich is cut up politically into Nazi party compartments, or Gaus, each headed by a minor Nazi dictator called Gauleiter, or Gau Leader, who is directly responsible to nobody except the Führer. Geographically, a province may contain several Gaus. But, notwithstanding the smaller size of his domain, a Nazi Gauleiter is more influential in Third Reich affairs than the governmental head of a province. Thus Herr Ludwig Siebert, the gray-haired, sagacious President of the Bavarian State Ministry, is less powerful than one-legged Adolf Wagner, who is twenty years his junior and who technically is boss merely of Gau Upper Bavaria, which occupies about one third of Siebert's territory. Wagner is the virtual, if not virtuous, dictator of Bavaria. Siebert is his puppet, left to do the dirty work in the Bavarian household. Thanks to his close association with Hitler, Gauleiter Wagner's importance in the destiny of Nazi Germany is at least as great as that of some Third Reich government ministers in Berlin.

Of the three dozen odd Gauleiters in the Reich who impose the Nazi will on their German pawns, Adolf Wagner is by far the most colorful, prominent, and dangerous. His powers are absolute in the heart of the Nazi stronghold. His sociological views are pagan. His personal influence on Hitler is considerably greater than most people realize.

An Alsatian by birth, Wagner came to Munich after flunking out of a university in western Germany, enlisting in World War One, and losing his right leg below the knee. When Hitler began his National

Socialist movement in the early twenties, Wagner began making the rounds of the Munich beer halls, literally as well as figuratively stumping for the Führer's party. His courage in the face of flying beer mugs, his inexhaustible voice, and his ability to outdrink, outsmart, and out-throw-out his political opponents won him the Führer's gratitude and appointment as Gauleiter of Upper Bavaria, which is reverently called the "Traditional Gau" of Germany by the Nazis as the birthplace of their party. The job of Gauleiter alone did not quite satisfy ambitious Adolf Number Two. He felt capable of better things than the mere collection and spending of party funds or the political policing of Bavaria. After all, didn't he have an impressive, gaping scar across his left cheek from one of his many student dueling battles? This was surely the trademark of a higher education, even if he had failed to pass his examinations. So Wagner dressed himself in the clothes of another office: that of Bavarian State Minister of Education, Culture, and the Interior. He enthroned himself in his dual capacity as Gauleiter and State Minister in a building only a stone's throw away from the home of his sworn enemy: Archbishop and Cardinal Faulhaber, the Pope's aged but fearless Bavarian apostle.

Over several glasses of beer, Wagner once told me in boasting, yet perfectly sincere tones, that he believed: "If more school systems in this world were run by men who had busted out of college, education would be the better for it." Munich schoolboys are inclined to agree with him, for one of Adolf ü's school measures was to give the pupils an extra half holiday every week, while he made the Bavarian teachers write essays on the purpose of education in the Third Reich. Wagner gleefully read these themes, severely reprimanding those unfortunate pedagogues who failed to agree with his own views about learning.

There are Gauleiters and Gauleiters in the Third Reich. Although Germany and the world would be better without these creations of the Hitler regime, all Gauleiters are not uniformly vicious. Some even have a decent streak or two in them. The lower order is represented by Franconia's rabid, low-browed, Jew-baiting racketeer, Julius Streicher. The higher type of Gauleiter is exemplified by Hitler's Other Voice. Adolf Wagner is not so ostentatious about his grafting; his vocabulary is larger; he can hold his liquor better; he attempts in his limited way to promote the arts; he dispenses a certain amount of justice and charity among the poor of his domain; he can understand a joke; and through his contact with the foreign tourists, correspondents, and diplomats in picturesque Munich, Wagner has acquired a degree of tact and diplomacy. He really would not be such a bad fellow if he only stopped persecuting the Church, hounding his personal enemies, pocketing other people's money, drinking excessively, and—despite his game leg—overstepping the bounds of matrimony.

Give the Bavarian Gauleiter his due. Not every Nazi boss would have been so astute as Adolf Wagner in dealing with foreign correspondents, as the story below shows.

In the summer of 1937, Adolf Wagner was engaged in a campaign to liquidate the Catholic schools in Bavaria. His self-appointed task was to "persuade" German parents to send their children to the Nazified state schools, rather than to the numerous private schools conducted by the clergy throughout Catholic Bavaria. Wagner followed the standard Nazi formula for gaining his ends: taking action first, then making it palatable or at least plausible to the public by oratory and the stuffed ballot box. This is what Hitler did in the 1938 Anschluss, first sending his troops into Austria, then making speeches and announcing that 99% of the people had voted their approval of his action. In the anti-Catholic school drive, Wagner closed confessional schools, staged rallies with all the Nazi ritual of showmanship and noise, attacked the Catholics during these rallies while praising secular education in the Third Reich, and finally announced in the Bavarian press and on the radio that an "overwhelming majority" of parents had elected to take their children out of the Catholic schools.

After one such rally, Boss Wagner invited me and three of my colleagues to a private luncheon in the little town of Fürstenfeldbruck, about twenty miles north of Munich. It was a very convivial affair. Wagner was proud of his speech ("I sure gave it to the Cardinal that time!" he chortled). The day was warm and sunny, so that his stump did not bother him. His deputy, Otto Niepold, had praised his "good work." So the six of us sat down to a square meal in the private room of the local inn, and cooled off from the hot morning with a steady stream of Bavaria's best brew.

The beer was so refreshing that it reminded me of a letter I had just received from my ninety-two-year-old grandfather back home.

"You lucky fellow," he had written, "working there at the source of the world's best beer. Wish I could have some too." I quoied this passage to my brown-shirted host.

"What's your grandfather's address? I'll send him some," Wagner exclaimed, flushed with Bacchus-inspired generosity. I wrote my nonagenarian's address on a slip of paper and handed it to the Bavarian potentate.

"Make a note of that, Niepold. Send a case of Lowenbrau's best Export to Herr Pope's grandfather," Adolf directed his deputy.

Familiar with Nazi promises, I dismissed the matter from my mind. But, incredible as it may seem, a case in the blue and white colors of Bavaria was left on the doorstep of my home in New York State a few weeks later. My grandfather was so overcome that he carried the heavy liquid load up to his room all by himself. Inside was a diplomatic toast written by none other than the Nazi chieftain. The sun never sets on the activities of the Nazis!

My grandfather naturally wished to thank the unknown donor, who had left no return address. Two weeks after the beer had been delivered, a letter with the following address dropped into my Munich Reuters-office mailbox:

Herr Gauleiter and State MinisterAdolf Wagnerc/o Ernest R. Pope
Mandlstrasse 9Munich, Germany

(German mailmen are very conscientious. Theirs is not to reason why, but to follow the rules blindly.)

Since Wagner was giving one of his numerous "teas" for the German and foreign press in the House of German Art that afternoon, I stuck my grandfather's letter into my pocket and handed it to Hitler's Voice personally.

"You see, Herr Gauleiter," I ventured to wisecrack, several glasses of Adolf's "tea" having emboldened me, "you could not be in better hands than care of the foreign press." Since Adolf also had consumed quantities of the beverage, he was in a jovial mood and roared at the joke.

Amid all the bluntness, stupidity, brow-beating, crudeness, and tactlessness that characterize Teutonic officialdom at its worst under the Nazi regime, Adolf Wagner's cordial effort to gain the good will of a foreign correspondent by sending his grandfather twenty-four pints of Munich beer stands out like a picnic bonfire in a blitzkrieg blackout. When his time comes, may he burn less painfully for this deed in the Inferno of the Catholics whom he has relentlessly persecuted all his life.

In return for so many parties, our foreign press association at Munich invited the Gauleiter one evening to a typical German function, known informally as a "Beer Evening." We had reserved the private room of his favorite Munich restaurant. A score of us played host to Wagner, his deputy Otto Niepold, his adjutant Herr Oberhuber, and two Munich press officials. The party developed into a contest to see who could drink the most. It not only emptied the funds of our little association, but forced us to make an additional levy on our members to pay the bill for entertaining the Nazis. While Wagner, Oberhuber, and I were content to pace each other in downing beer, his deputy Otto felt more aristocratic about the matter, and ordered champagne. So the polite correspondents at his table were compelled to keep him company in this expensive intoxicant.

During this beer evening, Wagner enlarged on his sociological theories, discussing everything from popular art to ghettos. But his favorite subject was the population problem. For one thing, he believed Germany should have still more children.

"The trouble with you foreigners from the democracies im that you don't have enough babies," he chided Mrs. Stanley Simpson, wife of the London *Times* correspondent and herself correspondent for two news agencies and two London papers.

"Well, I have four children," Mrs. Simpson replied quietly. Wagner, who has not done so well in wedlock, had no rejoinder. But he continued with a grandiose scheme of his for founding a luxurious, rent-free Munich Home for Unmarried Mothers, who he thought were still not getting a fair enough deal in spite of all that the Third Reich has done to raise the status of bastards. We did our best to keep a straight face while listening to the charitable chief, knowing that his interest in the welfare of these girl-mothers was doubtless increased by certain adventures he had had with his secretaries (one of whom has had three Wagner-inspired children) and with members of the theatrical and art world in his sphere of influence.

By three o'clock in the morning, friend Adolf had promised to guide us personally through the notorious Dachau Concentration Camp and every other point of interest around Bavaria. Oberhuber obediently made notes of all his boss's promises. But although Wagner did take the foreign press up the 10,000-foot Zugspitze Mountain near Garmisch a few months later to see the scenery, the tour of the concentration camp and other trips with a real news value somehow never materialized. Nevertheless, the beer evening proved successful in oiling the relations between foreign correspondents and their hosts in the Reich. It also gained for me the veteran's respect for my fluid capacity. Since that night, whenever I entered the restaurant while Wagner was dining with his associates, he would actually stand up and salute me as I passed his table.

On more than one occasion, Hitler's Bavarian playmate has failed to appear with his chief at public functions as scheduled. Officially, the Munich press then explains that the Gauleiter is ill, with complications from his old war wound. Unofficially, we know that he again had several too many at a beer evening or at one of his all-night parties in the Artists' House. Adolf Wagner and Robert Ley, the German Labor Leader, are two of the heaviest drinkers in all Nazi officialdom. I have seen them make speeches when they could hardly find the words they needed or the speaker's rostrum from which to deliver them.

Wagner's drinking is partly a result of the severe pains in his stump. He suffers from neuritis at frequent intervals, the more intense because he refuses to diet and cannot, despite his might, change the damp Munich climate. When Boss Wagner's stump hurts, there's hell to pay around his Ministry. Petitioners avoid his offices on rainy days, or when they suspect a hangover from some party jamboree. Adolf ü is extremely choleric in temperament. Woe to the subaltern or favor-seeking citizen sho crosses him when his face is bloated and the remnant of his right leg is filled with shooting pains. It was while in the throes of one of these spells that Wagner arrested Munich's most popular priest, Father Rupert Mayr, and sent him to concentration camp.

Catch him in a jolly mood, on the other hand, and you are a made man or woman. Embryo Munich artists and actresses who are willing to sacrifice everything to their careers spend most of their time and money in the Artist's House. For Adolf Wagner is the official Nazi patron of the City of German Art. He may be found almost every evening in this Nazi night club, talking and drinking to Bavarian beauties. If my grandfather could get a case of beer out of my quoting his letter to one-legged Adolf, imagine what a role a gorgeous Munich blonde can be given in one of the city's state theaters for saying nice things to a state dictator who has a fat, elderly wife at home and who finds himself in a private tête-à-tête at the "dangerous age." Wagner is magnanimous with his power and the party's money. He loves to make others happy, provided the philanthropy adds to his personal pleasure.

As Gauleiter of the most important political section of the Third Reich, Boss Wagner has numerous duties to perform for Hitler. He is responsible for putting across the latest party decrees. If the party launches a campaign for old bones and toothpaste tubes, Wagner guarantees that the local Labor Front, Hitler Youth, Women's Organization, Storm Troopers, and other Nazi groups collect and deposit these materials in a hurry. If Hitler wants to stage a triumphal entry into Munich after a Polish blitzkrieg or an Austrian

Anschluss or the Fall of France, Wagner orders handbills proclaiming the "greatness of the day" to be showered all over the city, and organizes the street cordons, torchlight parades, fireworks, and even the "Heiling" crowds to render homage to his Führer. If Hitler wants a building torn down or erected in any part of the city, Wagner gets the money somehow and has the job done. When Big Adolf takes a fancy to an actress or dancer, Peg-Leg (who knows them all) does the introducing and other arrangements. When the Führer wants a squadron of 'planes or baby carriages as a symbolic birthday present, Wagner orders the party in his Gau to raise the necessary Reichsmarks. No matter what information is required by Hitler, whether it concerns the number of Jewish stores in town, the number of Jews in Dachau, the activities of Reuters Munich correspondent, the political reliability of a Munich professor, what Bavarian bus drivers think of their Führer or with whom Hitler's English girl friend, Unity Mitford, has been associating, Adolf Wagner is ready to serve his master. Each Gau in the Third Reich is a little Naziland, with its local party leaders—minor Himmlers, Leys, Rosenbergs, Baldur von Schirachs, and Scholtz-Klinks—all of whom are responsible to the Gauleiter as well as to their national leaders. Thus the Gauleiter can regiment his entire domain as the Führer wills it, while the Führer needs merely assemble his Gauleiters at Munich or Berlin to know all about the nation of which he is the supreme dictator.

Raising money for his own and the party's coffers through street collections, taxes, paid admissions to rallies and circuses, sequestrations and expropriations of church and other properties, naturally is one of Boss Wagner's main functions, as well as the awarding of political patronage to promising young Nazis. A good illustration is provided by the sequel to the anti-Jewish pogrom in November, 1938. Together with his stable-boy subordinate, grafter Christian Weber, Adolf Wagner and two Munich lawyers formed a "corporation" to transfer the ownership of Munich apartment houses from Jews to Aryans. The Jews were given a small cash settlement for their houses. The Aryans paid a good price for their new acquisitions. Wagner's "corporation" pocketed the difference, netting one million Reichsmarks in less than one month. Each lawyer was given 10% of the spoils, while Wagner and Weber split the 800,000 marks fifty-fifty. Due to the fact that Weber is a political inferior to Wagner, and that one likes horses while the other likes the theater and paintings, Hitler's two Munich henchmen despise each other. They only co-operate when there is graft from the party system to divide, or for the sake of a united front when Chief Hitler is in town for a party ceremony of his Old Guard, such as the annual celebration of the Beer-Hall Putsch on November 8 and 9.

Hitler's Voice is also exploited as a sounding board or trial balloon by the Führer, to see how much more Nazüsm the German people can stand. When Hitler has some specially preposterous or drastic statement or action in mind, he will often make Wagner try it out on the Bavarians first. If they manage to swallow the statement without choking, the Führer can risk broadcasting it to the entire nation. If the thickheaded Bavarians can pull their belts up one more notch, it is safe for Hitler to ration the entire Reich accordingly. The Bavarian Gauleiter's province has often been the testing ground for the countless Nazi measures that have marked the cataclysmic rise of the Third Reich. For this reason alone, Adolf Wagner's importance should not be underrated. Similarly, Wagner's actions and speeches, as reported by Munich correspondents in the foreign press, gave Hitler, Goebbels, and Ribbentrop a clue to the reaction which foreign countries would have to official government action subsequently taken at Berlin.

Two months after England had declared war on the Third Reich, as I stood between two hatchet-faced Gestapo in the bombed Munich beer hall, Adolph Wagner stomped in with his deputy and retinue to inspect the wreckage of the night's "attempt" on Hitler's life. He gave a barely perceptible start when he first saw me, then marched up to one of the Gestapo, mid without a sign of recognition thundered, "Who is this man?" The agent informed him that I was an American journalist. Bavaria's boss himself knew that I was an American citizen, but his followers had always connected me exclusively with the British press, and therefore assumed that their efficient Gestapo had caught this "Englishman" red-handed at the scene of his Secret-Service-inspired crime. No wonder that Wagner, who had been given supreme powers—and responsibilities—in Munich and Bavaria by Hitler, could not afford to recognize the former Reuters correspondent while the Nazis were attempting to blame Chamberlain for the unsuccessful assassination of their Führer.

Sticking his scarred face within six inches of my nose, Wagner growled, "Young man, keep this out of the papers. This is our business, and only ours, to investigate and report. If you know what's healthy for you, get out of here as fast as you can!" He then limped grimly into the hall, leaving me to the Gestapo. That was the last time I ever saw Adolf Wagner, Dictator of Bavaria, Hitler's Confidant, and Beer Purveyor to Foreign Correspondents' Grandfathers.

***

CATHOLICISM IN THE NAZI CAPITAL

New Year's Eve in Munich. Every tavern, beer hall, and night club is jammed. Loud-mouthed, intoxicated local Nazi leaders push pigs' knuckles into their cavernous maws, washing it all down with quarts of beer or pints of champagne. Then they stagger to their feet to push equally porcine mistresses around the dance floors to the blaring of army or Storm-Troop bands. Or they clumsily attempt to keep time, with feet accustomed only to goose-stepping in hobnailed boots, to the smoother music of Hitler-approved German jazz orchestras in the more exclusive night clubs.

The night is *wunderbar* for indulging in all the pleasures dear to the pagan Nazi heart: waltzing around a smoke-filled beer hall with a buxom, uninhibited female; stuffing yourself with manly, strength-giving meat and potato salad; raising your elbow to down a quart of Lowenbrau or to greet a *Kamerad* with the Hitler salute; roaring some lusty *Kampf* song at the top of your top sergeant's voice; dragging your giggling *Madchen* to a dim nook or stairway as a triumphant gesture for the benefit of sturdy legions of a coming postwar generation. Hitler meanwhile has climbed his mountain one hundred miles away, secretly to consult his astrologer in the innermost recesses of his Berchtesgaden home about the prospects for a new year of blitzing.

But tonight not only the beer halls are filled to overflowing in the capital of the Nazi movement. Ten thousand devout Munich Catholics peacefully squeeze against one another, so that all may hear their beloved Cardinal, venerable Archbishop Faulhaber, deliver his New Year's Sermon to his oppressed followers in the historic Church of Our Lady. While marching songs and tobacco smoke fill the air of the Nazi night clubs as the carousers await their first nude show, the hushed chorus of Catholic prayers mingles with incense and candle light as the faithful Bavarians prepare their souls to receive the reverent words of their fearless, gray-haired Cardinal.

As Adolf Hitler, the high priest of National Socialism, climbs the stairs to his astrological room on the Third Reich's holy mountain at Berchtesgaden, the aging Bavarian Archbishop slowly ascends the circular steps around a pillar of the twin-domed Frauenkirche to his pulpit.

"Dear fellow worshipers," he begins, "in the coming year you must be brave, very brave. No matter how much our Church is being persecuted, no matter how often my sermons will be censored by state authority, no matter how many of your German brothers turn from the path of Godliness to paganism, keep the faith of your fathers and of the Holy Father."

A sea of upturned faces surges below the Cardinal's pulpit. Quiet, deep devotion and martyrdom are reflected in them—a tribute which the Führer, with all his *Wehrmacht* and propaganda will never be able to exact. His voice trembling at times with age, years of struggle against powerful forces of evil, and at times with a righteous anger at the fate of his suffering congregation, Archbishop Faulhaber enumerates the injustices perpetrated against religion in the Reich during the past year. He warns his flock of further trials to come, cautions them to conduct themselves as true Christians in the face of adversity, and finally gives them his and the Vatican's blessing. Silently, with bowed heads, the Bavarians leave the Cathedral.

Hedy Simpson and I attempt as speedy an exit as is possible without offending the throngs of worshipers. We have been taking notes on Faulhaber's sermon, as inconspicuously as conditions permit, with the added handicaps of dim lighting and no elbow room. The Cardinal's voice, crying in the wilderness of the paganized Reich, must be heard in London. As we crowd our way through the heavy wooden doors of the Frauenkirche, a young German brushes past us. We recognize him as another note taker.

"Heil Hitler!" he grins, giving us the familiar salute. Then he strides off in the direction of the Brienner Strasse. The youth has mistaken us for fellow-colleagues, taking notes on the Archbishop's New Year's Eve Sermon for the files of the Gestapo!

Our reports will bring sympathy from the outside world for the valiant struggle of Christianity in the Nazi camp. His report will bring severe censorship of sermons and confiscation of pastoral letters for Cardinal Faulhaber, the next time he attempts to perform the arduous duties of his ecclesiastical office at the birthplace of National Socialism.

Seventy-three-year-old Michael Cardinal von Faulhaber is rightly looked upon as a modern saint by the Bavarian Catholics, whose creed is percentually the greatest of any religion remaining in southern Germany. On the night of January 27, 1934, an irate Nazi heathen fired a revolver at the Cardinal, missing him by inches. On November 11, 1938, a group of Nazis, incited by the circus-building speech of their boss, Adolf Wagner, besieged the Munich Archbishopric, firing rifles at the Cardinal's apartment and smashing his windows. Some of these heathen troopers were hungry children back in 1923, when the Cardinal fed them with the food he had obtained for his diocese from funds he had raised during a visit to the United States. Chicago's Cardinal Mundelein personally had donated $1,000 to Faulhaber for his Bavarian children, who literally tried to stone him fifteen years later. No wonder that deep lines furrow the brow of Cardinal Faulhaber as, bearing the Cross, he runs the gauntlet of Swastikas in Nazi Munich during the traditional Corpus Christi processions.

Seldom could the aging crusader officiate in an atmosphere free from note-taking Gestapo, hissing Hitler Youths, or other insults to the Church. The little chapel of Nymphenburg Palace was one of the few places where Faulhaber enjoyed the peaceful Bavarian atmosphere of pre-Hitler days. It was in this chapel that the Archbishop performed his last "Royal Wedding" ceremonies.

In August, 1937, Crown Prince Rupprecht of Bavaria, living the secluded life of an exile in a wing of his own Nymphenburg Palace, escorted his royal guests to their seats in the little chapel. Ex-King Alfonso of Spain was one of these guests, assembled in Munich to witness the marriage of twenty-two-year-old Princess Marie of Bavaria to the Pretender to the Throne of Brazil, Crown Prince Henry of Orleans Btaganza. Cardinal Faulhaber, resplendent in his robes, tied the royal knot. During his blessing, the saintly Archbishop could not refrain from stressing the sanctity of Christian marriage vows in a world where such sanctity was being "flagrantly violated by statesmen-biologists whose sole thought is to breed a race of physically superior Nordics." The royal wedding ceremony was performed only a few yards from the scene, two weeks previously, of Christian Weber's libidinous "Night of the Amazons."

There are countless examples of Nazi persecution of the Church in Munich. Many of them, such as the "sex trials" of monks, nuns, and priests, are too unsavory to mention. An idea of the sufferings endured by churchgoers may be gained from the words of the Cardinal himself, as quoted from my dispatch to the *Morning Post* on February 14, 1937: "Cardinal Faulhaber, doughty defender of the Catholic faith, delivered the most vigorous broadside against Nazi 'excesses' of his vigorous career here today. His catalogue of violations of the Concordat (Herr Hitler's 1933 treaty with the Pope) caused repeated angry exclamations in the huge Cathedral of St. Michael, filled to its capacity with a congregation of 8,000.

"Cardinal Faulhaber first revealed that one of his own sermons had been censored by local Nazi authorities last week. His remark that he had been treated 'like a schoolboy' roused the congregation to unanimous irritation.

"He then mentioned infractions of the Concordat which cover nearly every paragraph of the treaty: confiscation of pastoral letters; interference with communications between bishops; arrest and detainment of priests; confiscation of Church schools; sequestration of Church moneys and taxes; discharge of thousands of Catholic nuns and teachers; prohibition of the world-famous Corpus Christi procession; and 'the flood of calumniations against even the highest princes of the Church' in the Nazi press. Here he indirectly referred to the scurrilous charges made against himself and the Archbishop of Freiburg during the tumultuous struggle 'to end all Church schools' in the January school elections.

"'The Concordat,' Cardinal Faulhaber drove home repeatedly, 'was signed as a free and voluntary treaty. Therefore, this is a treaty which cannot be simply torn up, without serious loss of honor.'

"He described the desperation of high Church officials as follows. 'Many say,' he declared, 'with the Concordat we shall lose our heads;

without it we shall be beheaded, drawn and quartered, and dragged through the streets. What is the difference?' He carefully pointed out Herr Hitler's friendly telegram to the Pope of last week as holding out hope of a reconciliation between 'the Fatherland and Mother Church.' But he emphasized the great loss of both State and Church if the Concordat should be renounced.

"'The greatest part of three years' work of reconstruction will crash in ruins,' he stated, 'if the Concordat is torn up by the State alone. It would be a severe shock to foreign nations now attempting to find confidence in the new Germany. Such an action would leave the shield and buckler of German honor—of which we speak so much these days—with a deep dent in it.'

"The special service was ceremoniously ended by the 8,000 members of the congregation swearing 'eternal fealty to the Church and adhesion to the Concordat so long as it lasts.' Cardinal Faulhaber was given a rousing ovation as he left the crowded church—despite his own expressed wish that no demonstration should be made."

The death of Pope Pius in 1939, instead of producing a lull, was the signal for renewed persecution. The Nazi-Roman Catholic controversy, which had been dormant in Bavaria since the beginning of the year, flared up suddenly in Munich the day that a High Mass for the late Pope was held in the cathedral. The Catholic Faculty of Theology at Munich University was closed by State decree the same afternoon on the order of the Reich Minister for Education, Herr Rust, and with the approval of the Church Minister, Herr Kerrl.

In the announcement of this drastic measure, it was claimed by the Nazis that Munich theological students had boycotted the lectures of a visiting professor of theology called to the Munich Chair by Herr Rust himself, and it was alleged that the boycott order came from the Catholic Ordinarius of Munich. No further explanation was given, except to state that the measure was made necessary by Catholic "interference with the freedom of science." This unexpected move coincided with the absence of Cardinal Faulhaber, who, was attending the Conclave at Rome.

That morning, in the greatest public display of Bavarian ex-royalty and aristocracy since 1933, 7,000 Roman Catholics, including practically all members of the House of Wittelsbach and the ex-Crown Prince Rupprecht, went to the Cathedral of Our Lady to attend High Mass. Although it was a working day, many laborers also went to the mass. But top hats and monocles were as much in evidence as uniforms were conspicuous by their absence.

Even the war, six months later, did not put a stop to the persecution of the loyal Bavarian Catholics. Oppressed not only by the Hitler regime, but also by the hardships of rationing and other wartime measures, to say nothing of the deaths of their sons, husbands, and brothers in the Führer's blitzkrieg campaigns, the Bavarians sought comfort through prayer in the many churches dotting the south-German landscape. Gathered together in worship, kneeling on the stone floors of these churches, the worshipers were interrupted by squads of Gestapo raiders bursting into the church. Often the entire congregation was herded roughly into trucks and driven to Gestapo headquarters for a grueling ordeal of questioning and intimidation. All because Heinrich Himmler's henchmen, not satisfied with tapping telephones, censoring domestic mail, spying, and denouncing, accused the Catholics of plotting revolution from the only remaining sanctuary in which they had still enjoyed the "right of assembly," the Church.

These Church arrests, incidentally, shed a new light on the murder of Storm Troop Leader Ernst Roehm by Hitler in the 1934 Blood Purge. Here is one explanation offered me by a staunch Bavarian Catholic, an ex-member of the Nazi party.

When Hitler was still in the vote-seeking stage of his double-crossing career, he promised Bavarians that he would remain true not only to the Bavarian Monarchy, but also to the Catholic Church. As proof, he even paraded his Storm Troopers past a reviewing stand occupied by Crown Prince Rupprecht and his followers in the Royal House. The same promises were made by the Führer's closest associate, Ernst Roehm. Despite his much-publicized failings, which Hitler concealed until he was ready to liquidate his Storm Troop Leader, Roehm was a loyal Catholic to the very end. His loyalty brought about his death. For, by keeping his faith, Roehm kept the support of Catholic Bavaria. Knowing the power of south-German Catholicism, Hitler was determined to break it and a possible separatist movement by killing Ernst Roehm. The persecution of the Catholics can be dated back to June 30, 1934. For the Führer knows only too well that the Bavarians will never forget his treachery to the Church.

Hitler's fears of a Catholic-Monarchist uprising in Bavaria also explain why his favorite Gauleiter, Adolf Wagner, is the Reich's foremost Catholic baiter. Not from his inner convictions: merely to prevent Hitler's playground from becoming the cradle of the Fourth Reich.

Protestant Pastor Niemoller,[5] the famous Nazi prisoner in Berlin, has a fellow sufferer in Munich. Niemoller was a submarine commander in World War One. For speaking the truth from the pulpit, he was clapped into jail by order of the Führer. In Catholic Bavaria, the most popular priest under Cardinal Faulhaber was Father Rupert Mayr, whose sermons in the Church of St. Michael did much to bolster the spirits of his flock. Angered at Mayr's courage, one-legged Nazi Boss Wagner peremptorily put this one-legged Catholic priest (Mayr lost his leg as a German officer in the First War) into a concentration camp. With their beloved priest taken from them, the Munich churchgoers spent night after night at St. Michael's, the Frauenkirche, and the other churches, praying for his safety. They even passed out typewritten slips of paper after every mass, containing the words "We pray every night for Father Mayr."

[5]*Friedrich Gustav Emil Martin Niemöller (1892–1984) was a Christian theologian and anti-Nazi activist. For his opposition, Niemöller was imprisoned in Sachsenhausen and Dachau concentration camps from 1937 to 1945. However, views of him today are mixed due to statements he made about the guilt of Jews, failure to protect them, and for his initial support of Hitler.*

I attended the mock trial of the priest, several months after he had been sent to prison. Forced to stand at attention (with the aid of his crutches), the pale martyr was ordered never again to ascend the pulpit. But, since his congregation still clamored for him, Gauleiter Wagner once more ordered his arrest. Thereafter, Nazi authorities refused to tell me where they had finally imprisoned Father Rupert Mayr.

Only one phase of Catholic life did Hitler's Gauleiter leave unmolested in his anti-Church, anti-confessional school drives. The best Bavarian liqueur is brewed by the monks of Cloister Ettal, near Garmisch; the best dark beer by the monks at Andechs Monastery, thirty miles from Munich. Hard-drinking Boss Wagner placed these and other monastery breweries under his personal protection! He sees to it that they obtain all of the necessary hops and other ingredients, despite war-time rationing.

While Cardinal Faulhaber was striving in vain to intercede for Father Rupert Mayr, on trial at the Munich Palace of Justice after an ordeal in Dachau Concentration Camp, and while other Munich priests were praying that they might be spared the fate of Father Mayr, candles were burning brightly in another Munich church. Hitler's own Bodyguard stood at attention near these candles, which shone on the bier of Abbot Albanus Schachleiter. The seventy-six-year-old abbot had joined the Nazi party in 1926. He had preached vigorous sermons to further the Nazi cause, praising Hitler as a "Savior." In 1933, the Pope revoked his consecration powers.

As Third Reich judges were passing their fatal sentence on Father Mayr, Gauleiter Wagner was stumping with bowed head in the procession behind Schachleiter's body to a State Funeral for the Nazi abbot—by special decree of Reich Chancellor Adolf Hitler.

Five months after he had ordered this State Funeral for his privileged abbot, the Führer entered the Catholic hospital in which General Erich Ludendorff lay dying. Glancing about the room, Hitler's eyes encountered a large Crucifix on the wall. His face turned livid.

"But Herr General," stormed the Führer, "how can you tolerate this perfidious cross in your sickroom? I shall order it to be removed from your sight at once!"

Raising himself with a great effort on his pillows, the grizzled war lord raised his voice against Hitler's.

"No!" exclaimed General Ludendorff. "The Crucifix shall remain! I have always strenuously fought Catholicism as a result of my personal convictions. But a mere Crucifix can do me no harm. And the nurses here are good nurses. I do not want to hurt their feelings."

A man of uncompromising principles, Ludendorff never joined Hitler's National Socialist party.

Cardinal Michael von Faulhaber is today a controversial figure. While he did raise opposition to the Nazis where it concerned the rights of the church, he also praised Hitler at times and instructed German priests to honor the state. Some of his statements on the Jews are also questioned, as he seems to have supported the Old Testament view of the Chosen People but did not concern himself with the Jews in German.

***

LUNCH WITH JULIUS STREICHER

"So you're a foreign correspondent!" grunted Julius Streicher, sticking his aggressive jaw within a few inches of my face. Hitler's hellfire-and-brimstone Jew baiter looked me over carefully, searching desperately for a Semitic trait in my features.

"You know," Streicher growled, "I've had bad luck with foreign journalists. Most of them are *Schweinehunde,* pig-dogs. And if you distort this interview, you're also a *Schweine-hund!"*

He paused. I laughed in his face.

"But you won't—You're too much of a Nordic for that," concluded the boss of the world's greatest race-hatred racket. Then he grinned and banged his silver-handled walking stick on the table so that the soup almost spilled into the lap of the German general sitting opposite me.

It was a hot Sunday noon in the summer of 1938. I had arrived in the picturesque little town of Dinkelsbühl in Franconia, some fifty miles from Streicher's Nuremberg stronghold, the previous evening, to get a feature story on the annual Nazi revivalist jamboree staged by the Number One showman of Third-Reich anti-Semitism on the Hesselberg, the "Holy Mountain" of Franconian Nazis.

I had left Munich Saturday noon in my first German car, an Opel roadster. Just before Augsburg—fortunately near a small railway station—my ersatz clutch started slipping in ersatz oil. So I left my car at the station and finished the trip by rail.

Hitler's trusty Jew baiter is the Gauleiter of Franconia in Northern Bavaria. He calls himself the "Franconian Führer." I had telephoned his adjutant that I would attend the ceremonies on the Hesselberg. The Nuremberg Nazis were highly pleased at having a representative of one of the world's greatest news agencies in their midst. I was treated like visiting royalty, the more so since I was the only foreign correspondent present at this rally of 200,000 paganized Jew haters. A director of *MAN*, Nuremberg's largest Diesel-engine factory, and naturally a "P.G." (Partei-Genosse—party comrade), drove me up the Hesselberg Saturday evening in his high-powered Mercedes.

The Hesselberg, a few miles from Dinkelsbühl, is a flat-topped, barren mountain. Streicher had pounced upon this landmark as the ideal spot to promote both anti-Semitism and the sale of his sordid newspaper, *Der Stürmer*. Every last week end in June, the Franconian Gauleiter exhorts his disciples to "follow him up to the top of the Holy Germanic Mountain," rain or moon-shine. At midnight, he preaches his first "sermon" by the light of a blazing bonfire. His bellowing voice, amplified a thousandfold by loudspeakers, booms across the Bavarian countryside. The boys and girls of the Hitler Youth organizations bring blankets. They spend the night bundling for Hitler. They awaken to the roaring of Streicher's own airplane squadron, which circles the mountain to announce the beginning of a morning of sport events on the Nazi Olympus. By early afternoon, more than 200,000 Germans have climbed the steep slopes of the Hesselberg to cheer themselves hoarse at Streicher's main address.

Some typical effusions from Streicher's "sermon on the mount" will illustrate his style of delivery. The Jew-baiting priest, wearing the Bavarian mountain costume of short leather trousers—forbidden to Jews in some parts of Germany—shouted:

"We need no men in black to make our confessions to. We have become our own priests, and get closer to God by climbing this mountain."

"We do not need the churches. God has always been with Germany, even hundreds of years before there were prophets or saints."

"I am in continuous contact with Jew haters all over the world, but I do not interfere in the internal affairs of the so-called democratic countries. If they don't realize the Jewish menace they will go to pieces on their own stupidity."

"All our sins were forgiven last night. The German youth on this mountain is much nearer to God than his Protestant or Roman Catholic parents were before Hitler came and united us. And the girls are beautiful with a godlike, natural beauty. Ugly girls and girls with lipstick or rouge should stay away from this holy mountain."

"Whoever recognizes the League of Nations has allied himself with the devil, and the devil is a Jew."

Streicher's bonfire sermon presented a weird contrast to the type of "fireside chat" with which all Americans are familiar. Except for the string of loudspeakers and the mass of brown uniforms that covered the mountaintop, the midnight ceremony on the Hesselberg might have taken place thousands of years ago. Indeed, Streicher reminded his audience that their holy mountain had been the scene of Germanic rituals long before Christianity.

The Teutonic high priest of anti-Semitism shouted to his followers with all the exhortations and long-windedness characteristic of primitive tribal chieftains. He painted the Jew in the most diabolical, lurid colors, as a terrifying black spirit that was responsible for all of the evils visited upon the German clan. I sat as inconspicuously as possible under a scrubby bush, taking notes with the help of a flashlight. Hitler Youths and Storm Troopers kept throwing pieces of wood from a huge pile of fuel on the flames, as Julius Streicher raved on ecstatically, telling them that all of their sins for the past year had been transferred to this wood and were being purified by the Germanic god of fire. The entire mob of Hesselberg pilgrims worked themselves into a pagan frenzy. Streicher spoke of the German war machine as of some supernatural magic, more powerful than any witchcraft of Germany's enemies, including the "hypocritical tomfoolery of organized Christianity."

With a final invocation to the great god Hitler, the Franconian rabble-rouser left his disciples to watch the glowing embers while he returned to his comfortable suite in the village to gather strength for the next day's powwow. I found my way back to the Mercedes, and was driven at breakneck speed to a tavern in Dinkelsbühl, where Storm-Troop captains attempted to flood me with drinks and questions about my reaction to their "wonderful ritual." I replied as tactfully as I could, bolstered in my attempt to show sincere appreciation by the fact that I really enjoy bonfires, picnics, and mountain climbing. But I was glad to get to sleep in a bed, rather than in the wholesale open-air flophouse of Hitler boys and girls on the bare rocks of a Nazi stamping ground. I suppose they were hardened—and preoccupied—enough not to mind the rainstorm that night. And if the adolescent couples felt a bit guilty about their unchaperoned bundling, they did not even need to confess their sins to a priest. They merely threw another stick on the fire to be purified from their carnal transgressions.

Most of the Franconian Führer's Nuremberg staff did not arise in time to attend the sport events Sunday morning. When I came down to breakfast in the little house where I had been quartered, I found myself seated next to two Germans dressed in Bavarian leather shorts. They were Streicher's deputy and his adjutant, but did not reveal their identity until they thought that they had sounded out my opinions about the bonfire revival meeting. I said all sorts of nice things about it. I like to see the childish pleasure that beams from a Nazi's face when you flatter him or his pet ideas.

I laid it on pretty thick, since I wanted an interview with the Franconian witch doctor. I told Hans Konig, Streicher's adjutant (who committed suicide six months later—Paragraph 175), all about the case of beer which Gauleiter Wagner had sent my grandfather, and how often I had been wined and dined by Adolf. There is little love lost between the northern and the southern Bavarian Gauleiters, who are jealous of Hitler's confidence in each of them. They are political rivals, with Wagner definitely the superior Gauleiter. I hinted that while I could see Wagner any time I cared to in Munich, it was a rare treat for this foreign correspondent to be so near to the great FrankenFührer. Konig scurried out to Streicher's hotel, and came back in fifteen minutes with an invitation for me to interview the Franconian fury as his luncheon guest.

At noon, I sat down with the editor of Streicher's daily *Frankische Tageszeitung* in the little beer garden in front of Julius's hotel, waiting for the Gauleiter.

"There he comes!" exclaimed the Nazi editor.

His bald head glistening in the sunlight, his barrel chest and hairy arms sticking out of an open white shirt, his knobby knees out of his leather panties, the notorious anti-Semite walked slowly down the little cobblestone street. A short, stocky man, Streicher still towered above the score of little kiddies whom he herded along like a kindly shepherd. He held one little girl by the hand. A little boy was riding on his "Uncle Streicher's" broad shoulders. It was a touching picture, staged to counteract the bloody reputation of the Tyrant of Nuremberg. But I could not help thinking about a wolf with twenty little Red Riding Hoods in tow. It would have been easy for any stranger to have shot Streicher with no danger of hitting the children. Yet Hitler's race expert knew that he was perfectly safe. For, if anyone had killed Streicher, the result would have been a ruthless massacre of Jews throughout the Reich and another Nazi would have carried on where he had left off.

Amid resounding "Heils," Streicher arrived at the hotel. He patted the kiddies' heads, then disappeared. When he came out again into the beer garden, he seated himself at the head of a long table. Konig introduced me. I was placed at Streicher's left, facing the general in command of the Nuremberg Army Corps.

After the blunt, rough-and-ready introductory remarks so characteristic of the "Aryan Crusader," Streicher told me to fire away with my questions while he wolfed his soup. He was in a jovial mood. Laughingly he denied all reports about his brutal persecutions. "I treat the Jews with an iron hand under a velvet glove," he boasted. I knew that this was a lie, since on other occasions he had boasted that he took great delight in personally whipping imprisoned Jews. But of course I did not contradict him, since that would have cost me the interview.

Most of our conversation was useless to me professionally. Some of Streicher's remarks were unprintable. To have quoted other statements would have meant my expulsion from the Reich.

"The trouble with Germany has always been that she is too honest," was one Streicher gem. "The reason the British are so successful is that they are the best liars in the world. But we'll learn. I know how hypocritical and deceitful the English are, for my son spent a year studying at a London college, and he told me how the British have perfected the fine art of lying."

"I suppose your son was learning how to lie for the Fatherland, Herr Gauleiter," I suggested. The Nazis certainly have surpassed their teachers!

After Streicher had repeated his phrases about "Jews are the source of all evil in this world; they are of no more benefit to humanity than leprosy; Germany can whip any nation in which Jews have a say in the government; it is fortunate for Germany to have lost the first world war, since anti-Semitism never develops in a victorious country," etc., I felt that I had enough material for the interview. So I decided to risk having a bit of fun with my host.

"The more I see of National Socialism, Herr Streicher," I remarked, "the less difference I see between Herr Hitler and Moses."

"What!" he exclaimed at this sacrilege.

"I said I think the Führer and Moses are very much alike."

"What do you mean by comparing our beloved Führer with that Jewish criminal?" he thundered.

"Well," I explained, "the Jews in Egyptian captivity were living on foreign fleshpots. After Germany lost the war, she was living on the fleshpots of foreign capital. Then along came the Führer, Moses, who said 'Let my people go'—from the Treaty of Versailles. Moses and Herr Hitler told their people to sever ties with alien peoples and follow him through the desert—of the Four Year Plan. Moses told his people that they must put aside their mates of another race to keep their blood pure. So did the Führer. As Moses led his people through the wilderness, manna rained from heaven. In the Third Reich, cut off from foreign raw materials, it rains Ersatz. Moses struck a rock, and water spurted forth. Hitler strikes German coal with Göring's wand, and from it gushes benzine. See what I mean?"

"*Donnerwetter! Ja,* you are right," Streicher burst out, slapping his thigh. "Moses also told his people not to worship strange gods and idols. And we National Socialists worship nobody but Hitler and the God who sent him to deliver us from bondage. We learned one thing from the Jews: what racial integrity means, and we are going to beat them at their own game. *Jawohl!*"

Despite all his oratory, Streicher had succeeded in stowing away an oversize pig's knuckle with plenty of potatoes and sauerkraut. In emulation of his Führer, however, he had not touched any beer or wine. Instead, the most brutal race bigot in the Third Reich drank a large glass of milk.

"*Nun,*" said gruff Julius, "I must hurry up to the Hesselberg. My adjutant will drive you up there. I was very glad to speak to such an Aryan-looking member of the international Jewish press. Too bad you aren't in the Führer's *Leibstandarte!*"

He shook my hand and left for his holy mountain. I left, to wash my hand.

The one road leading to the summit of the Hesselberg was festooned with banners screaming: "The Jews are our misfortune," "Read the *Stürmer,*" "The Devil is a Jew," "Fight the Jew—Buy a *Stürmer.*" Newsstands along the road sold Streicher's lurid, Jew-baiting *Stürmer* weekly and anti-Semitic books printed by his Stürmer Verlag publishing house in Nuremberg. Julius has made more money campaigning against Hebrews in Aryanized Germany than any high-pressure revivalist fighting the Devil in Christian countries.

I was given a seat a few feet away from the Franconian Führer, surrounded by uniforms of all descriptions. Streicher raved for three solid hours about the Hesselberg ritual, castigating the Church and praising the Nazi approach to godliness through the climbing of his holy mountain. I thought of Moses ascending Mt. Sinai alone to receive the Ten Commandments, and compared the simple Biblical account with Streicher's roaring up the Hesselberg in a grafted $10,000 Mercedes to harangue 200,000 pagan citizens of the Third Reich, blaspheme the Church, and praise the morality of the new, uninhibited German youth of today.

"A member of a great foreign news agency is with us this afternoon," Julius proudly announced to his flattered audience. "I spoke with him this noon as man to man. He has seen us purifying our souls in the Hesselberg fire. He has admired your clean-cut, strong and healthy appearance. I am sure that he is convinced that the Day of the Franconians has helped make us the most honest and moral people in the world!"

When I arrived at the station that evening to pick up my crippled Opel, I discovered that it had been stolen. Evidently the thieves had not climbed the Hesselberg to have their souls purified by Julius Streicher! Next day the police found my car, minus most accessories. It had been stolen by three young Franconians, disciples of Streicher's religion: pure Aryanism.

The war has curtailed the Gauleiter's activities slightly, since the Englishman now is Hitler's greatest enemy. But Streicher merely puts a Semitic twist on the face of John Bull in his publications, and continues to run his profitable hate-the-Hebrew business. There have been reports that the Franconian inquisitor has fallen from grace in the eyes of his hero, Adolf, that he has been imprisoned, muzzled, and, according to some rumors, shot. Knowing the fate of a former intimate of the Führer, Ernst Roehm, such reports seem plausible. But Roehm was a dangerous power in southern Germany, whereas Streicher has no ambitions in the way of reforming the Reich. He is content to run his anti-Semitic racket. The silence surrounding the FrankenFührer is due merely to the fact that he is now resting on his laurels. He has accomplished most of his main objectives: to kill, expel, or crush the Jews in the Third Reich, and to place them in ghettos wherever the first three alternatives are not used, and to convince Hitler that international Jewry was plotting the downfall of Nazi Germany. Now Adolf no longer needs to ferret out famous Hebrews in other lands as "warmongers," to be held up to the German people as frustrating Hitler's plans for a "peaceful new order." But he has no apparent reason to liquidate Streicher, whom he is saving—Julius hopes—to spread the Nazi gospel of anti-Semitism after the war wherever his armies may succeed in planting the Swastika flag.

The true strength of Streicher's position is his warm personal connection with Hitler. On Streicher's fiftieth birthday, Hitler publicly proclaimed this undying friendship. At a gala birthday party, the Führer ceremoniously declared: "In Streicher I have a comrade who I know has never wavered for a moment, and who at all times stands firm behind me."

Hitler's gratitude has a basis that is more than sentimental. If he is the father of the Nazi movement, Streicher may justly be labeled its first nurse. In 1922, Streicher's unvarnished, bellowing speeches against the Jews, the Catholics, the capitalists, foreigners, and all other discernible "exploiters of the German workers" had won him 3,500 voters and his own private party (the German Labor Brotherhood) in Nuremberg. When Hitler first started his own movement in Munich, Streicher unconditionally yielded his own organization to Hitler. At that time, the gain meant more to the struggling Führer than any later triumph.

Hitler was quick to turn Streicher's rare capacity as a rabble-rouser to account. In the abortive Munich Beer Putsch, stentorian Streicher was summoned from Nuremberg with the special assignment of "whipping up the masses in the Munich streets." It was not Julius's fault that the coup failed. He marched boldly and noisily in the front ranks of Hitler's Storm Troops into a withering fire from government troops massed in Munich's Odeon Platz. Ten minutes later he was still haranguing an astonished multitude from atop a monument in front of the Town Hall, two blocks away.

The imprisonment of Streicher and Hitler, side by side, for the next eighteen months in Landsberg Fortress firmly cemented their mutual friendship and admiration. Today Streicher honors Hitler not only in word, but even in gesture, diet, and haberdashery. Though himself so vigorous as to be almost a pugilist type, Streicher now drinks no alcohol and uses no tobacco—in public—for his Führer is an abstainer. Beneath his strongly beaked Roman nose lurks a tiny Hitler mustache. His hand habitually flourishes a light leather whip, such as the Führer constantly carried for self-defense in his pre-Chancellor days.

His personal press is no less crude than his notorious anti-Semitic propaganda. A front-page article of his own daily paper, the *Fränkische Tageszeitung,* declared: "Children on the street hasten to him, cuddle up to him, and trustingly gaze up with beaming eyes. The dishonest man avoids him and the traitor trembles before him.

For the upright German Streicher is the symbol of all the virtues of a fighting nation."

The Jew baiter's baby kissing serves a double purpose. Like his Hesselberg sermons, it is designed not only to increase his prestige as the leader, of Nazi Franconians, but also to swell the circulation of his Stürmer publications. For his Nuremberg publishing house prints a steady stream of anti-Semitic books to reach every available market, from schoolteachers and Nazi scientists to the countless kiddies in the large families of the Third Reich. As soon as a German child has learned to read, a Stürmer picture book is put in his little hands by Nazi schoolteachers. In this book, the price of which flows into Streicher's pocket, the Jew has taken the place of the goblin. A blond Nordic girl is the Streicher substitute for the traditional fairy princess.

Here is my literal translation of two illustrated nursery rhymes from Streicher's book, *Trust Not the Fox:*

The Race Shamer*

What a sorry fellow is the Kike:
His own race of women he just doesn't like.
He thinks it's clever as can be,
To steal himself a German "she."
But take a look at this Jew here;
With this blond girl he looks most queer!
Beside her, gracious, what a fright:
The Jew looks like an awful sight!
The Jew would do much better now,
To go back to his Jewish sow.
Hands off our German girls—and how!

The picture shows a fat, hook-nosed, and leering villain attempting to seduce an unreceptive blond maiden with a string of imitation pearls (footnote in original).

The Jewish Butcher†

The Hebrew, Isaac Blumenstine,
Earns money in the butcher line.
But take a closer look at him,
This fellow carving limb from limb:

Herr Isaac is a dirty boor;
He sells, not meat, but cheap manure.
One piece lies on the floor, A cat drags off some more.
The Jewish butcher thinks "That's great!"
For dirt on meat adds to its weight.
And—bear in mind—this blood-stained cheat
Won't have to eat his own foul meat.
How vile! Such filthy stew: The product of a Jew!
The moral of this little scene:
Trust not the fox on meadows green,
Nor Jew who swears his heart is clean!

†*A repulsive man with a dirty apron and a big cigar is shown at work in a filthy butcher shop (footnote in original).*

Publisher Streicher considers himself to be a great authority on religion. The famous Passion Plays in Oberammergau interest him greatly, because he claims that Christ was an Aryan who was "murdered by the Jews." Oberammergau's scenic beauty also appeals to the Jew baiter, who spends some of his holidays painting water colors of the Alps near his own villa, not far from the historic Bavarian village. Julius often slipped down to southern Bavaria incognito, to avoid his public and relax from his unnatural pose as a teetotaler.

On one of these weekend binges, Streicher dropped into a secluded Oberammergau tavern. After several beers, he could not resist voicing his pet theories to a group of bearded natives. As usual, his speech became more and more violent, until he climaxed his tirade by swearing: "All Catholics are *Schweinehunde.*" In a body, the bearded Passion Play extras pounced on the Franconian Gauleiter and gave him a drubbing that might have killed him if he had not possessed the physique of a cave man.

Beards proved useful for more things than acting in passion plays. When Streicher regained consciousness, the tavern was empty. The Oberammergau police protested their inability to identify any of the Gauleiter's assailants. He was in rival Wagner's territory, not his own Gau. Julius limped out of town in furious disgrace. A few days later his Nuremberg newspaper announced: "The Franconians' beloved Gauleiter is resting comfortably in a sanatorium, recovering from an operation for a leg injury sustained in the too vigorous pursuit of a strenuous sport by our youthful, fifty-two-year-old FrankenFührer."

If it is possible to classify Nazi Gauleiters according to their lack of virtues, I would place Julius Streicher at the head of the list. Streicher proclaims that "The Devil is a Jew." If this were true, I am convinced that when Hitler's supreme inquisitor lies on his deathbed, Satan will pack his Infernal Scepter in a hurry, and clear out before Julius arrives with his whip to take over Mephisto's throne.

***

NON-ARYANS

According to Propaganda Minister Goebbels and Reich Photographer Heinrich Hoffmann, Hitler loves German kiddies. Countless pictures and descriptions have been published in the Nazi press, showing the Führer embracing blond children, accepting bouquets from miniature Nordics, and, to use an actual paraphrase from the Third Reich press, "suffering little children to come unto him."

To supply the German magazines and newspapers with a steady stream of baby-kissing propaganda, Hitler poses frequently with German boys and girls. One sunny afternoon, on a drive along the foothills of the Alps from Berchtesgaden to Munich, the Führer wished to relax in the meadows above a Bavarian summer resort. Hoffmann sized up the situation as ideal for taking pictures of the Reich's Supreme Child Fancier. So a dozen SS Bodyguards were detailed from the Führer's entourage to round up suitable young Nordic material.

The Bodyguards invaded the town, collecting a score of youngsters from their playgrounds. The SS men told the children's relatives or nursemaids that they could call for their charges at five P.M. on Hitler's meadow.

"You are highly honored to have the Führer wish to see your children," they were reminded, if they hesitated.

Hitler and the kiddies spent a busy hour posing for photographer Hoffmann. Toward five o'clock Adolf was photogenically playing "horse" with a little blond girl riding on his knee. Across the meadow walked a dark, curly-haired boy. Timidly, and as obviously ill at ease as he was non-Aryan, the lad approached the Führer group.

"What are you doing here, you pig-dog Jewish brat?" snarled two SS Bodyguards.

Hitler's knee stopped rocking as he became aware of the interruption.

"I came to get my kid sister, please."

"What the hell! Where is your sow-Jew sister?"

"There, on the Führer's knee!"

Hitler, flabbergasted, dropped the blond child like a live coal. The dark-haired boy grabbed her arm and fled, followed by the, curses of Hitler's Bodyguards. The picture-taking picnic ended in confusion. Biological laws of race and heredity sometimes play queer tricks on the Nazis.

The German Museum in Munich for decades has enjoyed an international reputation among engineers and scientists as a remarkable institution. It houses fascinating models and exhibits of every branch of science, from steam engines to astronomy. It includes a large library and also several lecture halls and auditoriums for scientific meetings. The German Museum was founded by Oscar von Miller, whose antecedents were not all Aryans.

In November, 1937, the Nazis took over the German Museum to inaugurate a gigantic exhibition "for the education of German citizens." This exhibition was entitled "The Eternal Jew." A thirty-foot-high, yellow and black picture of Shylock was prominently displayed on the outside of the building to advertise the show.

Where schoolchildren as well as adults had once flocked to study the operation of internal combustion engines, X-ray machines, mining, or aviation, they now beheld displays such as "Jewish ritual knives used for circumcisions," "Talmud torture instruments for the killing of Gentiles," "Moving pictures of Kosher butchers massacring defenseless cattle," and a weird chamber of horrors, replete with seven-pronged candlesticks, blood-stained ceremonial robes, and a goodly number of skeletons. This room was described as "A true replica of the inside of a Masonic Temple."

By contrast with the accurate scientific exhibits of the German Museum, the displays in the "Eternal Jew" were so carelessly slapped together that they were often ludicrous. For example, Munichers scratched their heads when they read "Photostatic copies of the criminal records of Jewish concentration-camp inmates." Three records were shown, all with long lists of rape, murder, robbery, arson, and other crimes. Yet the clumsy exhibitors had failed to notice that the names of two of these three villains were "Adolf Hiller" and "Rudolf Hess"!

"Scientific" maps, diagrams, and charts, all claiming to illustrate "the sinister influences of Jewry throughout the world and throughout the centuries," supplemented the more graphic exhibits. Cracked, scratchy phonograph records of Richard Tauber's songs, Jehudi Menuhin's violin solos, and Toscanini's orchestras were played incessantly on slightly off-center turntables as illustrations of "degenerate Jewish music."

One hall was devoted to the showing of banned, pre-Hitler films. (It was difficult to find a seat here. Munichers flocked to the "Eternal Jew" movies, roaring with laughter at the antics of Jewish comedians whom they had missed on the screen since 1933.)

A section of one room was devoted to "that evil American Jew, Charles Chaplin." It included an oversize portrait of the American comedian. But the Nazi exhibitors had been very careful to eradicate every vestige of Chaplin's mustache! Mayor La Guardia, President Roosevelt, and Secretary Morgenthau shared honors with Disraeli in another Nazi "Rogues' Gallery of Notorious Jews."

It took me more than four hours to examine all the exhibits. Still under the influence of the plaster heads, photos and paintings of "typical Jews," I walked through the streets of Munich, suspiciously peering at every German face.

I could not seem to find an Aryan among them! I looked at a picture of the Number One Nazi Jew baiter, Julius Streicher. His facial and phrenological traits coincided perfectly with the pseudoscientific descriptions of non-Aryans presented in the exhibition "The Eternal Jew."

One year after the opening of the "Eternal Jew," the Nazis exploited the murder of Secretary vom Rath in the German Embassy at Paris by the young Polish Jew, Grynspan, to launch a far more violent campaign of anti-Semitism: the November 1938 Pogrom. Hitler, Goebbels, Streicher, and other Brown-Shirt leaders had just concluded their annual Old Guard celebration which commemorates the 1923 Putsch. At ten P.M. on the night of November 10th, Goebbels summoned Adolf Wagner and the local Storm-Troop leaders.

"Starting this minute," exclaimed Joseph, "the hunting season on Jews is officially opened. Go forth and see how much game you can bag!"

Goebbels' announcement was the signal for instant action. A complete list of Jewish-owned or -operated stores in Munich was already in the hands of the local party chiefs. Headquarters for the organized pillaging and window smashing were established in a centrally located Nazi stronghold—Hitler's night club, the Artists' House! Every half hour a squad of Storm Troopers would stomp into a hall of the Artists' House, brushing glass splinters from their uniforms and putting adhesive tape on cut hands and fingers.

"Orders executed!" they reported triumphantly. Their pockets were bulging with rings, bracelets, silverware, and other spoils of their midnight frolic. They would gulp several drinks, then dash out to smash Jewish stores in some other street. The festival of destruction lasted all night. Fires broke out in several of the ruined shops from short-circuited window-lighting fixtures. The entire Munich fire department was out in the streets. The firemen extinguished the flames, then stood by idly, grinning as they watched the looters snatching furs, radios, earrings, shoes, jewelry, or whatever else they could lay hands on for themselves or their girlfriends.

I rushed stories of the opening scenes of the Pogrom to London, then returned to the business section of town to collect further evidence for the next day's dispatches. Finally policemen were posted in front of the cavernous, debris-littered shops to prevent further pillaging. But one could still hear the crashing of plate glass and the jubilant shouts of Storm Troopers around as yet unpatrolled corners. By six o'clock in the morning, the streets were filled with brown-uniformed vandals. All were drunk, cut and bleeding, but bubbling over with a primitive happiness—and much richer than they had been before Goebbels had fired the starting gun.

A terrific fight took place in front of one large Munich store. The battle was waged between brown-uniformed Storm Troopers and the black-uniformed SS Guards. The store specialized in oriental rugs, valuable tapestries, vases, and other antiques. Its owner was Herr Bernheimer—the only "Honor-Aryan" in Munich. Field Marshal Hermann Göring had placed this Jewish dealer under his personal protection, since Bernheimer supplied him with luxurious furnishings for his Karinhal estate. The Storm Troopers had just smashed a window of the Bernheimer store, shattered one beautiful vase, and slit a gobelin tapestry with their "Daggers of Honor" (part of their standard equipment), when a group of SS Göring Bodyguards appeared. They made straight for the looters. One Storm Trooper was killed, several were hospitalized, and a few of the black uniforms injured. SS Guards can be just as ruthless in protecting Göring's Jewish property as they are in torturing Jewish inmates of Dachau Concentration Camp.

While city employees were sweeping up all the broken glass they could find the next day, dumping it into refuse trucks, the Gestapo was equally active in scouring Munich for its entire male Jewish population (about 3,000), which was unceremoniously dumped into concentration camp. While Storm Troopers were nursing the superficial cuts which they had received from too eager window breaking, Jews in the party capital turned on the gas, cut their throats, or jumped out of their windows. Pillaging gave way to sequestration. Trios composed of one member of the Gestapo, one member of Adolf Wagner's Bavarian party organization, and one member of the municipal "Chamber of Culture" toured the city in cars followed by moving vans. The trios entered Jewish homes, examining all private property. Any valuable painting, piece of silverware, rug, or piece of furniture was summarily confiscated, loaded into the vans, and taken to the cellars of Munich museums and art galleries "to be preserved for German citizens."

The Pogrom continued for several weeks. Some Jewish friends of mine, including a former professor at Munich University, wandered around in the mountains, or hid along the banks of the Isar, begging food from sympathetic peasants. Many appealed to foreign correspondents and consuls for help. There was little I could do except store some of their valuables, but some of my consular friends housed a few Jews in their own homes—until the Gestapo knocked at the door and took them away.

The Jewish Old Women's Home on the Kaulbach Strasse was raided. The Brown Shirts confiscated the bedding and pitiful belongings of women from fifty to ninety years of age, then turned them out of the house to seek refuge wherever they could among the private Jewish homes.

I heard many authentic reports of men beaten to death by raiding Storm Troopers. In one case, the Nazis entered a Jewish home, to find the lady of the house in tears. They ransacked the living room, then made for the door to the bedroom.

"Please don't go in there," begged the sobbing woman. "My husband is in bed. He is very ill."

"Don't lie to us. Out of our way," snapped the biggest Trooper, bursting in the door. A form, covered with blankets, was lying on the bed.

"Hey, you, you pig-Jew, get the hell out of there!" barked the Nazi, kicking the prostrate figure as hard as he could with his heavy boots.

No response.

The Storm Trooper yanked back the blankets.

The Jew was dead.

After Nazi rage had spent itself in several weeks of Jew baiting, some of the male Pogrom victims were allowed to return to Munich from Dachau Concentration Camp. Shaved heads made their daily appearances at the British and American Consulates. But the shorn Jewish men were not permitted to leave Dachau if their wounds were still visible. Nor did all of them go from the concentration camp to visa-granting consulates. I counted an average of seven fresh graves daily in Munich's Jewish Cemetery two months after the beginning of the Pogrom.

Hitler's anti-Semitism has been horrifying the civilized world ever since the Nazis came to power. Foreign correspondents have sent many dispatches out of the Reich on this subject. But there were some stories that I had to keep secret until now.

An Italian Jew living in Munich was a member of the Fascist party—not by choice, but of necessity. When Hitler staged a grand parade of his army and party formations for his guest, Benito Mussolini, in the Bavarian capital, this Italian—because he was the tallest Fascist in Munich—was ordered to command the group of local Black Shirts who greeted the Duce and helped him review the parade. The entire procession was headed by none other than Streicher, who saluted as he passed the reviewing stands. Thus Julius unwittingly paid tribute to his sworn enemy by marching past a Jewish captain!

A certain German woman, wealthy and the wearer of Hitler's "Golden Party Button," which is awarded only to the most deserving Nazis, was in Vienna, where the Pogrom also raged. This woman had helped Hitler with her home and money at the beginning of his party career. She was still a close associate of the Führer, and so ardent a Nazi that she even refused to greet me, a foreign correspondent, with anything except a grim "Heil Hitler." Yet this same Führer-sponsor, seventy years old, stormed through Vienna, scolding and slapping the faces—not of Jews—but of fifteen-year-old Hitler Youth vandals who were pillaging Jewish homes. Secretly, by the most devious routes, this bearer of the Golden Party Button also sent packages of food and clothing to destitute Austrian Jews. But she dared not ask Hitler to stop the Pogrom.

Nazi ideology and the doctrines of Nordic purity are hammered into the minds of all German boys and girls. "Race-shaming" is a cardinal sin in the Third Reich. For a German girl to have an affair with a Jew is as heinous a crime as it is praiseworthy of her to bear Aryan children. But young Nazis do not always interpret their lessons accurately.

Dressed in a smart Fascist uniform, and driving an expensive Italian car, a Black-Shirt officer picked up a blond, twenty-year-old leader of the "League of German Girls," the female counterpart of the Hitler Youth. He was returning from a reception for Italian war veterans in the Munich Town Hall. A lively conversation followed. The German girl leader was enthusiastic about her career in National Socialism. She also praised the Rome-Berlin Axis.

"We Fascist and Nazi women know that our men are far too busy working for the good of the party and the Axis to court us with idle compliments, flowers, presents, and the other decadent methods of wooing prevalent in the pluto-democracies," she volunteered to her new Italian friend. "We are simply here to serve our men in whatever way they think best. We are no false hypocrites or prudes."

Taking the hint, the dark-haired Fascist drove to his apartment. Nature, unimpeded by any artificiality, took its course.

"It is the will of the Führer and of the Duce," the blond girl exclaimed, as she climbed back into her girl leader's uniform.

Fascinated by the eight-cylinder Fiat, the dark eyes, the snappy Fascist uniform, and the bright future of the Axis, the Nordic blonde had completely forgotten that some Italians are Jews. Now her child is a constant reminder.

My landlord Fritz volunteered in the First World War. At first, like Hitler, he was a messenger. Then, like Göring, an aviator. Fritz was finally shot down, but managed to drift back to earth. A machine-gun bullet had plowed through his right forearm, permanently crippling his middle finger. But, after seeing more active service than most Nazis, Fritz managed to establish his medical practice in Munich after the war, and refused to forsake his beloved Bavaria even after the advent of the Third Reich.

Fritz was the only non-Aryan member of the household. His wife and stepchildren each had Aryan parents and grand-parents, so were officially "Germans." Fritz's parents were Jews, therefore—by Nazi decree—only Jews and foreigners were permitted to rent rooms in his house. But Fritz was more Aryan in appearance than Goebbels or Streicher. When we went skiing together, be was constantly being embarrassed by Nazis who ranted against the Jews in his presence, and even asked him what he thought of "the swine."

Despite Hitler's repeated assurances that Jewish war veterans could continue their professions unmolested, the Herr Doktor's practice was filched from him until he was treating only the poorest members of the working class, whom party doctors spurned as unprofitable patients. Only the rent and his savings kept the household together.

Munich's fanatic drive against Jewish physicians produced, timing other things, placards that covered the walls of the city's Compulsory Sickness Insurance offices. Every worker is required to call at these offices in order to receive permission for medical treatment. The placards, four feet square, read as follows:

Remember you are a German!The Jews are our misfortune!You betray your people if you go to a Jewish physician!German women, you dishonor your people when you entrust your body to a Jewish doctor!

In 1932, Fritz had a large practice and drove a respectable automobile. In 1937, he was reduced to pedaling thirty miles daily, winter and summer, on an antiquated lady's bicycle to make the rounds of a few sick patients in the poorest sections of town.

Came November. A special edition of Streicher's *Stürmer,* posted on every prominent street corner, castigated Jewish doctors and brought threats of impending Reich action to wipe out the non-Aryan medical profession. Simultaneously, announcements of the exhibition, "The Eternal Jew," were plastered all over the city. And, as the last straw, the annual celebration of Hitler's 1923 Putsch was due, with promises of more persecution and forecasts of more severe measures against Jews and their families for the next year.

On November 4th I said "Hello" to Fritz as I returned to the house for a moment to examine my noon mail. His family were out for the day. When Frau Doktor came back in the evening, she could not find Fritz, so, fearing the usual fate of Munich Jews, she went to Gestapo Headquarters to see whether her husband had been arrested. The Gestapo knew nothing, but kept her several hours for an investigation.

As I drove up to the house again after dark, a policeman was standing at the door.

"What do you want here?" he asked.

Pale and trembling, Fritz's stepson came to the door. "Herr Pope lives here, let him in, Officer," he said, then blurted out: "Ernie, I found Fritz!"

"Where is he?"

"Down in the cellar."

I hurried down the stone steps. At first I did not see him. Then, in the room where we kept our skis, I discovered Fritz. He was slumped down against my skis, a bullet hole in his left temple. His automatic lay in a pool of blood near his good hand.

We managed to intercept Frau Doktor before she reached the house, and got friends to take care of her for the night. I helped the coroner carry Fritz to the ambulance that took him to the City Morgue.

The next three days I used all my influence in obtaining permission to have Fritz buried in the municipal North Cemetery. I finally succeeded, after much red tape, entreating, and wire pulling.

But Fritz's wedding ring was gold. That was too valuable to the Reich to be buried with him. But at last that special permit was also obtained. To make sure, I put the ring back on Fritz's finger myself, just before the cemetery attendants placed him in his coffin.

Fritz was loved and respected by all his neighbors, friends, and patients in our section of Munich. So when he was buried, the Gestapo took photographs of one of the largest crowds that ever attended a funeral in the North Cemetery. The four municipal cemetery guards performed their routine duties, stolidly, like automatons. When they had lowered the casket into the freshly dug grave, they stood for a moment at attention. Over Fritz's body, the guards stretched out their right arms—in the Hitler salute!

***

THE BROWN-SHIRT PRESS

When Hitler flew through the night to Munich to murder his trusty Storm Troop Leader, Ernst Roehm, and to direct the rest of the Blood Purge of June 30, 1934, the international spotlight again was focused on the cradle of National Socialism. The installation of the Nazi regime at Berlin during the previous year had brought about a temporary eclipse of Munich as a news center. After organizing his party in the Bavarian capital, and attempting to seize power there in 1923, the Führer finally waged a successful political blitzkrieg on the Prussian capital of the Reich, which ended with the surrender of the German Republic to the Nazis on January 30, 1933. Devoting all his energy to launching his new regime at Berlin, Hitler neglected Munich—until the night of June 30, 1934.

The Blood Purge marks the revival of the party capital as a source of Third Reich news. After this fateful night, during which hundreds of unsuspecting Nazi followers were slaughtered by order of their Führer, Hitler began to spend an increasing amount of time in Bavaria. He expanded his mountain retreat at Berchtesgaden, transforming it into a second Reich Chancellery, from which he could control his government without any lengthy stays in ugly Berlin.

With the Führer redirecting his activities to southern Germany, foreign correspondents began to migrate to Munich. At first they were lone wolves, snatching bits of news as best they could, but at the mercy of the pack of watchdogs that guarded the Brown House and other Nazi strongholds. It was not until the initiative of an American journalist finally rallied these correspondents into an organized group that the foreign press could cope successfully with all the problems imposed on them by uncivil Nazi officialdom.

This wide-awake American was Charles E. Hewitt Jr., who left the Berlin office of the Chicago *Daily News* in September, 1934, to organize the Munich Reuters Bureau. Charlie became acquainted with the heterogeneous group of foreign correspondents who made the daily rounds of the Nazi press offices. Some were seasoned reporters who could tell the difference between brown and white.

Others were young Turks, Brazilians, Rumanians, or Hindus, who not infrequently became the dupes of Nazi propaganda in their attempts to supply their home papers. A few, like the Bulgarian reporter, Keyhayeff, deliberately passed on Goebbels' propaganda as "news." Charlie, assisted by my predecessor, Ralph Hartell, rounded up the entire group, and founded the first Foreign Press Club in Munich. To impress officialdom, it was called *"Die Arbeitsgemeinschaft der ausländischen Journalisten in Munchen."* (The Co-operative Society of Foreign Journalists in Munich.)

Our club created a standard press card, which gave us official recognition in the Reich. We numbered approximately thirty members, with Charlie as president. Our club was the only democratic institution still functioning in Munich with official Nazi sanction. It presented a united front to the Swastika, increasing our bargaining power in obtaining permission to attend party functions, acquiring press facilities and other privileges that are taken for granted by reporters in democratic countries. Our organization helped remove some of the friction with the local press chiefs, and also provided each of us with a greater feeling of security, since the arrest of one of our number could not escape the attention of the others.

By protesting in a body, we succeeded in improving the treatment previously given to foreign correspondents in Hitler's Munich. At our weekly luncheons and evening meetings, we were able to exchange valuable rumors, tips, and information. Moreover, the foreign press club provided an oasis of welcome social intercourse in the grim desert of our goose-stepping hosts. It helped us to remember that there were still many free countries beyond the Nazi horizon that marked the limits of our professional life. When we reserved a dining room and bowling alley at one of the numerous little inns around Munich, we could relax and forget for the moment that we were marooned in a totalitarian state.

Charlie and I combined forces to cover southern Germany and Munich for Reuters news agency and for the London newspapers, *Daily Express* and *Morning Post,* which was later merged with the *Daily Telegraph.* In our spare time we explored new ski trails in the

Alps. Early in 1937, Charlie packed his bags, strapped his trusty hickory skis firmly together, and turned his back on the Führer's territory for a triumphal return to God's Own Country, leaving me in sole charge of the three-ring circus we had been handling for the British public.

At the top of the list of my colleagues, in length of service, experience, and journalistic importance were Stanley and Hedy Simpson, a delightful young English couple who had come to Munich when Hitler still was only too eager to grant an interview to a foreign correspondent for the sake of publicity for his little-known National Socialist party. Stan represented the New York and London *Times.* Hedy, small but extremely efficient, fed news to four big interests (The London *Daily Mail,* the *News Chronicle,* the Associated Press, and the Exchange-Telegraph), and food to her four small children.

When the Duke and Duchess of Windsor were vacationing in Austria before their marriage—and before the Anschluss—Hedy climbed into her little four-cylinder Opel and drove down to the White Horse Inn for a story. The frontier guard stopped her for the customary examination.

"May I see your passport, please?" he asked.

Hedy handed it over, the passport of "Mrs. Simpson."

"Pass, Your Royal Highness!" the awed guard exclaimed, bowing deeply and then saluting with all the eloquence his primitive Alpine training could muster.

One evening, while Stan was out on an important assignment, Hedy was 'phoning a long story to London. In the middle of it she suddenly broke off:

"Must stop now; will call you back later with the rest of the story," she told the stenographer at the other end of the trunk line. Half an hour later, she called her London office and gave them the rest of her report.

"Why did you cut off?" she was asked when she had finished dictating.

"Oh, I have just given birth to a baby girl!" she replied. Hedy had asked the nurse to plug in her telephone next to her maternity bed to enable her to send the story. This incident characterizes the spirit of foreign correspondent Mrs. Hedy Simpson, who took the last peacetime train out of Germany to dodge Nazi bombs in London with her husband while serving their country via the short waves of the British Broadcasting Corporation.

In addition to his wife and his writing ability, Stan had two important assets for a Munich correspondent's job. One was a liquid capacity equal to that of the hard-drinking Nazi officials. The other was a long list of reliable sources, which he managed to keep secret with the true British trait of pokerfaced reserve. When the three of us combined forces on a big piece of news, or shared a story that one of us had discovered independently, there was very little happening in Hitler's haunts that escaped our attention.

My Italian colleague, Dr. Emiliano Enenkel, a staff member of the Italian Consulate-General in Munich, held—and probably still holds—the post of correspondent at the capital of the National Socialist movement for the official Italian news agency, *Stefani*. The Doctor is the exception that proves the rule when it comes to describing a Fascist. Emiliano was one of the most pleasant colleagues with whom a foreign correspondent could co-operate or compete.

Dr. Enenkel would stretch to the limit the bonds imposed upon him by his position in the Axis, in order to give me news made available to him by virtue of this position. When non-Axis correspondents failed to get satisfaction from Reich Press Chief Dietrich or other Nazi contacts, my Italian colleague very often succeeded in persuading them to confide in him. Then he would contrive to drop a hint that I was not slow to pick up. If the news was intended exclusively for Italian consumption, I had recourse to the vacant telephone booth adjoining the one in which the Doctor was shouting his story into the receiver for the Fascist stenographer in Rome.

I also made occasional use of the British Fascist, Phillip Spranklin, Munich correspondent for Sir Oswald Mosley's Fascist newspaper,

Action, a close friend of Unity Mitford's, and wearer of Heinrich Himmler's SS badge for privileged Nazi sympathizers from abroad. In return for lucre or liquor, Spranklin would lift the veil of Unity's love life with Hitler, or other goings-on within the walls of inaccessible Nazidom. Young and boastful, Phillip enjoyed proving how close he stood to the Nazi leaders.

In his endeavors to obtain news, the Munich correspondent must deal with a wide variety of sources and officials. Besides the effusions of the Nazi press, there are numerous "press chiefs" to contend with, from Hitler's publicity agent, Reich Press Chief Dr. Otto Dietrich, all the way down to the press chief of the local Hitler Youth organization. All prominent Brown Shirts and all the subdivisions of the complex Nazi machine have their own press agents. The foreign correspondent must learn how and when to approach them without wasting more time than he can avoid in the bureaucratic Third Reich. Each chief is a little dictator, jealous of the others and not very eager to serve the needs of the democratic press.

When Joseph Goebbels built his Berlin Propaganda Ministry on the Wilhelmstrasse, he also established a branch office in Munich. With symbolic consistency, the club-footed dictator of German public opinion enthroned a crippled running mate in the luxurious Bavarian propaganda bureau. His name is Adolf Dresler; the main difference between him and his senior partner is that, while Goebbels cannot wiggle the toes of his left foot because he was born that way, Dresler cannot wiggle the fingers of his right hand because an Allied projectile tore off the tendons of his forearm in World War One. Thanks to his subordinate position and to a more honorable deformity, Adolf Dresler is the lesser of the two evils. But he is still the most powerful Nazi press official in the southern half of the Third Reich.

Adolf Dresler is directly responsible to Goebbels as the boss of the Nazi propaganda machine in Bavaria. Like his Prussian master, Dresler organizes press conferences, arranges inspection trips and excursions for German and foreign correspondents, signs the press cards accrediting reporters to southern Germany, and issues releases that are usually published faithfully by my German colleagues and consigned to the wastebasket by the foreign correspondents looking for news.

Dresler suffers from an inferiority complex. He has been compelled to serve two bosses. In the Reich he is known as "Goebbels' Slave," and in Munich society as "Frau Dresler's Husband." He is anything but a Siegfried, whereas Frau Ciska Dresler is a buck-toothed Brunhilde. Paradoxical as it may seem, Adolf Dresler is the "Caspar Milquetoast" among Nazi dictators. His numerous speeches on the "fighting spirit of heroic Nazidom" are delivered in the anemic voice of a henpecked husband who spends an agonized life under the dual shadow of a concentration camp and a rolling pin. Despite these handicaps, Little Adolf occasionally manages to imitate the private life of his Berlin chief and have some extra-marital fun. I know, because I got the goods on him several times, but promised not to tell Ciska.

Once, for example, I was deep down in the cellars of the Deutsches Theater, restoking my metabolic furnace with sausage and beer around four A.M. of Christian Weber's carnal carnival party. I had seen Ciska leave the festivities in the billowing wave of a mink-and-ermine coat. Sipping the beer and waging a private blitzkrieg on the *Weisswurst,* I gazed about at the Nazi bacchanalia described in a previous chapter. The voice of a man with his back turned seemed familiar. On his lap were a blonde and a brunette. His stooped shoulders were even more suspicious. Sure enough, it was none other than Milquetoast Dresler himself, exploiting his wife's early departure to indulge in a bit of much-needed variety. As hush money for his escapade, the Bavarian press dictator bought me another beer and transferred the brunette to my own lap. Thus is a *modus vivendi* between foreign correspondent and Nazi official attained in the playground of the party.

Goebbels' flunkey figured out other methods of circumventing the onerous regimentation of his professional and home lives. One method was to arrange press trips to Bavarian breweries outside Munich, thus maintaining an official and educational character while providing Dresler and the underpaid German reporters with an excuse for a stag party at the expense of the Reich. Another escape mechanism employed by Little Adolf centered around raft trips on the Isar River. These annual cruises, to my knowledge, were the only effective good-will tours ever instituted by any branch of the Nazi fleet.

Timber from the wooded Alps is floated to Bavarian sawmills on the numerous streams that cross this region on their way into the Danube. One of these major tributaries, the Isar River, traverses Munich, for which lumbermen and fold-boat fans are grateful. Rustic Bavarian axmen pilot the rafts through the shoals and down the sluices of the Isar, only too glad to make some extra cash by taking passengers. The National Socialist Press Raft is the flagship of this tree-trunk fleet.

At five A.M., Dresler and his two chubby deputies, brothers Fritz ("Tweedle-Dum") and Eugene ("Tweedle-Dee") Meier, welcomed two score Munich correspondents of the domestic and foreign varieties at the Munich railway station, ready to take the early morning train to Bad Tölz. The little resort town of Tölz lies on the Isar River at no great distance from the 1936 Winter-Olympic town of Garmisch. Dresler had made arrangements for a special car, hitched to the regular train. As we puffed out of the station in this car, a Bavarian brass band hired by the propaganda chief struck up a tune to start the day off in the proper atmosphere. The female reporters were in great demand for waltzes in our special coach as we lurched to our destination, two hours from Munich on a branch line.

On one of these excursions, our car was identified by two red flags bearing the name of the travel bureau through which Dresler had arranged the trip. Alighting at Tölz, with the brass band heralding our arrival by heading our procession through the streets to the river, my Danish colleague, Franz Willemoes, grabbed the flags and executed a sham goose step in front of the band, much to the embarrassment of Dresler and the surprise of the rudely awakened burghers of Raz, who stuck their faces out of their bedroom windows and scratched their heads at the sight of red flags devoid of Swastikas being borne proudly down the streets of the Third Reich.

Before boarding the raft, of course, we turned in at a beer garden for a breakfast of sausages and Tölz's native brew. With this additional ballast stowed away, we then resumed our triumphal march to the water's edge, where a huge raft had been warped to the shore of the swirling water. For Dresler's honored guests, the logs had been covered with planks. A railing had been added, to keep several kegs of beer —and their prospective consumers—from rolling overboard. And at the stern of the flagship, a carefully camouflaged rustic institution dispelled the fears of the thirsty passengers that the long voyage ahead of us would present a serious problem to their modesty. To the Teutonic equivalent of "Anchors Aweigh" as rendered by the brass band, the raft was poled into midstream, and shot Munichward under bridges lined with the cheering populace of Tölz.

The 1937 Nazi raft trip was my first experience with dive-bombing Stukas. As we floated serenely on the green waters of the Isar, two representatives of the *Luftwaffe* roared over our heads. They escorted us for thirty minutes, zooming out of the sky directly at our craft, then looping up again at the last moment, fortunately without dropping any bombs. Even a raft provided a practice target for training death-dealing Nazi pilots. Not even on this sunny Sunday morning excursion in scenic prewar Bavaria could one escape the prophetic signs of Hitler's war, as heralded by these mechanized birds!

After shooting down the sluices of several dams along the Isar, holding tight to our mugs and kegs, we tied up near a monastery for a fish fry. We also restocked our supplies from the monastery's cellars and cast loose once more. Sunburned and as tired as if we had been on a serious assignment, we finally left the raft and brass band near Munich's Isar swimming hole, the Germans to write glowing accounts of the trip, with high praises for Adolf Dresler, the foreign correspondents to rush to their offices to find out whether Hitler had pulled any fast ones on us while we were at sea.

Goebbels' Munich propaganda office has some queer ideas about press trips. I did not mind exploring breweries or rivers. But I refused to be herded into a bus with my sheepish German colleagues for a long and tiresome drive to Nuremberg, merely to watch steam shovels excavating ground for another marble party building. The Munich newspapers published enthusiastic reports the next day regarding the number of cubic meters of dirt moved for a Nazi stadium. This information was of no more interest to London than Dresler's inspection tours of Bavarian tree nurseries. I did permit myself to be driven out to the Bavaria Film Studios a few miles outside of Munich. There I could see German actresses and Benjamino Gigli sweating under the spotlights for a new Italo-German film. Gigli sighed as he told me that he would rather be singing at the Metropolitan again, but had sold his soul to the Axis.

When pressure from Berlin or from Ciska kept Dresler anchored in Munich, he would delegate his powers as guide through Bavaria to one or both of the Meier brothers. These boys lived a soft life, thanks to their participation in Hitler's 1923 Putsch. Close associates of the Führer, they would sometimes give me whatever information they could about him without risking their well-padded necks. Admitted to the innermost circles of Hitler's anniversary beer-hall parties for his Old Guard Nazis, Tweedle-Dum and Tweedle-Dee supplied me with much local color on the secret rituals from which foreign correspondents were invariably excluded. Beer is a wonderful lubricant!

Through Adolf Dresler, the Munich branch of the Propaganda Ministry performed another function, of equal importance to that of chaperoning the south German press: it serviced the Rome-Berlin Axis. During the critical days leading up to the Italo-German military alliance, Dresler, a personal friend of Il Duce and Count Ciano, contributed much toward the Axis in his Milquetoast way, while carefully avoiding the international spotlight focused on the meetings of Hitler and Goebbels with their Fascist partners.

The Axis began as a nonmilitary union of the Fascist-Nazi ideologies. Munich was the birthplace of National Socialism; Mussolini's first trip to Germany took him to Munich as a stone mason long before the Third Reich had come into its own. Consequently, Munich's propagandist Dresler was the logical go-between for the German and Italian governments. Half a dozen times annually, Dresler has taken flying trips to Italy, sometimes to see Mussolini privately, sometimes to guide his Bavarian scriveners and return to praise the southern neighbor in the Nazi newspapers. When Benito paid his first visit to the Third Reich, in September, 1937, he headed straight for Munich. It was *Reichshauptamtsleiter* Witherfingers who supervised the Duce's publicity and informed the Germans that their guest had once earned his living by building houses in the capital of the Nazi movement.

Whenever the steadily increasing delegations of Italians—blackshirt war veterans, *dopo lavoro* workers, athletes, economists, and students—came to the Reich, their first and last port of call was Munich and Adolf Dresler. Dresler was the official who supplied me with ringside tickets for the triumphal entries, stays, and departures of Mussolini, Ciano, and their ilk in the years 1937-1940, including the fateful Munich conference. When Hitler thought it inopportune for himself or his minister to make a widely publicized trip to Italy, Dresler would quietly slip across the Brenner to Rome in the interests of the Axis, thus supplying Munich correspondents with useful information while everything seemed quiet in Berlin.

During the Czech crisis of September, 1938, Adolf Dresler was a very worried little Nazi. Goebbels was leaving his junior partner in the dark about the latest developments. War seemed imminent. Little Adolf was phoning his chief frantically for orders to pass on to the Bavarian press. The Berlin Propaganda Ministry had enough cares of its own without keeping Munich posted until the situation could be clarified. In despair, Dresler herded the Munich reporters into a banquet hall of the Artists' House, where he fed them and plied them with drinks and with broadcasts from the Berlin-controlled radio. Knowing that I was in constant communication with London—something forbidden him—Dresler begged me to come to the banquet as soon as I could. So I dropped in at the Nazi night club, hoping to obtain some news from the Bavarian press chief. Instead, I gave him information withheld from him by his own chief, Goebbels.

"Herr Pope," Dresler queried tremulously as I entered, "for heaven's sake, tell me what's new!"

"The British fleet has just been mobilized," I replied.

You should have seen his jaw drop! Dresler had been through one war, and that was enough. The Bavarian newspapermen looked no happier when their boss passed on this information. They had all been led to believe that England would take no action in the Czech affair. The Nazi press is so severely censored that even such an important official as the head of the Munich propaganda office was left in the dark concerning international developments. In return for past favors, I later put Dresler's mind at ease by breaking the news to him that Chamberlain, Daladier, and his pal, Mussolini, were coming to Munich for a probable appeasement—hours before Dresler was told this all-important fact by his own headquarters in Berlin. On several other occasions, my professional Nazi host came to me for off-the-record news of the outside world, until Goebbels's wartime laws made such confidences a criminal act.

Any information relating to the Führer's presence in Bavaria was naturally preferred grist for the mill of a news agency like Reuters. Consequently, I was compelled to be on the alert at all times of day and night, to follow his movements around Munich, Berchtesgaden, and his other Bavarian haunts. The impregnable fortress of his mountain chalet, the "Berghof," at Berchtesgaden made this task very difficult. I relied mainly on his Reich Press Chief, Dr. Otto Dietrich, or the latter's assistant, Herr Lorenz, for any information about the dictator that I could not obtain from other sources. Like Mary's little lamb, Lorenz trailed Hitler wherever he went. And Lorenz was often no more communicative than the lamb, which could only say "Baaaah."

Dietrich and Lorenz are Hitler's press agents. One of them is always in Hitler's entourage, along with the Führer's adjutants, official photographer Heinrich Hoffmann, and his Elite Bodyguards. If I could not reach the senior or junior press chief at the "Berghof," (the Führer's unlisted Berchtesgaden telephone "number"), I knew that I must sleuth for Hitler elsewhere. Calling Berchtesgaden was the most unsavory job that I had to perform at frequent intervals from my Munich office. I could visualize the grim SS Guard at the Berghof switchboard, a heavy-caliber automatic at his side, gruffly cursing the "insolence" of a foreigner attempting to pry into the Nazi holy of holies.

Late evening. My work done for the day—I hope. Suddenly, the long, irregular "Brrrr" on my 'phone, meaning long distance.

"Is this Munich 35 669?"

"*Jahwohl, Fräulein.*"

"*Ein Moment, here calls you London.*"

"Hello, this is Pope in Munich."

"Look here, Pope old boy, find out what Hitler's doing, and call us back."

"Okay."

Reluctantly I dial long distance.

"*Fraulein,* this is Munich five-and-thirty, six nine-and-sixty. *Bitte* give me Berchtesgaden, Berghof."

I hang up. The Berghof is just one hundred miles from Munich, but even such a short call requires from ten to thirty minutes for the connection, in the Third Reich.

"Br-r-r-r."

A rasping voice: "Here is the Berghof. Heil Hitler!"

The "Heil Hitler" sounds just like "Hands up." I'll be damned if I'll "Heil," just the same. But it is a terrifically painful moment, like refusing to shake hands or to advance and give the countersign.

"Here is the British news agency, Reuters. I wish to speak to the Reich Press Chief or Herr Lorenz."

More painful moments of silence.

Then: "Here is *der Reichspressechef,* Heil Hitler!"

"*Guten Abend, Herr Doktor.* This is Pope in Munich. Pardon me for troubling you, but will the Führer stay at the Berghof tomorrow?"

"*Ich weiss nicht.* The Führer's plans are unknown."

"Is he staying at Berchtesgaden tonight?"

"Probably."

"Did he have any important visitors this afternoon?"

"Not that I know of. Der Führer had a simple supper and then went for a walk with his dogs. Heil Hitler!"

"Danke schan, Herr Doktor."

I call London with this scant information, but at least have confirmed the presence of Hitler in his mountain nest, and know that I must keep an eye, or at least an ear on him tomorrow. Over an hour, and ten dollars in telephone tolls, to tell the world that Hitler walked with his police dogs and is sleeping in his Berchtesgaden fortress.

Reluctant to give out any solicited news, the Reich Press Chief can be only too voluble on his own initiative. Shortly before the Austrian Anschluss, he called me up from Hitler's house late one night.

"Herr Pope," Dr. Dietrich pleaded, "some irresponsible British newspapers are printing shocking reports about German troops massing at the Austrian border. You represent a reliable news agency, and I have always respected your integrity. Please be so good as to deny these false rumors to Reuters. There is not one word of truth in them. The Führer went to bed two hours ago. There are no troops along the southern frontier, etc., etc...."

Sometimes Dietrich or Lorenz volunteered a good feature story about Hitler having tea in his mountaintop eagle's nest on the Kehlstein, reached through a hidden elevator from the Berghof. They would describe the Führer's clothes minutely, and add that Goebbels and Göring were in the party. This was fairly good copy. But when Hitler was brow-beating important visitors, or haranguing at conferences, there was little information to be obtained. Dietrich or Lorenz would issue a terse communique to the German news agency, containing a minimum amount of real news.

Two infallible signs always revealed Hitler's presence in Munich. I merely had to drive past his apartment on the Prinzregenten Platz.

Even if no shiny black Mercedes were parked there, the fact that a policeman stood before the entrance to the building was a sure indication that Adolf was doing the town. No guards of any description were placed on sentry duty outside the apartment when the Führer was away, although black-uniformed SS Guards and Gestapo teemed in the floors below and above Hitler's apartment. The other sign was young Herr Lorenz. I would run into him at the Nazi hotel, Vier Jahreszeiten, or at the offices of the German news agency. Or I would simply ask for him by telephone. If Lorenz was registered there, I knew that Hitler could not be far off, so made preparations accordingly to attend the performance of the *Merry Widow* or some other show that evening.

Face to face with Press Chief Dietrich or his buddy, it was much easier to obtain information about the Führer than via the Berchtesgaden telephone. Enenkel and I would corner him over a drink, and he would talk quite freely about Hitler's Munich schedule of visits to the House of German Art, dinner at the Osteria Bavaria or the Artists' House, and a "surprise" visit to a play by Shaw, opera by Wagner, or his beloved *Merry Widow*. He might even divulge the Führer's plans for the next day, provided they were not a state secret.

Like the other Nazi leaders, the Reich Press Chief did a considerable amount of lavish entertaining. The purpose of these extravagant parties was not merely to present an opulent front to the outside world, but was also intended to appease the dissatisfied native hirelings of the controlled Third Reich Press, who still remembered what good food was like in the, old pre-rationing days.

A few months before the war, Dietrich gave a special banquet for the Bavarian press. He chartered the swankiest country hotel near Munich, the Kaiserin Elizabeth at Feldafing on Lake Starnberg. This hotel was von Ribbentrop's favorite Bavarian hideout, complete with a golf course and an English fireplace. Busses were provided for those journalists who could not catch a ride in a colleague's car. I drove out with Stan Simpson. Hedy, knowing what these banquets were like, stayed home. So did the other journalists' wives.

The main dining room with adjoining terrace was festively decorated. Dietrich and his fellow Nazis were decked out in their smartest white summer uniforms. Before dinner, the waiters passed around excellent Manhattan cocktails. The Press Chief had provided for every conceivable comfort for his guests. Two busses had brought out the prettiest mannikins from the Reich Fashion School at Munich, as partners for the German and foreign correspondents.

I picked a lovely brunette. Stan had his eyes on a sleek blonde. Together we sat down to a dinner of lobster, pheasant, steak, imported vegetables, fruits, wines, champagnes, cognacs, Mochas, as well as the best German victuals and beverages. After the ice cream, Dietrich made a short speech, paying a left-handed compliment to the Bavarian press that had helped the Nazis to power before Goebbels became Propaganda Minister in Berlin, and flattering the foreign correspondents assigned to Munich. He told us how we should work together with our German colleagues for Hitler's dearest wish: "Peace." Enenkel gave a short response for our club, polite and noncommittal. Then, to the swing music of a smooth orchestra, we began a long evening of dancing and champagning, interrupted only by chasing fireflies in the park with our hostesses. The girls' busses went back to Munich—empty.

DNB stands for Deutsches Nachrichten-Büro (German News Agency). My German colleagues have nicknamed it *"Darf Nichts Bringen"* (Can't publish anything). Dietrich and Lorenz feed this agency with news about the Führer whenever they see fit. In censored, secretive Naziland, foreign correspondents have been compelled to turn to DNB for much of their news about Third Reich affairs.

When Hitler made speeches to his Old Guard Nazis at their secret beer-hall sessions, DNB was the only source available for the Führer's talks. We knew that Lorenz or Dietrich had deleted Hitler's strongest statements before releasing a report of the speech to the German news agency, and therefore pounced eagerly on whatever meaty passages the Reich Press Chief had not censored. I would wait restlessly at the DNB office, scanning each sheet on an important Nazi speech as it came off the machine, then rush to my office with the DNB pages to write and send my story. Sometimes DNB was careless. On one occasion, for example, I sent a story about a wild speech Goebbels had made at Nuremberg. Scarcely had I finished dictating to London, when there was a violent pounding at my door, and a member of the DNB staff dashed breathlessly into my office.

"Herr Pope," he exclaimed, "I must take back those sheets on Goebbels' speech! Please give them to me."

"What's the trouble; you put them out, didn't you?"

"*Ja, Ja.* But that's the wrong version! We will have the corrected version for you in two hours."

"Okay, here you are. But bring me the speech as soon as you can. It is very important."

I did not tell him that a report of the Goebbels outburst was already going to press in London. Two hours later, the DNB slave brought me the revised version. I thanked him, pretending to snatch it eagerly from him. The new report was an emasculated edition of the first. I read it with mild amusement, then tossed it in the wastebasket.

The great Nazi news bottleneck, DNB, presumably is first in the Reich with any important stories. Its members, headed by Dietrich and Lorenz, are given access to conferences, speeches, ceremonies, and rallies from which other reporters, especially foreign correspondents, have been barred. Consequently the German agency occupies a monopoly position in Third Reich news. Its members are given precedence in making long-distance calls. Yet I have beaten DNB.

Once I jumped out of the press bus returning from a saber-rattling speech made by Hitler at Ratisbon, and hurried to the nearest telephone while the DNB reporter dutifully continued his ride with his colleagues. When General Ludendorff died in Munich, I not only beat all foreign competition with a bulletin on his death, but also the official German news agency.

General Ludendorff was lying critically ill in the private Catholic Hospital of St. Joseph, across the street from Munich Army

Headquarters. Reuters cautioned me three times to be first with the news of his death, ahead of the Associated Press, the British United Press (represented in Munich by a smart German journalist, Dr. Falkner), Exchange-Telegraph, Havas, Stefani, and the others.

Two weeks before the famous World-War fighter lost his last battle—for his life—I called on the head nurse at the St. Joseph. She was a dear little old woman, neatly dressed in the quaint cape and gown of her order, with a large Crucifix hanging over her clean, starched front. I carefully explained my sad mission: that Ludendorff's death was a vital matter to me, that I must be the first to learn of any crisis, and the first to know when his heart stopped beating. She understood. I took a twenty-mark bill from my pocket, and pressed it into her hand.

"I know, Sister, that your needs are not of an earthly nature," I said solemnly. "But pray take this money for your church."

"May God reward you," Little Sister replied fervently and gratefully. At four A.M. on December 21, 1937, I was awakened by the insistent ringing of my telephone.

"Herr Pope," the nurse announced in a hushed voice, "the General has taken a turn for the worse. His family are gathered around him. The Doctor has given injections and a transfusion. But he is not expected to live more than a few hours. *Grüiss Gott!*"

"God bless you," I replied, and at once flashed the message to Reuters' London and Berlin offices. At 8:22 A.M. Little Sister called again:

"General Ludendorff passed away peacefully at 8:20 this morning."

Again I bulletined London and Berlin, then hurried to the hospital. The DNB and other German reporters sneered as I entered.

"Late again, Meester Popey!" they jeered. Some were still telephoning from the hospital switchboard.

"Says you," I replied in my best Bavarian dialect. "I beat you boys easy. But I won't tell you how."

Twenty marks to the persecuted Catholic Church in Nazi Germany had proved far more effective than any compulsion from the regimented official German news agency, upon which my press-club colleagues had relied for their own belated bulletins of Ludendorff's death. Reuters rated my Ludendorff beat among the twelve best in their world-wide organization for the year. In gratitude for Little Sister's faithfulness, I gave her another twenty marks for her church.

German newspapers are another news source which the foreign correspondent cannot neglect. To be sure, most of their space is taken by DNB reports of the previous evening. The German agency even dictates to the local newspaper editors, heading an item with the implied command: "We request the right honorable editors to print this report in heavy type on Page One." Now and then, however, an important story would be printed by a Munich newspaper before it came to the attention of DNB, which sometimes refused to distribute local news that might alarm Germans in other parts of the Reich, especially if it concerned serious accidents, local rationing restrictions, or outbreaks of epidemics.

Four important dailies were published in Munich, headed of course by the Munich edition of the party's *Volkischer Beobachter*. The local reporters for these papers diligently attended Dresler's press conferences, Wagner's rallies, Hitler's Munich speeches and shows, and Weber's banquets. Their main task seemed to consist of recording the names of as many Nazis attending the function as they could identify, and describing the affair in the most laudatory general terms. But automobile accidents and fires helped them feel that they were still reporters, despite taboos on any investigations of local graft, scandals, or political crimes.

Even the dramatic critics walked a perilous tightrope, as illustrated by the sad case of the *Volkischer Beobachter's* theater specialist.

This young German had been sent to cover a new musical comedy at the Deutsches Theater. It was a good show, there were no hitches, and a smooth performance with well-rehearsed chorus girls was presented to the first-nighters. The Munich reporter turned in an enthusiastic review to his Nazi managing editor. The next day the editor of the *Volkischer Beobachter* assembled the entire staff of the newspaper. Then he summoned the unfortunate theater critic, and attacked him with all the vehemence of which Teutonic oratory is capable.

"How dare you use a phrase of the Führer's in reviewing a musical comedy!" he stormed. "If this happens once more, I shall fire you, and have you arrested for blaspheming Adolf Hitler. Let this be a warning to all of you!"

What had caused this terrific outburst? In praising the musical comedy, the "sacrilegious" reporter had written:

"The stage manager had rehearsed his cast so well that all he needed to do was to say 'Begin,' and the show ran itself with no coaching from the wings." Three years before that, while inaugurating work on his new highway from Munich to Salzburg, Hitler had concluded his speech to the laborers with the words *"Fanget an"* (Begin)!

Yet the Führer himself had stolen this phrase from Richard Wagner's *Meistersinger*.

Because the German reporters were often given access to Nazi meetings and certain press conferences from which the foreign correspondents were excluded, and because in the course of their duties they often picked up highly interesting information that they could not use themselves, they were of great help to me. I won the confidence of several of them, who, at the risk of a term in concentration camp, would tip me off about arrests, troop movements, anti-Jewish measures, and other Nazi lore which they dared not report to their own editors, but which was meat for my chiefs in London. I was extremely cautious not to reveal my "reliable sources," nor to contact them by tapped telephones or wherever there might be unwelcome ears in the vicinity. They had enough troubles as it was.

Take the case of the reporter for the *Münchener Neueste Nachrichten*. Less than a year before Ribbentrop perpetrated the Berlin-Moscow Pact, this journalist was watching the dynamiting of the Church of St. Matthew, the largest Protestant Church in Munich.

Hitler had ordered it to be razed to make room for a parking lot near the center of the town.

"Germany is getting to be just like Russia," the reporter remarked to a neighbor in Bavarian leather shorts; "except that the Soviets leave the churches standing and use them for movie houses."

The supposed Bavarian peasant grabbed the reporter. "Your name! Your passport! Your vocation! Your address!" he thundered, showing his Gestapo shield.

The horrified Munich journalist complied.

"Report to Brienner Strasse Headquarters tomorrow morning at eleven o'clock," grimly warned the agent, then turned abruptly on his hobnailed heel and left.

The reporter fearfully whispered an account of the incident to his colleagues that evening at his newspaper office.

"You've done something terrible," they sympathized. "We'll probably never see you again!"

They didn't. He slashed his jugular vein that same night.

The Munich press photographers likewise led a life full of hazards and discomforts. They were compelled to wear gray uniforms and an official arm band which could be revoked at a moment's notice by the Reich for "bad conduct" in the presence of prominent Nazis, or for taking uncomplimentary pictures of these leaders. The authorities did little to facilitate their risky jobs. The German newspapers paid them a pittance for their photographs. On top of all these professional burdens, the news photographers had to face the competition from Heinrich Hoffmann. Hitler's official photographer has turned his job into a monopoly racket. His string of cameramen are supplied with Mercedes cars, privileged places, and expensive cameras, while the "independent" German press photographer is forced to get to the scene as best he can, and to take his pictures from wherever he can squeeze room for himself with whatever apparatus he can afford to scrape together.

Hoffmann distributes his pictures to all the German magazines and newspapers, as well as forcing them on the postcard and propaganda markets. Here is a typical Hoffmann trick of his trade. If an ordinary German photographer had resorted to it, he would have been summarily sentenced to death for desecrating the Führer. Hoffmann took a picture of Hitler standing on his veranda in the Alps, laying his hands on the upturned palms of two little girls. In the right foreground stood a plain evergreen tree. Behind the Führer one could see the arm of his adjutant, while through the glass windows and the opening of the veranda the outline of the mountains against the sky was visible. Hoffmann printed "Berchtesgaden children congratulate the Führer" (on his birthday, April 20th) on the bottom of the picture. He made thousands of postcards from this picture, and sold them for the spring trade. Then, to save himself and Hitler the trouble of posing again, the Führer's official photographer blacked out the sky and mountains to make it look like night, effaced the adjutant's arm, painted tinsel and burning candles on the tree, then wrote in large letters above Hitler: "Merry Christmas." Again he sold thousands of the faked postcards to the gullible German public for his Christmas trade!

When I had exhausted the rationed supplies of news furnished by the Reich Press Chief or Dresler, I would turn to the press chiefs of each local potentate, such as Gauleiter Adolf Wagner's publicity agent, the press representative of Munich Police Headquarters on the Ett Strasse, the press chief of Munich Gestapo Headquarters on the Brienner Strasse, the municipal press chief of the city, the Hitler Youth press chief, and a dozen other minor heel-clicking Brown Shirts in the various party organizations.

Until the war called him to active service in the Seventh Army Corps, Adolf Wagner's press chief was a vest-pocket Göring by the name of Dr. Max Werner. After several midnight sessions over pewter mugs, corpulent Maxie took the liberty of addressing me as "Sonny Boy." Ordinarily, he would supply me with useful information regarding Boss Wagner's activities. But when the Gauleiter tore down the Munich synagogue for Hitler, when Archbishop Cardinal Faulhaber's windows were smashed, when the

Nazis were on the march toward Austria, or on other momentous occasions for a foreign correspondent, the only advice I could obtain from Maxie was: "Run along and play, Sonny Boy. Everything is normal. You must have been listening to idle gossip again."

Nazi officials are experts at buck-passing. Because he disliked Dresler's office and salary, Werner would often feign ignorance about some touchy subject in Bavaria and send me over to Dresler. The *Reichshauptamtsleiter* in turn would recommend me to Gestapo Headquarters, which would curtly advise me to call on the municipal police headquarters. Each press chief was afraid to risk his job by telling the correspondent what he knew, and at the same time hoped that some rival press chief might let the cat out of the bag and thereby get into hot water with Berlin.

The municipal press chief of the Bavarian capital contributes his share to the orientation and feeding of Munich correspondents. His office is in the Town Hall on picturesque Marienplatz. His boss is the Mayor, *Reichsleiter Burger-meister* Dr. Karl Fiehler, an ex-clerk who rules over the city with the help (or rather interference) of Christian Weber, the chairman of the Town Council of aldermen. While I was stationed at Munich, the municipal press chief was Herr Georg Freudenberger.

"Georgie," as he was universally called, was very popular with the undernourished German reporters. For one of his jobs was to reserve the press table at the numerous banquets held in the Town Hall. No visiting delegation of foreigners ever came to Munich without being wined and dined by Fiehler or Weber. No important municipal function took place in fun-loving Munich without an accompanying celebration in the Town Hall. Even the "Junior Year" students from American universities were given banquets, soft soap, and expensive books advertising the beauties of Nazi Bavaria when their year of study at Munich University ended. The rest of the Reich might starve, yet the banquet hall in Mayor Fiehler's building would still resemble the first-class dining room of a luxury liner.

Freudenberger issued invitations to the press for all functions at which a member of the municipal government officiated, as well as releases on the work of the party in Munich. He diligently clipped all foreign newspaper stories that mentioned Munich or his boss.

While the Führer was still the sworn enemy of the Soviets, and his *Luftwaffe* was practicing for the blitzkrieg in Spain, a delegation of Generalissimo Franco's youth leaders paid a visit to the Munich shrine of Naziism. Again the banquet tables were set, and a crack SS Guard orchestra was commandeered to play Fascist songs. An interpreter told the leader of the Spanish delegation that the orchestra was about to play Franco's national anthem, so they arose and gave their Fascist salute. Imagine their surprise when their German brothers struck up the tune of their Red enemies, the *loyalist* anthem! The stupid SS orchestra, unfamiliar with any Spanish anthems, had picked the wrong sheet music.

The 115 Spanish Fascists' arms wavered awkwardly from the salute. "That is the Bolshevik song!" the boys whispered to one another. After moments of painful fidgeting, the Soviet song ended. Tactfully, the leader of Franco's representatives spoke up:

"To thank you for the splendid reception you have accorded us in the capital of the Nazi movement," he said, addressing Mayor Fiehler, "we will now sing for you our Spanish national anthem."

The 115 young men then burst out lustily into their "Cara al Sol." Not a hand wavered this time. The SS bandmaster hastily fussed through his music. As the Franco followers filed out of the banquet hall, the Black Guard orchestra tried again, striking up a different Spanish anthem. This time they improved a trifle: they played the anthem of ex-King Alphonso's monarchy!

The incident made a wonderful story for the British press at that time. I flashed it to London, which gave it a good play. A few days later, at another Town Hall banquet, Georgie Freudenberger grabbed my arm and took me aside.

"Herr Pope," he expostulated, "that was very unkind of you, to send that unfortunate story about our mistaken music, after the nice feast which you enjoyed in our Town Hall."

I patted him on the back. "Listen, Georgie," I consoled him, "if you promise to play no more of those nasty Bolshevik songs in the capital of the Nazis, I promise to send no more stories about them."

The ubiquitous seventeen-year-old press chief of Bavaria's Hitler Youth deserves to be mentioned, even if he never furnished any news fit for foreign consumption. For he typifies the Nazi youth of today: arrogant, swaggering, prematurely worldly-wise, with no scruples whatsoever. Claiming to be a pure German, he had a Polish-sounding name which I never could spell or remember exactly, something like "Buttinski." He attended every press banquet, conference, and excursion in full brown uniform, with loaded boots designed to give the impression that the entire German army was on the march.

While gray-haired German journalists who had survived the preceding Reich and Weimar Republic sipped their wine, smoked their pipes, and talked in low voices, Buttinski would puff furiously at a big cigar, pour down one glass after another, force his way into everybody's conversation at the top of his recently changed voice, and describe his numerous love affairs in graphic detail.

Shortly before the war, Buttinski, in his cups, boasted to me that while in England with a group of Hitler Youths at a British exchange camp, the Nazi boys spent much of their time drawing maps and becoming familiar with the English terrain, avowedly for a possible invasion of their hosts at a later date. If I had sent Buttinski's startling confession to London, the German authorities immediately would have denied it, and probably would have expelled me for "malicious, hateful, democratic journalism."

Another Brown-Shirt press executive in Munich is familiar, at least in name, to many Americans: Rolf Hofmann. Hoffmann sent tons of his "News from Germany" to the United States—via Siberia—to carry on Nazi propaganda at any price, and to compensate for the curtailment by the war of his activities among tourists and foreign correspondents in Munich. Reputedly a former hosiery salesman, a fashion plate with a winning manner and an excellent English accent, young Rolf's assignment before the war was to ingratiate himself and the Reich with foreigners from the Anglo-Saxon countries, especially students and tourists. He also headed the foreign section of Dresler's propaganda bureau, diligently clipping, translating, and filing the reports which we sent to England and America from Munich. When British newspapers with my own stories were banned from the Reich, I still could find them in Hofmann's office.

Keeping a record of our dispatches was only one of Rolf's varied jobs. Another was to reserve accommodations, special press cards, and tickets for us at the annual party congresses in Nuremberg every September, providing us with transportation to and from Hitler's official "City of the Reich's Party Congresses." Hofmann's obliging manner often reminded me of the suave floor walker in a department store, who puts his best foot forward to volunteer his assistance when you know that he really wants to examine you more closely to see whether you have been shoplifting.

On the same low-grade paper in various colors, and with the same cheap mimeographing used in his bulk propaganda shipments to America, I received Rolf's news about the Third Reich from his Starnberg home near Munich at my Reuters office. I always glanced at it before throwing the news in the wastebasket, for it sometimes contained harmless little items that I could use for Reuters' filler service: descriptions of Germany's largest salt mines, beer kegs, buildings, or the top speed of the Nazis' newest electric locomotive.

Handsome Rolf also acted as official Nazi pimp for unsuspecting American and British tourists, in much the same way as those persistent slickers who proposition male tourists with, "Want to see the town; want me to show you very nice girls, mister?" He or his agents would waylay parties at Munich travel bureaus and hotels, engage them in conversation and reminiscences about "the good old U.S.A.," then invite the people to attend some celebration. His enticements included free trips to Nuremberg rallies, tours of Nazi institutions in the Reich, visits to Brown-Shirt festivals and sport meets—anything to overwhelm the tourists with the accomplishments of the Reich.

At one summer festival organized for the Day of German Art by Reich Press Chief Dr. Dietrich, Hofmann turned up with a dozen

American tourists fresh from Switzerland. During a lull in the program, he excused himself from his guests and drew me aside.

"I would like you to meet these people," he whispered. "They are very nice Americans. Could you please find out their names, and let me know who they are?"

Most of the Munich correspondents avoided Hofmann whenever possible, except for the pro-Axis hirelings from Bulgaria, Spain, etc. There was one notable exception among the Anglo-Saxons. His name was Phillip Spranklin. He and Hofmann were the best of friends!

***

TEA FOR TWO

As I was walking past the Regina Palace Hotel one afternoon, about a year after Neville Chamberlain had checked out of the hotel upon signing the Munich Conference agreements, I almost bumped into a tall blonde who had just left the Regina beauty parlor.

"Why hello, Unity! Are you back from the Berchtesgaden mountains already?" I exclaimed. "Did you see the write-up I gave you in the *Express?* Tell me all about your visit and I'll give you another one."

"You don't know the half of it, Ernest Pope, and you never will," replied Miss Unity Freeman-Mitford, daughter of Great Britain's Lord Redesdale, sister-in-law of the British Fascist leader, Sir Oswald Mosley, and former sweetheart of Reich Chancellor Adolf Hitler. But she gave me a friendly smile and added, "Excuse me, but I must dash off to have tea with the Gauleiter."

Nobody will ever know all about the strange affair between the supreme Nazi dictator and this statuesque English girl—the only British woman who has spent weekends on the Ohersalzberg at Berchtesgaden as Hitler's guest. But I learned quiite a bit about Unity during my frequent encounters with her and her associates in the party capital.

"Next to my wife, Miss Mitford is the most beautiful Nordic woman I have ever seen," Marshal Hermann Göring once declared. This remark explains in part why, next to Chamberlain, Unity was also the most successful appeaser Hitler ever met. For Lord Redesdale's daughter was a very selfish person, who used all of her influence over the Führer to prevent a war between Germany and England. Such a war meant the end of her happiness and personal ambitions. When it came in spite of her efforts, Unity faked a suicide attempt, and has not yet recovered from the blow to her own ego.

In *Life* magazine of March 17, 1941, there is a picture of an embittered, much older-looking Unity. The caption under the photograph reads: "Unity Freeman-Mitford, 'the woman who trusted Hitler,' was in Cotswold last fortnight apparently recovered from a mysterious illness which confined her for more than a year. Jilted by Hitler when the war broke, she collapsed, was landed in England with armed escort. Note sagging stockings." Unity doesn't care any more. She cannot live the life she gloried in during the prewar days of the Third Reich. From her point of view, it was a wonderful life.

Whenever Unity stayed in Bavaria, I was constantly getting queries from my London chiefs about rumors that Hitler's English girl friend was about to become a German citizen. Although I knew the answer in advance, I would interview Unity about the matter, and she would always reply "Not this year!" The explanation of her paradoxical reluctance is simple.

Unity Mitford would never consent to becoming a German citizen except as Hitler's wife. For a while she even hoped secretly that the Führer would propose. Until the Czech crisis in 1938, Adolf openly advocated an Anglo-German entente, in which England was to control the seas, while the Reich, with a "free hand in the East," was to police the Continent. Had such a European policy been embraced by Great Britain and Germany, it is quite possible that Hitler might have embraced Unity before the altar and consummated a union between this member of the English nobility and the lord of the National Socialist German Labor Party. But England spurned Hitler's advances, so the Führer's love for his Blond Britain cooled.

Without a Swastika engagement ring on her finger, Unity was much better off as one of His Majesty's subjects. She could travel back and forth between the Reich and the Isles as a British tourist. By keeping her residence in England, she could convert her pounds sterling into Reichsmarks at the tourist rate of exchange, which gave her twice as much spending money in her beloved Naziland as the official rate which she would be required to apply to convert her English pounds if she were a German citizen. She could run important errands for the Nazis as she traveled around Czechoslovakia and other adjoining countries in her British car, with British license plates and British papers. And she could make pro-Nazi speeches in Hyde Park with the party button given her by Hitler nestling in the lapel of her Munich-made sport jacket. In the

Reich she also could address Nazi rallies and have her talks appear in the German newspapers the next day as representing "the real British attitude."

More than one young German owes his life to Unity—his life in Dachau Concentration Camp. Before the war, there was a large colony of Britishers in the picturesque Bavarian capital, most of them students from wealthy English families. Teas and cocktail parties were the order of the day. The English girls would invite their German acquaintances to these parties. In a democratic atmosphere, with liberal expressions of opinions in the King's English encouraged by dry Martinis and Johnny Walker highballs, the pent-up Germans would loosen their regimented tongues to tell their friends from across the Channel what they really thought of Hitler and Nazüsm. Woe to them if Unity overheard their remarks and took exception to them! Miss Mitford saw to it that the indiscreet anti-Nazi was sent to Dachau. In young Munich society she was known as "the most dangerous woman in Munich."

The anti-Fascist members of the British colony studiously avoided Hitler's girlfriend. Yet they forced Lord Redesdale's daughter to buy Swastika flags wholesale. She was compelled to keep a large supply of the Third Reich emblems in her boardinghouse on the Schack Strasse. For her automobile carried British license plates, yet flew the Nazi flags from standards above them. The English students at Munich University resented this brazen display of Nazi sympathies, and surreptitiously ripped off the Swastikas from Unity's parked car.

In the summer of the 1938 Czech crisis which led to the September Munich conference, Unity Mitford and Phillip Spranklin, both British Fascists and wearers of Himmler's honorary SS badges, toured Czechoslovakia in Unity's car. They were arrested and searched. Among the items confiscated from Unity by the Czech police were an autographed picture of Hitler, an expensive camera which he had given her, and her highly treasured Storm-Trooper Dagger, which had been presented to her by none other than the man Hitler had murdered exactly four years previously—Ernst Roehm! Finally, after a bodily visitation by a police matron, Unity was released. So was Spranklin.

The British Nazis headed straight for Nuremberg, where they were received by Julius Streicher. The Franconian Gauleiter put them up at the Deutscher Hof, the hotel reserved for the Führer and his retinue whenever he visits Nuremberg. Spranklin, in an unguarded moment, later told me the following story about Unity's adventure at the Deutscher Hof.

The Führer's blonde came down to breakfast the next morning looking very upset and pale. She complained to the management that a man had come into her room while she was sleeping, and that she struggled with him in the dark. She did not reveal the outcome of the fight. The Gestapo manager of the hotel apologized profusely, and promised an immediate investigation. But his sleuthing ended as abruptly as it had begun. For Unity's midnight visitor turned out to be "a very high official in the Gestapo." Heinrich Himmler is a fanatic worshiper of blond Nordic womanhood.

Unity's Czech adventure, with the resulting publicity, brought her a flood of protesting letters from indignant Britishers. She told me that some of these letters threatened her safety. She told the same story to Adolf. So her hero gave Unity permission to carry both a sub-machine gun and a revolver with her in her car, a privilege usually reserved for SS Guards. She graciously declined the machine gun. But she accepted Hitler's revolver. It was this gun which she used to muss up her skin when Hitler jilted her at the start of the war.

Unity remained in Bavaria only long enough to attend the September Party Congress with her father, as guests of honor of the Führer. Then she left the country for a long and mysterious absence—until May of the following year.

In July, 1939, Miss Mitford and her sister were very much in evidence at the reviewing stand of the Reich's guests for the procession "2,000 Years of German Culture" during the Führer's Day of German Art. I watched Unity taking pictures of the procession—with the $300 camera given her by boy friend Adolf to replace the one confiscated by the Czechs.

Whenever the British Brunhilde returned to Munich from abroad, I would look her up for a story. She usually received me in the presence of a huge, black Great Dane, who seemed as suspicious of my visit as did Unity. Hitler's companion has lovely hair, a beautiful complexion, and a tall, erect, and full figure. But two features mar her Nordic beauty. Her eyes give an impression of chronic severity amounting almost to crossness. And when she smiles, which is seldom, Unity reveals a miserable set of irregular, dark teeth. Arrived in Munich, Unity would fret about the town, calling on Adolf Wagner and letting her presence be known to the inner Nazi circle, then fidget in her Pension Dörnberg apartment like a schoolgirl waiting for her date, until a call from the Berghof informed her that Hitler was ready to welcome her to his mountain villa.

Unity has spent everything from an afternoon to several days at Berchtesgaden, appeasing Adolf and also clinging to his every word. Spranklin once showed me a photograph of the would-be Mrs. Hitler with Adolf in a very informal tête-a-tête over some tea in the Führer's home on the Obersalzberg. Phillip had obtained this candid-camera shot from triumphant Unity herself, who wanted to prove to her sister, Sir Mosley's wife, that she too could snare a Fascist leader.

Hitler's Deputy, Rudolf Hess, did not share his master's affection for the British blonde. At one banquet of the Nazi inner circle, which the Führer was too busy to attend, Hess turned to his neighbor and, pointing to Unity, remarked: "I wish someone would throw that painted — out of here!"

Joachim von Ribbentrop and Unity have also hated each other cordially, ever since Ribbentrop was Nazi ambassador to the Court of St. James. For Unity and Ribbentrop quarreled about the methods of advancing the Fascist movement in England.

For several years, Hitler's English girlfriend managed to hold his attentions. But in 1939 the calls from Berchtesgaden to her boardinghouse became less frequent. Adolf was turning again to his native love, buxom Evi Braun, whom he had met years before, when Evi was an assistant to photographer Heinrich Hoffmann. Nor did it please the Führer that Unity was often seen with Munich relatives of

"Putzi" Hanfstängel, who had already fallen from Hitler's graces. Ribbentrop and Hess used their influence to secure a cold shoulder for Unity from other leading Nazis who had been her friends in earlier days. As a further affront to her female ego, Miss Mitford learned that Hitler had provided Evi Braun with a furnished house at 12 Wasserburger Strasse, just a few blocks away from his own apartment.

The fury of a woman spurned was not the only reason which induced Great Britain's ace female pro-Nazi to make such a scene in Munich that Hitler, exasperated, gave her an armed escort to get her out of his Reich. It is true that Evi Braun was now living with the Führer in his bomb-proof Chancellery at Berlin. But there were other factors that led to Unity's complete frustration. The war put an automatic stop to Miss Mitford's career as the star English actress on the Third Reich stage, toasted by Streicher, Wagner, and other important Nazis. The German Foreign Minister, von Ribbentrop, may be credited with delivering one of the fatal blows to Unity's Swastika-permeated spirit. For, by forging the Berlin-Moscow pact, Ribbentrop shattered some of her most cherished ideals. I wonder whether she pieced them together again when Germany invaded Russia!

For years Unity had swallowed her dear Adolf's words with passionate credulity as Hitler raved against Bolshevism, Soviet Russia, Red-Jewish Communism, etc. She had made his anti-Moscow doctrines her own, believing in them implicitly. Suddenly everything was different. Hitler not only renounced his love, but also his hate. He left Munich for Berlin, Unity for Evi Braun—and Chamberlain for Stalin. Had Lord Redesdale's Nazi daughter not been so inherently selfish, egocentric, and stubborn, she—like Madame Butterfly in the opera—might actually have killed herself in Munich. Instead, she was found merely unconscious, with a superficial bullet wound, on a Munich park bench—in the English Garden. After a brief stay in a Munich hospital, she was shipped off to England by her angry Nazi god.

Hitler's affairs with other women are more numerous than protracted. I learned on the best authority that when the Führer was spending a few days at Berchtesgaden, young German actresses were flown to his private landing field in his private 'plane from Berlin. If they pleased Adolf, they were immediately given a leading role by Nazi film czar Goebbels upon their return. It was not until early in 1938, however, that Hitler developed this taste for Third Reich glamour girls. When it did develop, the Führer carried his new interests to characteristic Teutonic extremes. He not only insisted on naked beauties in his favorite comic operas. He even introduced them into his Wagnerian specialties, which in previous years had been kept somber and dignified so that the Mauer might dream his megalomanic dreams while watching Germanic heroes and heroines strutting across the Bayreuth stage. For example in 1939, just before the war, a special performance of *Tannhäuser* was ordered by Hitler in the State Opera House at Munich. Two new features made their appearance for Adolf's benefit at this performance. One was a nude girl posing as "Europa" on a bull. The other, inspired by Hitler's admiration for the erotic painting described in a previous chapter, was a living, unclad Leda with her swan.

Before the Nazis had come to power, and before Berchtesgaden had developed into a combination week-end Reich Chancellery and love nest, Hitler's Munich apartment was the scene of clandestine wooing whenever the Führer felt it safe to take time off from the needs and the watchful eyes of his struggling party. One sinister incident, that is still being whispered around Munich, remains a mystery.

There is one room in Adolf's Munich residence which he has not entered, and which has been sealed, for more than fifteen years. According to trusted Munichers who knew Hitler when he was just one of several hundred politicians in the Weimar Republic, it was in this room that Hitler's niece shot herself—after an unwilling incestual night with her wild-eyed uncle.

Since the war, Hitler has settled down with Evi Braun. She cooks elegant meals for him in the Berlin Chancellery, and serves him in every way expected of a German Frau. It is occasionally rumored that the Führer has actually married Evi. I doubt this. There can be only one Hitler. Nazi law even prohibits Germans from naming their children after the Chancellor. And Nazi propaganda has decreed with a severity greater than any religious doctrine of chastity that no mortal woman is worthy to become a Frau Hitler, wife of "the divinely inspired Führer of eighty million Germans."

***

DEATH TAKES A HOLIDAY

Exactly two months before Hitler issued the fateful proclamation to his troops that the Third Reich was at war with Great Britain, England's largest newspaper, Lord Beaverbrook's *Daily Express,* published the following short editorial, based on a message I had telephoned the *Express* from Munich:

Kept Out of Mischief

"Hitler confers with architects on plans for a new opera house in Munich. It is an excellent task, a splendid operation, an admirable project. If he concerns himself with these interests, he will achieve something in his life that we can praise. And it provides employment for a man who should never have his hands idle. Satan finds mischief for idle hands."

Hitler was in Berlin when he ordered his *Wehrmacht* to invade Bohemia and Moravia. He was in Berlin when he commanded his troops and *Luftwaffe* to massacre Poland. But Hitler was in Munich when he permitted himself to be appeased, and withdrew his plans to fight the Czechs. It is in Bavaria that Brown Death takes a holiday.

The midsummer Day of German Art is one of the major events on the Führer's vacation calendar. His annual celebration of the November Beer-Hall Putsch is another. His frequent oglings of the *Merry Widow* are also an important item in his holiday schedules. Throughout the year Hitler finds many, albeit not enough things to do in Bavaria to rest his hands from the numerous tasks imposed on them by Beelzebub.

Bavaria and Munich form an ideal playground for people from seven to seventy, from tourists to dictators. If Prussia could be flooded to make a second Zuider Zee, and south Germany fenced off into a human wild-life sanctuary, the Teutonic thorn would forever be removed from the flesh of suffering humanity. The peaceful little villages, with their painted houses, the snow-covered Alps with their majestic scenery, and Munich with its hedonistic tradition of art and music have nothing in common with the infernal blitzkrieg machine controlled from the odious Third Reich ministries at Berlin.

This contrast between Prussia and Bavaria explains why Adolf Hitler spends most of his leisure moments in southern Germany. Even a fanatic Führer must relax and change his pace occasionally, if he is to push his plans for totalitarianism, conquest, and German domination to the limit. That is why he chose Berchtesgaden for his vacation headquarters, and Munich for his playground, where Nazi money and Nazi men are requisitioned for Hitler's hobbies with the same extravagance as for his fanatic ventures as the German Chancellor.

Many of the criminally insane harbor a great passion for music. In the occupational therapy shops of psychiatric clinics, one can find maniacs quietly building model houses and making pencil sketches. Ruthless paranoiacs often are kind to little children. Incurable lunatics spend much of their time outdoors in country hospitals, so that nature may help soothe their abnormal nervous system. Hitler's leisure moments are divided among his interests in music, architecture, German children, and the Bavarian countryside.

When Adolf takes leave of his governmental war machinery in Berlin, his bombproof train is waiting at Anhalter Bahnhof to sneak him overnight to his mountain resort in Berchtesgaden. There, at the Berghof, everything is in readiness for the dictator's holiday. A tall, blond young SS Guard, who has been killing time during his master's absence by dancing with Berchtesgaden girls in the bar of the Grand Hotel, has kept Adolf's leather shorts and other informal Alpine haberdashery spic and span, since he is Hitler's permanent valet on the Obersalzberg. Fat little Herr Kannenberg, head chef of the Berghof, is ready to serve his Führer a meatless breakfast of rolls, peppermint tea, grits, and an apple on the sun porch of Haus Wachenfeld, or, if Adolf wishes to eat at a higher altitude, in the glass-walled "Eagle's Nest" on the peak of the Kehlstein, 1,000 yards above the Obersalzberg.

To help dispel the Prussian-Berlin atmosphere from Hitler's mind and make him feel at home once more, Hitler's cook may oblige with some command performances of Bavarian folk songs rendered on his accordion, which he plays as well as he makes salads. Herr Kannenberg frequently has been taken along on Adolf's automobile trips through the countryside, not merely to pack and unpack the picnic baskets, but to supply the dictatorial cortege with accordion music and tenor singing as Adolf sinks his gold-capped canine teeth into a defenseless *Käsebrot*. Adolf himself plans the route of these trips, often ordering his chauffeur to leave the highways and drive through a lonely forest, so that he can listen among the trees like Joan of Arc to his inner voice, while he meditatively peels an orange with his six-inch hunting knife.

After breakfast, Hitler takes his three police dogs (two four-legged *Wolfshunde* plus Heinrich Himmler) for a walk along the slopes of the Obersalzberg. He may drop in to chat with Hermann Göring. Göring invites Adolf to try his luck with a bow and arrow. The Führer usually misses the target, Göring seldom. Adolf does not practice as much as Hermann. Or—if photographer Hoffmann is one of the hikers—Hitler may stop and chat with a weather-beaten peasant, whose white hair and stooped shoulders will look well in a propaganda picture of the "gregarious" Führer. Hitler's hikes are the most strenuous exercise the Führer has taken—except for his jaw muscles and the shoulder muscles of his right arm—since he came to power. Adolf, once a messenger boy in the Kaiser's army, can still strut along at a good pace.

After his walk, he returns to the Berghof for his first bath. Hitler normally takes three baths daily. Not so much from a sense of cleanliness, as due to the persuasive influence of his erstwhile physician, Professor Bummke, the doctor in charge of the psychiatric ward of Munich University's College of Medicine. Septuagenarian Bummke, having had a life-long experience with manic-depressive patients, prescribed this schedule of baths for the Führer as part of a program to keep Hitler's unstable nervous system under control. For a while Bummke was Hitler's personal physician. In 1937 they quarreled. Bummke, whose brother is chief justice of the State Court at Leipzig, refused to treat the Führer any longer, and rejected all "invitations" to return to the Berghof. He seems to have preferred less famous, more tractable patients. But Hitler keeps on with his three baths daily, while Bummke keeps on with his other patients, ranging from those who can only say "Heil Hitler" to those who think they are Hitler.

After his bath, while Kannenberg is preparing his special vegetarian lunch, Adolf reviews the press reports submitted to him by Dr. Dietrich. Then he eats, with a few guests such as Göring, Goebbels, Adolf Wagner, or whatever other Nazi happens to be staying on the Obersalzberg. His guests can order what they like from the Berghof kitchen, even if dictator Adolf sticks to the diet of a Casper Milquetoast. Adolf prefers to eat lightly, letting his eyes rove over the mountains or haranguing his fellow diners with the latest political ideas revolving around inside his Bummke-renovated head.

Berchtesgaden has developed into the Mecca of all loyal Nazis. "Strength-through-Joy" hotels have sprung up near the Obersalzberg. Robert Ley's Labor-Front busses form an endless procession to and from this little Alpine town, which still operates the salt mine underneath Hitler's mountain. Whenever Adolf is in residence at the Berghof, he takes a daily ride through Berchtesgaden around the noon hour, in order that his pilgrims may see their hero riding in the juggernaut of the armed SS Bodyguard automobile caravan. Little girls with bouquets are permitted to slip through the SS cordons to be patted on the head by Hitler from the front seat of his car. Adolf knows that his "Strength-through-Joy" admirers will return to all parts of the Reich to tell their comrades proudly: "Just think! I actually saw the Führer when I was at Berchtesgaden!" Adolf also knows that his daily exhibitionism, as the star attraction of a trip to Berchtesgaden, will help his "Greatest Idealist," Ley, to sell "Strength-through-Joy" tickets to his thirty million underlings in the German Labor Front.

Hitler never ventures outside his mountain home without escorts. His party adjutant Bruckner is always at his side, unless Adolf substitutes one of his military adjutants. His most frequent other companion on his mountain hikes is Gestapo Chief Himmler. Occasionally he will ride around the little Königsee lake in a motorboat, below the towering cliffs of the Watzmann Mountain. Then no other boat is permitted to ripple the surface of the Königsee. Adolf gets most of his exercise vicariously. He will glue his eyes to a powerful telescope to watch intrepid mountain climbers ascending the Watzmann. Once three young men climbed its vertical cliffs until they were caught and could neither advance nor retreat. Hitler immediately ordered a squadron of army 'planes to drop them supplies, commanded a troop of the Alpine soldiers who later conquered Norway to rescue the climbers, turned three of his six-wheeled Obersalzberg winter cars over to the troops to assist in the operations, and finally invited the rescued young mountaineers to the Berghof for dinner. Reich Press Chief Dietrich issued equally sweeping orders to all German newspapers to play up his stories of Adolf as "the discoverer of the mountain climbers' plight and the director of their thrilling rescue?"

Inside his villa, Adolf spends much of his time in his library. Brückner claims that the Führer has read more than six thousand of its books, most of them late at night after the staff of the Berghof had already retired. History, architecture, and the other branches of the arts take up the greatest space in Hitler's five-meter shelves. In one recess of the building, inaccessible to the members of his staff, is his Astrological Room. Hitler is said to keep a mysterious astrologer—a certain Karl Ossietz—employed on a full-time job here. All my efforts to establish the identity of this man and to obtain a reliable description of the Astrological Room in the Berghof were frustrated by the impregnable wall of Nazi secrecy.

My luck was better in discovering the facts about at least one of Hitler's astrologers (he has several of them—there is no all-powerful "Rasputin" controlling the Führer's destiny. Like his generals and his personal physicians, Hitler's astrologers are never sure how long they will hold their jobs.) Fraulein Elvira Luft, a little old woman whose fingers and frame are almost crippled by arthritis, is frequently called to see the Führer at Berchtesgaden and Munich. She lives on the Nymphenburger Strasse, and was listed in the Munich telephone directory as a "graphologist," since "astrologist" is a prohibited profession in the Third Reich. Fraulein Luft gave astrological advice to many prominent Nazis, including Rudolf Hess, Alfred Rosenberg, and directors of heavy industries such as Krupp. Her clandestine meetings with men at the top of the Nazi machine were more useful to her in counseling Hitler than her charts and stars. These men confided in her; she knew several things about conditions in the Reich that even Heinrich Himmler and his Gestapo were unable to ferret out.

Another of Adolf's mystic advisers was an ugly, toothless woman of fifty who was simply known as "Elsa." She was not an astrologist, or even a graphologist. Her specialty was a pack of grimy black rubber cards with no markings whatsoever on them. I managed to arrange a seance with Elsa in a house opposite the Führer's Munich apartment a short time before the Munich Conference. Through an intermediary I was introduced as a trusted foreign adviser of the Reich Press Chief. Elsa began to mumble, and to shuffle her black cards. Then she grunted: "The question in your mind has the following answer: there will be no war this year in the East." That was all she said. She motioned me to leave, to make room for her next client, a member of Adolf Wagner's staff. From him I learned that Elsa had seen the Führer that same morning. Hitler must have dropped a hint that he did not intend to force the issue to the point of attacking the Czechs. Probably Fraulein Luft had advised him against war that fall, and he had wished to compare her astrological findings with the recommendations of Elsa's black cards. (When some of Adolf's advisers like Göring find it hard to influence him by the direct method, they plant their own opinions in the mouth of Elvira Luft. Göring was against waging war on Czechoslovakia in 1938.)

The Berghof contains all of the latest scientific luxuries for Adolf's private enjoyment of films (foreign as well as German), broadcasts, and gramophone records. But when Adolf is not entertaining his ministers or female visitors, he actually does spend most of his time reading his books or discussing Nazi architecture (with emphasis on new types of bunkers, pill boxes, and coastal gun emplacements since the war began) with specialists summoned to the Berghof whenever Hitler feels like exercising his drawing board and pencil again.

Adolf soon grows restless in his mountain retreat. The Berghof is conveniently located as a jumping-off point for several of his favorite excursions around Bavaria. Nearest of these is Salzburg, a half-hour drive, on the former Austrian frontier. Since its Nazification, Hitler often has motored to this famous city, the birthplace of Mozart, to enjoy an opera after dining on the Obersalzberg. Half encircled by mountains, Salzburg is almost as difficult a target for RAF bombers as Berchtesgaden. In its theater, entranced by Mozart's *Il Seraglio*, Adolf can relax completely and forget all about his blitzkrieg.

Hitler's private Ainring Airport, only a few miles from the foot of the Obersalzberg, enables him to hop up to Nuremberg in an hour to lunch with his Franconian Gauleiter. In the afternoon, Julius Streicher escorts his boss around the Party Rallying Grounds, where new stadiums, arenas, and other gargantuan buildings are constantly under construction for the permanent glorification of the Nazi party. Adolf averaged two trips per month to these building sites in 1938 and 1939.

Before the war, Hitler strayed farther afield to the northernmost part of Bavaria, to Bayreuth and its famous Wagner Festivals. Repeated attempts were made to link his name with that of Winifred Wagner, his hostess in charge of the festivals. With four children, Frau Wagner was the ideal German mother from the Nazi standpoint. Adolf's fondness for the *Ring of the Nibelung* and for Bayreuth at the height of the tourist season, however, matched his fondness for Frau Winifred. This Wagner friendship remained platonic. And Bayreuth Festivals remained Wagnerian, Hitler or no Hitler.

The Führer also would attend operas at the Augsburg State Theater, or festivals at Ratisbon in honor of the Austrian composer Bruckner. Führer Adolf has been the guest of honor in every Bavarian city that boasts a symphony orchestra or an opera house, and there are many of them.

Of all the cities in Germany, Hitler likes Munich best. He may trot north to Bayreuth or east to Salzburg for some musical entertainment, but he spends most of his time in the capital of his movement. After a Himmler stroll around the Obersalzberg, a Bummke bath, and a Kannenberg luncheon at the Berghof, Adolf likes to head northwest at the steady speed of fifty miles per hour to the home of his operettas, art galleries, architectural creations, and the cradle of National Socialism, only two hours away from Berchtesgaden. The three to five Mercedes that carry him, his staff, and the omnipresent SS Bodyguards along the four-lane *Autobahn* are capable of almost twice the speed, but Hitler has given strict orders for his drivers never to exceed eighty kilometers per hour. Nor do they often proceed more slowly. Before the war brought about the rationing of benzine, there was no speed limit on the *Autobahns*. If a faster car overtook the Führer convoy, two of the Mercedes would swing out of line to the left of Hitler's car as a moving wall to protect it from any possible "accident." Head-on collisions are out of the question, since there is only one-way traffic on each of the double lanes of the highway. Except in very wet weather, Adolf takes the Berchtesgaden-Munich trip with the top down, a habit he formed while campaigning for his Nazi party in the twenties. He is driven straight to his Munich apartment on the periphery of the city near the end of the *Autobahn,* so that few Munichers have occasion to observe his arrivals or departures.

Hitler's recreation in Munich varies with his moods, the time of year and the time of day. There are several fairly constant factors. He usually pays a visit to the House of German Art in the afternoon, staying there to have tea with Gauleiter Wagner. During the first half of the year, the High Priest of Nazi Art rummages in the basement for paintings to be hung in the annual exhibition. In the autumn months, Adolf inspects the architectural models, for his art gallery also stages a winter exhibition of Nazi architecture. On these occasions he is accompanied by Professor Albert Speer, his favorite architect, who succeeded widow Gerdy Troost's husband. Hitler himself borrows a ruler, pencil, calipers, and compasses to inflict his ideas on his sycophantic advisers. Large-scale models of Robert Ley's mass bathing establishments for "Strength-through-Joy" workers, of the luxurious Führer Schools for Hitler Youths, of the Fallersleben People's Car Factory, which was converted in 1939 to turn out German panzer cars by the thousands, of new party buildings for Nuremberg, of fantastic opera houses, railway stations, super-hotels for workers, subways, and other projects abandoned at the outset of the war, to say nothing of the same *Autobahns* over which Adolf already had traveled countless times before, are the mainstays of this exhibition, which gives Adolf an excuse to speak twice annually in his Art Temple. Hitler has spent innumerable hours in this super-building-block nursery, playing at being what Gauleiter Wagner publicly calls him: "The World's Greatest Architect."

The Führer frequents three restaurants in Munich. The Italian-style Osteria Bavaria in Schwabing is one. It was his favorite eating house before he came to power, as the Carleton Cafe on the Brienner Strasse is his favorite tea room. The Osteria Bavaria contains a little patio with a tinkling fountain and bright frescoes, where Adolf can sip his vegetable broth and dream that he is a Caesar supping in ancient Pompeii. If the Nazi waiters know you well, they will seat you near enough to see "him" eat turnips while Adjutant Bruckner and Press Chief Dietrich carve their way through juicy steaks. The waiter expects a large tip for this privilege.

Adolf also enjoys eating at the renovated Preysing Palace Restaurant, which boasts several private halls for Nazi parties. This restaurant, which obtains Italian asparagus and other out-of-season vegetables by Swastika airplanes from all over Europe, lies directly behind the *Feldherrnhalle* (Hall of the Generals) on the Odeon Platz, between the parallel Theater Strasse and Residenz Strasse. It was at the Feldherrn-halle that Bavarian troops opened fire on Hitler and the other Putschists in 1923. A huge wreath hangs on the Residenz Strasse side of the monument. It is flanked day and night by two SS Guards with fixed bayonets, in honor of Adolf's abortive attempt to seize the reins of the Bavarian government. Pedestrians and bicyclists passing the monument on the wreathed side must raise their hands in the Hitler salute. Originally, the entrance to the Preysing Palace Restaurant was on the same side. But the management found business so poor that they bricked up this entrance and moved it over to the opposite side, facing the Theatiner Strasse and the Theatiner Church. Business improved immediately. Munichers like the church and the Theatiner Strasse. But many of them suffer from Residenz-Strasse phobia—they dislike walking between the desecrated former residence of Bavarian kings now housing Christian Weber's trucking business, and the grim SS Guards, compelled to salute no matter how many bundles they are carrying. Munichers have renamed the Residenz Strasse the "Druckeberger Strasse," the "Try-to-Get-Out-of-It Street."

Recently, Hitler has become especially fond of the restaurant in his Artists' House. For he can play draughtsman with half a dozen architects in his suite there, then repair with them to his dining room in the same building to continue discussing his plans for the Third Reich's "glorious symphony of stone," and after dinner stroll through the bars and dance halls to eye the cream of young Nazi beauties summoned to the Künstlerhaus by the Gestapo manager.

Sometimes the Führer dines privately with an Old Guard Nazi, as he did at the shotgun-wedding banquet of Hermann Esser. Esser, at present Secretary of State and Tourist Traffic in Goebbels' Propaganda Ministry, was a former Bavarian Communist turned Nazi. Thanks to his early efforts for Hitler's party, he was given the job of Bavarian Minister of Economics. In March, 1935, Adolf shelved him temporarily because Munich tongues were wagging too loudly with the stories of Hermann's scandalous affairs. Married and getting no younger, forty-year-old Esser had seduced Annie Bacherl, eighteen, daughter of the boss of Munich's most famous beer hall, the Hofbrau Haus. A child was born. For a while Adolf was too busy with the Anschluss and his own rape of Czechoslovakia to worry about the rape of a beer baron's daughter. At last, however, he lost his temper, and made Frau Esser divorce her errant husband. Then he forced the Munich Don Juan to marry Annie. On April 5, 1939, he was "guest of honor" at the private Esser-Bacherl wedding banquet in the Hotel Vier Jahreszeiten, even postponing a return trip to Berchtesgaden to put a friendly and artistic end to his self-assumed role as the shotgun father. No notice of the banquet appeared in German newspapers. The headwaiter told me that it was "intimate, and restricted to a small circle of Herr Esser's friends."

Unless urgent affairs of state detain the Führer in his Munich apartment or in the Brown House headquarters of the party, he invariably attends the theater in the evening. Early in 1939 he invited his entire Berchtesgaden staff to a performance of the *Merry Widow*—his own third visit to this show in less than one month. For a change from the comic operas at the Gärtnerplatz Theater, he will put on his tuxedo and see a classic opera at the National Theater on the Franz Joseph Platz, or at the Prinzregenten Theater just across the street from his apartment. Or, with mixed feelings as he muses over his affairs with England's Unity Mitford, Adolf will follow G.B. Shaw through *Caesar and Cleopatra* at Falkenberg's *Schauspiel Haus* opposite the Hotel Vier Jahreszeiten. After the theater, Evi Braun is ready to run over to her illustrious sugar daddy and kiss him good night.

Hitler devotes his Munich mornings to semiofficial business. He may confer with his architects, with Nazi artists, with Ribbentrop, Dietrich, Goebbels, and other ministers whom he has called overnight to his southern headquarters, with symphony conductors like Furtwangler, or even with heads of German jazz bands. Several times in 1939 he ordered private auditions from the leader of the Munich Radio Orchestra, to discuss with him Nazi dance music purged of "Jewish and negro influences." He also received Peter Kreuder, the German jazz king and piano virtuoso who put swing and trick melodies into Hitler's favorite versions of Lehar's *Merry Widow*.

Adolf punctuates his Munich stay with visits to the bedsides of Storm Troopers injured in private or political brawls, to the studios of Joseph Thorak and other Nazi artists specializing in sculptures, plaques, and posters for the Third Reich, to the BMW airplane-motor factory, to Oberwiesenfeld Airport to watch test flights of his private, four-motored 'plane, to near-by Landsberg Prison, where he wrote *Mein Kampf* after his arrest in 1923—and to Dachau when he is in a sadistic mood, to see his SS Guards administer a beating to one of his less fortunate political opponents.

The Bavarian capital is a favorite city for inaugurating Nazi exhibitions of all kinds. To vary his program, Adolf visits whatever new Nazi show has been opened. On such occasions, my press card and the fact that I knew several of the Führer's bodyguards and plainclothes Gestapo, enabled me to trail him through the exhibitions at close range, watching his facial expressions and overhearing his remarks to his adjutant. At Reich Minister Darre's Agricultural Exhibition on the Theresienwiese, I stood for several minutes so near to Hitler that I could have touched him as he commented on "the beautiful simplicity and *wunderbare* workmanship" of a model farmhouse. I admit that some strange, dynamic force seemed to radiate from his presence. But I am not sure whether I would have felt this magnetism if the medium-sized, homely-mustached man with the steel-blue eyes had been Adolf Schickelgruber, an ordinary German interior decorator, and not the Chancellor of the powerful Third Reich.

Hitler's regular beer-hall appearances are an integral part of his Munich holidays. February 24th finds Adolf atop a wooden table in the "Festival Hall" of the Hofbrau Haus. Three thousand five hundred Old Guard Nazis pack this hall and keep the buxom waitresses busy refilling their beer mugs as their Führer delivers an informal, impromptu speech that is as sharp and agreeable to the Brown Shirts as the Bavarian horse radishes served with their beer and pretzels. Here Adolf shakes hands with the members of his party who first heard him proclaim the twenty-five points of his program from the same table in 1920, the night that Rudolf Hess got conked on the head and permanently scarred by a stein thrown by a Communist who had forced his way into the Hofbrau rally. The night of November 8-9 finds Adolf rubbing shoulders with the same crowd at the Bürgerbräu Keller, commemorating his inauguration of the 1923 march through Munich streets from this beer hall to the Feldherrnhalle in the Putsch. Christmas Eve—unless he is at the front with "his boys in field gray"—finds teetotaling Hitler under a giant Christmas tree in the main hall of the Lowenbrau Keller, distributing gifts ranging from Mercedes cars to radios to some of the five thousand Storm Troopers and other deserving Nazis who do their best to drain the capacious barrels of the beer cellar. No urgent call from Mars or the government of the Third Reich can keep Hitler away from these annual festivities.

Adolf celebrates two birthdays in Bavaria. He was born on April 20, 1889, at Braunau on the Austrian side of the Inn River. He flies to Munich from Berlin every afternoon of April 20th for a brief rest from his birthday formalities at the Reich capital, and for an informal party in the Brown House. But Hitler considers another date to be as important as his nativity. It is the sixteenth of August.

April 20th is the birthday of Adolf Hitler, Reich Chancellor. August 16th marks the birth of *Freiwilliger* soldier Adolf Hitler, who enlisted on this date as a volunteer in the 16th Bavarian Reserve Infantry Regiment. In 1939, Hitler was fifty years old. Twenty-five years before, he first became a soldier. Thus in 1939, Adolf had spent exactly half of his life as a fighter, beginning and ending on the battlefront, with a period of political belligerency sandwiched in between the first and second world wars.

On August 16th, the Commander-in-Chief, the Chief of Staff of Hitler's *Wehrmacht,* and his fat Field-Marshal head of the *Luftwaffe,* call on their Führer to congratulate him and to wish him a happy "soldier's birthday." Hitler invites past and present officers and men of his former regiment to a special "birthday party" at Berchtesgaden. The Swastika battle flag is hoisted over the Munich headquarters of the Führer's old regiment—renamed the Adolf Hitler Barracks. It is a gala day in Hitler's program of rest and recreation!

***

BRASS HATS IN BAVARIA

Hitler's assistant dictators, like their chief, play hookey from Berlin to indulge in their own special brands of hobbies in their pet south German haunts. Thus Reich Foreign Minister Joachim von Ribbentrop plays golf on the Feldafing Course, fifteen miles from Munich; Reich Labor Leader Robert Ley whips his speedy motorboat around Lake Starnberg below Ribbentrop's golf course; Hermann Göring sticks boars in the Bavarian Forest; Rudolf Hess attends—or rather attended—concerts with his wife in Munich's "Tone Hall"; Goebbels retires to one of his luxurious Bavarian love nests; while Heinrich Himmler takes a day off from his Gestapo desk for some vigorous exercise—personally administering whippings to the inmates of Dachau Concentration Camp.

The Obersalzberg at Berchtesgaden is vacation headquarters for the Nazi chieftains. Most of them have their own private villas near Haus Wachenfeld. Needless to say, the zoning laws are severe, since the Berghof section of Hitler's mountain is reserved exclusively for the resort homes of his closest Third Reich associates. Their neighborly proximity makes it easy for Adolf to consult his ministers, who sun themselves on their front lawns on the Obersalzberg while waiting to be called to see their chief. If Führer Hitler does not believe that he will have need of their service immediately, he tells them to run along and play in other parts of Bavaria. In less than three hours, Adolf can have his henchmen assembled together from their various pleasurable pursuits for a plenary session of the Nazi government at the Berghof.

Gestapo Chief Himmler does not know how to play. I have not been able to discover him enjoying any of the lighter things of life. He seldom smiles. His hobby, if it could be so called, resembles most closely that of dog, horse, or cat fanciers, who spend their time breeding, training, and showing off their special race of animal. One must remember that Heinrich obtained his degree in *agriculture* after studying at Munich University. Himmler's Brown-Ribbon entries are young Nordics. His kennels, stables, or whatever you wish to call them are the barracks of his SS Guards. On the subject of breeding and propagating perfect physical specimens of Nordic

Germans, the Gestapo chief is a fanatic. Whenever his cold-blooded duties permit, he visits the barracks, Hitler Youth camps, and labor-service homes of the League of German Girls to inspect his stock, to preach the gospel of healthy reproduction, to award medals for the best male and female specimens, and to arrange facilities for encouraging the optimum number and quality of the Third Reich's postwar generation.

Himmler likes bonfires. He feels the blood of the ancient Druids coursing through his veins as he rallies his young SS men around a burning pyre at midnight. With a wild storm raging through a forest clearing or over an Alpine mountain top, he exhorts his guards to "keep the race pure," and swears in new recruits to eternal fealty to the Führer with Runic symbols, archaic German phrases, and special Teutonic rituals devised by himself in moments when he is not busy studying the latest scientific methods of sleuthing, document forging, and wire tapping.

Reich SS Führer Himmler's other forms of recreation are plain. Most of his time at Berchtesgaden is spent accompanying Hitler on his walks. Unlike Goebbels, Göring, and most of the other Nazi ministers, Black Heinrich lives simply. He cares little for the wine, women, and song extolled by German poets. In some respects he is much more ascetic than Adolf, who softened after five years in power. Himmler keeps himself in better physical trim than his Führer, whom he can outwalk on their Obersalzberg peregrinations. Whether Heinrich derives any aesthetic pleasure from his strolls through Berchtesgaden nature at its best is doubtful. He knows that exercise and fresh mountain air are good for him, whereas birds, flowers, and blue water are pitfalls for "degenerate poets" like his black-listed namesake, Heinrich (Heine).

Finally, the Gestapo chief's vacations are devoted to devising and testing new methods of punishment and torture for his concentration camps. Like a good leader, he does not expect his men to do anything that he would not do himself. Consequently, he himself takes the whip out of their hands to administer some *Kashumbo* to one of his prize catches whom he particularly hates.

There is a streak of sadism in Heinrich Himmler almost as strong as his paranoiac fanaticism for Nordic racial supremacy.

At the opposite extreme of pleasure-seeking Nazis we have Hitler's deputy, Rudolf Hess. Rudolf was called a *"guter Junge,"* a good boy, by the German people, who know something about their rulers. His hobbies were aviation and music. He was the most insipid of the Brown-Shirt leaders, and had become little more than the Munich watchdog of Nazi Party Headquarters, the Brown House, before he broke his chain and ran away from his master.

Born in Egypt, Hess has not quite succeeded in casting off the British influence of his early years. Perhaps a certain nostalgia brought him regularly to the symphony concerts conducted in the party capital before the war by the noted British composer and conductor, Sir Thomas Beecham. Perhaps certain pangs of conscience caused Hitler's deputy to shed his brown uniform, put on plain street clothes and take his wife to church services incognito in the more remote environs of Munich, where he would not be recognized by members of the party.

In public life, Rudolf Hess was the "yes-man" of the Third Reich. He took his cues for his deputized speeches from his boss and from other Nazi orators, and like a good boy said and did what he was told—for a while. His exalted position in the party was due to his pre-Third Reich services as Hitler's Paladin, when he dutifully took the hard knocks and flying missiles intended for the Führer, and to the fact that his life, compared to other party members, was sufficiently free from scandal to permit him to assume the role of the "irreproachable" Führer's deputy.

Hess's actual ability to rule the Third Reich with an iron hand, and his failing popularity among the other members of the Nazi "inner circle," were eloquently appraised by none other than his chief, who placed Hermann Göring ahead of his own deputy to assume the Swastika throne, should anything happen to Adolf Hitler. Rudolf Hess became little more than an ornament in the Nazi hierarchy. His main attributes, which distinguished him from more capable Third Reich leaders, were an apparently absolute subservience to the Führer, almost naïve physical courage, the type of manly handsomeness that bowls over the simple-minded female adherents of Hitlerism, and sufficient breeding to extend a cordial welcome to the Reich's guests whom busy Adolf turned over to his *Stellvertreter*.

Except for the party riches which enabled him to indulge in his favorite sport, flying (like Göring, Hess was an aviator in Kaiser Wilhelm's air force) and for his deputy functions, Rudolf lived the life of the average bourgeois German. The more conservative members of young Germany, especially university students, idolized him, not the radical Hitler Youth Leader, Baldur von Schirach. They would gladly have followed his example in parachuting to internment by the British rather than suffer the consequences of the Führer's berserk leadership.

I met bushy-eyed Rudolf on several occasions, notably in connection with the Beecham concerts. From my knowledge of the man and his position in the Reich, I could quite easily understand his dramatic flight from Naziland in May, 1941. I believe that the main motive that prompted Hess to "steal" a Messerschmitt 110 and and take French leave of Germany was to avoid the fate of another close associate of Hitler, Ernst Roehm. Just before his death, Roehm had argued with Hitler about Third Reich policies. And Roehm had remained loyal to his personal creeds. Just before his flight, Hess had had differences with the Führer about the conduct of the war. And Hess had remained loyal to his religion and to his belief that the war between the Anglo-Saxons and the German "brothers" was a ghastly mistake, to be terminated as quickly as possible. When Rudolf found that he was getting nowhere in his attempts to persuade his chief, he took the only way out, hoping to save his skin and, if possible, himself to take the initiative in bringing about a negotiated peace.

What about Frau Hess? Why did the Christian Nazi leave his family behind to the tender mercies of his erstwhile gang?

The answer is simple. Rudolf Hess was undertaking the most dangerous adventure of his career. If his family had accompanied him to that Augsburg airport from which he took off or England, this would have aroused suspicion among the uninitiated Nazis.

154

Furthermore, Rudolf, flying in the face of death from both German and British 'planes, preferred to die alone rather than to be instrumental in the death of his wife and child. In Germany, despite his deed, they would be safe. For once in the hands of the British, Hess knew that the Nazis could exert no pressure on him to return to the Reich to protect his family. And knowing the Hitler mentality, he could reckon with a "noble gesture" from the Führer, who would realize the propaganda effect on German morale of letting Frau Hess be seen in public, instead of stirring up still more resentment against himself by the Hess adherents for imprisoning or executing her. Knowing the British from his early youth, Hitler's deputy was sure of his personal safety once he landed on the Isles, even if his pacifist mission should fail.

One of Joachim von Ribbentrop's topcoats kept the hood of my roadster warm throughout the winter of 1937-1938, before deteriorating into a bed for one of my friend's doghouses. I did not intentionally take the Nazi Foreign Minister's coat. An American friend of mine on a tour of the Reich bears the brunt of the blame.

This college classmate turned up in Munich in the late summer of 1937, quite unprepared for the cool, damp evenings that every so often sneak down from the Alps without warning. I loaned him my topcoat. The British consul, Captain C.J. Phillips, and his wife had invited me to meet them for dinner at Feldafing's Kaiserin Elizabeth Hotel, a pleasant drive from Munich along the west bank of Lake Starnberg. "Bring your friend," said the hospitable Captain. I had no news for London that day; everything in Munich seemed quiet. So I switched my telephone to *Kundendienst,* whereby one of the *Reichspost* telephone operators automatically became my secretary, recording the names, numbers, and messages of all persons attempting to call my office. I used this service frequently. It enabled me to go skiing at Garmisch and other places, from which I could telephone the Munich operator to find out whether there had been any important calls for me.

Bob and I motored out to the little village of Feldafing and joined the Phillipses. The Kaiserin Elizabeth seemed deserted. Only half a dozen men, all in tuxedos, were dining at the table near our own.

The Captain and I exchanged significant winks. Both of us had had considerable experience in spotting SS Bodyguards. I excused myself for a moment from the dining room. First I called Munich to make sure that everything was still quiet. It wasn't. Reuters had been trying frantically to get me. I put in a call for the Berlin office. Then I slipped the hotel porter ten marks, whispering, "Who is your guest of honor?"

"Ribbentrop and his Frau! They arrived this afternoon, and have retired to their rooms. Herr von Ribbentrop plans to stay here for several days for a bit of golf. That's his coat, hanging next to yours. *Vielen Dank.*"

Telephone service in Germany is primitive, compared with American standards. I was able to finish my dessert and coffee before my Berlin call came through.

"What the hell are you doing out there, Pope?" an angry voice rasped. "We've been trying to get hold of you all evening. You are paid to be Reuters' *Munich* correspondent, not to go galavanting about the countryside!"

"What's up? What can I do for you?" I replied humbly, fearing that Hitler had crashed in a 'plane over Munich or that some other wonderful story had broken which my competitors were scooping from me. I was very worried.

"Ribbentrop is not in Berlin. We are not able to locate him. It is very important to know where he is. We think he is down your way somewhere, but can't find him. Drop everything, hurry back to Munich, and get busy on his trail. London is very displeased that you are not on the job at your office."

"Tell London that they never had a more wide-awake correspondent in the Nazi stronghold. I know what I'm doing all right. Your Ribbentrop is about twenty feet away from here over my head. What in hell did you think I came out to Feldafing for, anyway? I had my reasons!"

"Good boy!" old man Josten sighed into the Berlin end of the trunk line. "Excuse me for scolding you. I'll pass on your interesting information to London right away. That's all we want for tonight, but keep an eye on Rippy."

I was so relieved at the fortunate outcome of my unexpected trip to Ribbentrop's hiding place that I tipped the porter again. Then I joined Bob and the Phillipses in the *Bierstube,* a cozier place for social drinking than the large dining hall. We traded jokes about the Nazis, sang songs, and had a very convivial time.

One by one the tuxedos dropped into the beverage room. Gradually—and they may have thought imperceptibly—their conversation switched to English. Then it became louder. They began singing English songs, with a slight accent. After an hour or so, and several more rounds at each table, one of their number cam over, bowed, and asked whether he could sing with us.

"Perhaps we had better all be more quiet," I suggested. "Our singing might disturb the slumbers of someone upstairs."

"Don't worry. this place is deserted. In fact it is as dead as a cemetery upstairs!"

"Now, now! Come, come! What if your chief heard you say that! Isn't your job to keep tombstones off the gentleman who is now asleep in the best suite of the Kaiserin Elizabeth tonight?" I rejoined, unable to contain myself at their clumsy spying any longer. The British consul, his wife, Bob, and I beamed most pleasantly at the Gestapo lieutenant. He withdrew to his colleagues, after mumbling a confused "I do not comprehend you. There must be some error. Excuse me, please. Perhaps have I had too much wine."

The unmasked Gestapo tuxedos left the room as soon as they could without losing more face, and went upstairs to take up their night's vigil.

We were so pleased with ourselves that we stayed on a bit longer to celebrate the Gestapo's discomfort. Finally, however, it was time to go home. Even the porter had gone to bed. So we fetched out coats ourselves, then drove back through the crisp night to Munich.

The next morning Bob 'phoned to announce that he had bought himself a *Loden Frey* coat. I picked him up at his hotel for lunch.

There he handed me the topcoat which he had borrowed the previous evening. I looked at it, dumbfounded. The color was the same as mine. So was the weight. But it was not the one I had loaned him. *It was Ribbentop's.* Bob had grabbed the wrong coat in the dim cloakroom of the Hotel Kaiserin Elizabeth.

I called the hotel porter from Munich. With profuse apologies, I promised to exchange the coats as soon as possible. But somehow I never found time to drive out to Feldafing. I telephoned the hotel every few days, assuring the porter that I was coming out very soon, and at the same time inquiring about Ribbentrop's activities for the day. The last time I called the Elizabeth that month, the Nazi Foreign Minister (at that time German Ambassador to England) had just left for the north. I do not know to this day whether he took my topcoat with him, or threw it away in disgust. His own was too small for me, so I used it to cover the hood of my car when winter came. By spring it was only fit for the doghouse.

The Feldafing Golf Course is part of an exclusive country club reserved for distinguished foreign tourists, Ribbentrop, and the handful of Axis statesmen who know how to wield a niblick as well as the club of power politics. On its greens one has a clear view of the Alps forty miles to the south, of Lake Starnberg and the shore opposite Feldafing where King Ludwig the Second of Bavaria drowned himself and his personal physician, and of the Feldafing "Führer School," where fuzzy-cheeked Hitler Youths are being trained not only to replace kings, but also the present generation of Adolfs and Ribbentrops. Many informal conferences of Continental foreign ministers have been held at the Kaiserin Elizabeth, the nineteenth hole of the Nazi Foreign Minister's golf course. It was here that Hungary's Foreign Minister Count Czaky was wined and dined in the summer of 1939. Ribbentrop let the Count play through at Feldafing, and in return received Czaky's assurance that Hitler's troops could play through Hungary's *pustas* on their way to the next birdie in the Balkans.

Not content with chartering the Kaiserin Elizabeth for his golfing week ends, Ribbentrop exploited the Anschluss of Austria to acquire a second summer home one hundred miles to the southeast of

Munich, near Salzburg and the famous Wolfgang See, on which is situated the original White Horse Inn. The Nazi politician seized four-hundred-year-old Fuschl Castle, a beautiful lakeside estate owned by Herr Gustav von Remitz, a Jewish Legitimist, who was promptly thrown into Dachau Concentration Camp. It was here that Rippy sauntered along the shore with Fascist Foreign Minister Count Ciano, plotting the overthrow of the British Empire two weeks before the war. Since the Nazi Foreign Minister could not speak Italian, nor his Fascist colleague German, the Axis ministers discussed their intrigues against England *in English!*

When Hitler needs Joachim at his beck and call in Berchtesgaden, Rippy vacations at his Fuschl Castle, forty-five minutes from the Obersalzberg by car. When Adolf puts up at his apartment in Munich and wants Rippy close at hand, Joachim moves to his country-club hotel at Feldafing, likewise an easy three-quarter-hour drive from the Führer's temporary headquarters. Nothing like combining comfort with practicability!

When in Munich, through which Joachim von Ribbentrop frequenthy passes on his way to Berchtesgaden, Italy, and other excursion points, the Nazi Foreign Minister stays at Ilse Hotel Vier Jahreszeiten. It was here that President Roosevelt's telegram to Hitler caught up with him in April, 1939, proposing complete reciprocal pledges against aggression for at least ten years, to be followed by a world peace conference to discuss disarmament and economic readjustment. Mr. Roosevelt's appeal caught Ribbentrop in one of his frequent attacks of indigestion, which may have contributed to the belching character of his rejection of the American President's peace message.

On another occasion, after spending the afternoon with the Führer in the House of German Art, Rippy suddenly forsook the companionship of his chief and retired in pain to his hotel suite. That evening disappointed Adolf attended the *Merry Widow* without his foreign minister, to whom he had intended pointing out the juicy bits of the comic opera.

When the next chapter of history is written, Joachim von Ribbentrop's stomach deserves a paragraph near Hitler's manic-depressive nervous system. Probably as a result of drinking too much of his wife's Henkell champagne, which he peddled before he became Hitler's traveling salesman, Ribbentrop's digestive tract is always getting out of order, despite his golfing at Feldafing, his hikes around Fuschl Castle, and the internationally recognized talents of Herr Walterspiel. Walterspiel's Restaurant in the Hotel Vier Jahreszeiten is without question the finest cuisine in Germany. Herr Walterspiel has opened hotels in North and South America, in Africa, France, and Scandinavia. He has devoted a lifetime to the study of making food tasty for the most exacting palates. He speaks several languages; his dishes can talk in any language. That is why Ribbentrop nurses his stomach ulcers with Walterspiel's cooking whenever he is within earshot of the Munich dinner gong. If the Third Reich's Foreign Office could be moved to the Hotel Vier Jahreszeiten, or Walterspiel's Restaurant to the Wilhelmstrasse, Nazi foreign policy might be changed considerably. Walterspiel told me so himself—before he adopted the protective habit of wearing a Nazi party button.

Reich Propaganda Minister Goebbels is seen less in Bavaria than any of his Wilhelmstrasse colleagues. The clubfooted little dictator is the least popular of the high-ranking Nazis among the south Germans. He sometimes hobbles along as Hitler's shadow, but seldom ventures out in public on his own, unless it is to inflate his vanity and compensate himself for his private unpopularity by playing host to Bavarian officials and leading citizens at large and expensive formal banquets. Goebbels spends most of his time in the secluded heights of the Obersalzberg, to which he imports his feminine talent from Berlin. To be sure, his junior partner, *Reichshauptamtsleiter* Dr. Adolf Dresler, occasionally does a bit of clandestine procuring for Pal Joey among the less scrupulous career actresses of the Bavarian stage and screen, and joins him in private parties at the Artists' House. Goebbels' other Munich confrere whom he always looks up is Adolf Ziegler, President of the Reich Chamber of Arts, who has the inside track on Munich artists and their models.

Whenever he is in Munich, the Propaganda Minister never fails to see Dorothy van Bruck and the other blitz-teasers at the Theater am Gärtnerplatz. But he has little use for the beauties of Bavarian nature, unless represented by two legs and a grass skirt. Bavarian women flee in terror when Wotan's Mickey Mouse pops out of hiding.

Aside from introducing variety into his affairs, Goebbels disports himself in Bavaria by appearing on the lecture platforms of Munich University to justify his academic title of "Doctor." Attendance is compulsory for Munich students, so the Sage of Smear is always sure of a large audience. His subjects may range from anti-Bolshevism to pro-Sovietism.

Munich students delight in relating the story of two flies that ran a race from one corner of the Propaganda Minister's mouth to the other: One fly was conceded to be the faster runner of the two. Both started at the same time from the left corner of Goebbels' mouth. But, when the faster fly arrived at the right corner, his slower competitor was already there.

"How in the world did you get here ahead of me?" asked the astonished fly, who had been sure of victory.

"That was easy—I took the short cut around the back of Goebbels' head!"

Frau Magda Goebbels frequently comes to Munich for a vacation. A vacation from her embarrassing husband. She hides in a modest home in Munich-Schwabing, to which she retires in order to forget that the man she married is the noisiest and most active rake of the entire Nazi tribe.

Reich Labor Leader Robert Ley has as grand a time in Bavaria as his Führer permits. His whisky-tenor voice rings out repeatedly amidst his Brown-Shirt comrades in any one of several Munich beer halls. His summer home on the shore of Lake Starnberg is the height of luxury. A subterranean boathouse with a tunnel leading directly into his villa harbors his speedboats. In his idle hours, which are more numerous than most Germans are allowed to believe, Ley leads the life of a multi-millionaire playboy on the dues collected from the members of his Labor Front.

When his ostentation threatened to become too apparent, Hitler cracked down on Ley and confiscated one of his private palaces: a huge estate in the most expensive residential section of Munich, Grünwald on the right bank of the Isar River. Ley had hoped to outrival Göring's Karinhall, Ribbentrop's Fuschl Castle, and the other villas of the Third Reich plutocrats with this estate.

"This is going too far," Adolf warned him. "Remember, you are My Greatest Idealist. I command you to turn your Grünwald mansion over to the National Socialist Welfare Organization!"

The Reich Labor Leader was forced to obey. But he still owns half a dozen smaller, equally luxurious estates in various scenic parts of Bavaria.

For a real binge, with no danger of disillusioning any of the trusting Germans, Ley resorts to a simple suhterfuge. Three of his transport 'planes are warmed up at the Munich airport. Ley and his immediate staff enter the first. His "secretaries" enter the second. His Mercedes is rolled into the third. The Labor Front 'planes take off, supposedly on an important business trip to another part of the Reich. Instead, they land on an obscure airport in southern Italy, far from the prying eyes of the hard-working German laborers. In 1938, the champagne bill for Robert Ley's weekend party at the Dominico Hotel in Taormina, Sicily, paid the hotel's taxes for the entire year. After such an "arduous business trip devoted to the welfare of his fellow citizens," ordinary Germans must forgive their dynamic Labor Leader for taking a day off on Starnberg Lake and burning up some of the Reich's precious benzine!

Field Marshal Hermann Göring bears little resemblance to a rose. Yet he was born in the "Home of the Roses," the city of Rosenheim, halfway between Berchtesgaden and Munich on the Inn River and Hitler's *Autobahn*. "Uncle Hermann" enjoys returning to the land of his nativity for a change from his Prussian territory. I do not know how many mountain chamois have had to sacrifice their hides to furnish sufficient material for Göring's expensive leather shorts. But the fact remains that the Field Marshal likes this informal costume as much as any of his gaudy, bemedaled uniforms.

Bavaria is one more excuse for Hermann to indulge in his diverse outdoor sports. The woods of the Bavarian forests provide boars, deer, and other animals for Hitler's official Reich Master of the Hunt. The wooded trails are fine for his sleigh rides in winter, while the Chiem See, the large lake less than ten miles from his home town, is ideal for the Field Marshal's boating picnics. Anything from a bow and arrow to an elephant gun is the proper toy for Göring, who is the absolute dictator of German forests as well as the boss of the *Luftwaffe*. As Reich Game Warden, the fat huntsman picks his targets as he pleases. Unconfirmed local rumors even reported that Heinrich Himmler on occasion would flush some condemned two-legged game for the *Reichsjägermeister,* to lend additional zest to the chase. In Germany, you must obtain your hunting and fishing permits from the Espionage Division of the *Wehrmacht,* which makes sure that you steer clear of certain areas among the woods, fields, and streams of the Third Reich. What a wonderful opportunity for privileged characters to hunt "the most dangerous game"!

When Uncle Hermann is not waddling up and down the slopes of his estate above Hitler's villa on the Obersalzberg, or sticking boars in the *Bayerischer Wald,* he shops around Munich. The "City of German Art" has provided many masterpieces and interior furnishings for the Field Marshal's Prussian and Bavarian homes. Munichers agree with Shakespeare that "fat men, sleek men, men that sleep o' nights" are much more preferable than men with the "lean and hungry look" of Cassius and Goebbels. Therefore they cheer Göring whenever they see him riding through Munich streets, and form crowds outside the Hotel Vier Jahreszeiten whenever he is in residence there. The Bavarians appreciate Hermann's regular patronage of the state theaters in Munich, for opera-going is an integral part of Munich life.

Munichers also remember that Hermann's brother Albert[6] married a Bavarian and is south German at heart. Engineer Albert Göring tries to keep Bavaria from being treated like a stepchild by the Prussian administration in Berlin. At present he is the manager of the famous Skoda Munition Works near Prague, which were taken from the Czechs in March, 1939. Before that, he was head of the Italian branch of a German film company (*Tobis*). The Görings are a versatile family!

[6]*Albert Göring is known today for his many anti-Nazi actions and his aid to Jews in Germany.*

Every Third Reich boss has his own reasons for coming to Bavaria. Reich Minister of the Interior Frick spends his winter holidays skiing in the Alps. Reich Führer of Justice Franck, who later became the Nazi governor of Poland, putters around his House of German Justice on the Ludwig Strasse or, as a close friend of Il Duce, delves into Munich night life with members of the Italian colony, whom he treats to banquets in the Preysing Palace. Reich Youth Leader Baldur von Schirach leaves his Führer's boys and girls to visit his own wife and children on their country estate forty miles from Munich. General Ritter von Epp, leader of the Reich's Colonial League, has his head office and home on the Prinzregenten Strasse, two blocks from the House of German Art. They all recognize that Bavaria has more to offer in the way of enjoyable living than any other part of the Reich.

So do their blond secretaries.

It was in this informal atmosphere that the representatives of the foreign powers accredited to the Nazi playground worked and played with their Brown-Shirt hosts.

In Hitler's playground, diplomacy bore little resemblance to the Berlin brand. Ambassadors to the capital of the Reich constantly were struggling against the snobbish petulance of Joachim von Ribbentrop and his henchmen in the Foreign Office. They fidgeted at their unsavory social duties when Chancellor Hitler, Field Marshal Göring, and Propaganda Minister Goebbels invited them to the stiff, electricity-charged receptions of nouveau-riche Nazidom in the Chancellery and the other Berlin showrooms of the Third Reich. In Munich, the representatives of foreign powers contended with more congenial Nazi hosts: phlegmatic, white-haired little Bavarian

Prime Minister Siebert instead of an unpredictable, nasty-tempered Hitler; a country gentleman of the old school, jovial Baron Stengel, as the official host of the diplomats for the State of Bavaria, in place of the gangster prima donna Ribbentrop; sheepish Adolf Dresler rather than satanic Goebbels; beer-guzzling Adolf Wagner instead of the ex-dope fiend Göring.

Of all the consuls stationed in Munich, one in particular deserves special mention: My closest friend and associate, Captain Christopher J. Phillips of His Britannic Majesty's Consulate-General. In my opinion Consul Phillips was the most able man serving the interests of His Majesty in the capital of the Nazi party. When he left Munich for England, he left a very sad Reuters correspondent behind him. But the Nazis breathed a sigh of relief. If Great Britain had shaped her foreign policy in the light of work done by Captain Phillips, there never would have been a Greater Germany and a Hitler menace. But Parliament and postwar Prime Ministers up to—and to a certain extent including—Chamberlain failed to act on the information about Germany that was coming in a steady stream from British consuls like the Captain ever since the end of the First World War. What Captain Christopher J. Phillips did not know about Germany after spending eighteen years in the Reich was not worth knowing.

As a representative of the British press in Munich, I naturally kept in closer touch with His Majesty's Consulate-General than with my own, which I visited less frequently for professional reasons than for the sake of sociability. Occupying the second floor of an office building in the Pranner Strasse, the British Consulate defiantly fluttered its Union Jack in the face of the Swastika on "The House of the National Socialists," Gauleiter Adolf Wagner's Bavarian party building.

Part of my daily news-gathering routine consisted of dropping in at the British Consulate for a chat with the Captain or his colleague, Consul Frank Fulham. As a correspondent, I could snoop about Bavaria in places where a representative of His Majesty's foreign service would hesitate to be seen, while the latter often would be in possession of information inaccessible to a journalist without a diplomatic passport.

"Ernest old boy, what do you know?" was the Captain's customary greeting, after he had carefully closed the door to his office and offered me his etui of Gold Flakes.

"The supplies of ether in Munich have been requisitioned by the *Wehrmacht,* and the Munich surgeons told to use substitute anesthetics;" "Kung, the Chinese Minister of Finance, will see Hitler at Berchtesgaden tomorrow noon;" "Nazi tanks are holding maneuvers between Garmisch and Weilheim this week;" "the *Volkischer Beobachter* will publish a violent editorial about British mandated colonies in tomorrow's edition;" "Mr. So and So is seeing quite a bit of Unity Mitford"—might be my answer, depending on what I had learned from my private sources, personal observations, or colleagues during the past twenty-four hours. The Captain would take down some notes to include in his regular reports on the situation in Bavaria. In return he would tell me that the Duke and Duchess of Kent were due in Munich incognito on the Orient Express that evening; that Siegfried Aufhauser, the Swedish Consul-General, had reported to him that a Jew had been beaten to death by two drunken Storm Troopers in the—house at No.— on the —Strasse the previous night; that Lord Redesdale was coming to Munich to visit his daughter Unity; that the Munich home of Mrs.— had been raided by the Gestapo; that 479 British visas had been issued to Munich Jews in the past month; or other facts that I could telephone to my editors.

Dinner at the Phillipses was a bit of England in the heart of Nazi Germany. The best products of "Caterers to His Majesty the King," thanks to his diplomatic privileges, were served in the Captain's home by a maid whom Mrs. Phillips had trained to perfection in the duties of an English servant. Needless to say, Phillips's liquor cabinet was always stocked with all the favorites of a Sherwood Forester. After coffee and brandy, we would listen to the BBC News and talk about Adolf.

"Why that bloody scoundrel!" the Captain would exclaim. "We should have wiped him and his gangsters off the map the moment he became Chancellor. All he wants is war, and will do his darndest to get it. Yet all they do in London is sit on their tails and watch Germany grow stronger every day. I have sent in report after report. All they do is collect dust. Have another drink."

Together we explored practically every night club and beer hall in town, often getting into hot arguments with the Nazis. Phillips did not mince words. His friends feared that he would be asked to leave the Reich any day. But somehow, he managed to stay on. When he finally bade his formal adieu to Bavarian Prime Minister Siebert, his docket on Siebert's desk —which the Prime Minister would not permit him to examine—was almost half a foot thick. In it were recorded the places in which the Munich consul had been seen, his anti-Nazi remarks, his activities, the people, like myself, who had been observed in his company at all times of day and night in all parts of Bavaria, and other phases of the Captain's private life, carefully compiled by Gestapo agents, with some of whom we had doubtless downed beers in the early morning hours. Phillips knew that he was being watched. But that did not dampen his boyish enthusiasm for expressing his contempt of the Nazis.

One summer morning about five A.M., when we were feeling as rosy as the sky on the eastern horizon, the Captain and I walked arm in arm past the SS Guards and their sacred wreath at the Feldherrnhalle, our hats tilted at a racy angle, harmonizing Tipperary at the top of our voices. Phillips's tenor was his pride and joy; in exchange for American college songs, he taught me some of his cockney favorites which we practiced wherever we put in for a beer. Not content with demonstrating his disregard for the "hallowed" site where Nazi violence first had been frustrated, the Captain said:

"Come on, Ernest. Let's desecrate the corpses of these bloody Putschists!"

Somewhat hesitant, but consoling myself with the knowledge that my license plates were caked with mud, I permitted myself to be persuaded. We climbed into my roadster, and zoomed around on the Königlicher Platz in front of the two Third-Reich temples containing the coffins of the sixteen Brown Shirts killed in the 1923

Putsch. Nobody except Hitler and high-ranking officials or guests of the Reich are permitted to drive past these "sacred monuments." I breathed a sigh of relief when I had satisfied the Captain's whim without being caught or shot by the SS Guards posted at each temple.

In spite of his fondness for night life, Captain Phillips would be hard at work at his Consulate early every morning. Fifteen years my senior, he set a pace that I did not find easy to follow, yet enjoyed very thoroughly.

At the Consulate, the Captain discharged his duties with that quiet efficiency so characteristic of the British, and so different from the blustering efficiency of the Prussian *Geist*.

It is the difference between a silent, high-speed steam turbine and the ponderous hammering of a reciprocating engine. Writing reports on the economic, political, and military status of Bavaria was one of Phillips's jobs. Taking care of the interests and difficulties of British tourists and businessmen in Germany was another. Examining the cases of German Jews and Nazi agents disguised as refugees, who came begging for visas to England, was a third, Representing His Majesty's Government at Hitler's, Wagner's, and Mayor Fiehler's Nazinalia took a large part of the consul's time. But in between, he contrived to pick the right horses at Reim for extra Reichmarks, the right German acquaintances for extra information, and the right British tourists for the extra enjoyment of his kaleidoscopic post in the Nazi Stronghold.

Captain Phillips resigned from consular service in July, 1939, in order to assume the directorship of an armament factory in England. His departure from the Reich revealed his keen judgment, as well as one of the neatest tricks I have seen played on the Nazis. In 1938, his wife Anita still held considerable property in Germany in the form of Reichsmarks, which the German government refused to exchange for pounds. The Captain was well aware that Germany was headed for war with England, and that he could not long exercise his consular duties in Hitler's playground. He was nobody's fool, least of all the Nazis.' So he bought himself an expensive American car from a Munich dealer, then, then drove to England.

There he purchased an unfurnished cottage fifty miles from London, then returned to the Munich Consulate. He and Anita proceeded to buy up the most expensive household furnishings from Munich department stores, having them crated and shipped to England under his diplomat's privileges. In 1938 and 1939, the Captain made four trips to England, in a new car each time. The last automobile was one of the few remaining British models left in the Reich. In it, with all his property safely in the cottage, Christopher and Anita made their final diplomatic exit from Germany, two months before the war began and before the seizure of British property and the internment of British subjects (including consuls) in the Reich. A completely furnished cottage, plus four racy automobiles "somewhere in England" are material testimonials to Captain Phillips's ability to outsmart the Nazis.

The Consulate-General of the United States of America at Munich was one of the happy-go-luckiest clubs I have frequented. Until its removal to the Ott Strasse, and until his retirement in 1939, it was presided over by a lovable old character: Charles Hathaway, dean of the Munich diplomatic corps. White-haired, academic Hathaway was more interested in the Nazi-Church controversy than in any other phase of Third-Reich policy. We would hold lengthy discussions of Archbishop Faulhaber's sermons, the closing of confessional schools, and the philosophy behind the new German paganism. The American C.G. had a keen sense of humor. Kindly old Hathaway even forgave the crude Nazi officials who made him stand painfully for two long hours in the crowded "Hall of Fame" of the House of German Art one year, while Hitler inaugurated its annual exhibition as Storm Troop petty officers sat comfortably in chairs.

When "Papa" Hathaway—as he was affectionately called by the members of the British and American colonies in Munich—retired, he was succeeded by Consul-General Orsen Nielsen, a somewhat younger, very capable member of the State Department. Hathaway's retirement to a well-deserved rest in peaceful California marked the passing of the easygoing days of consular service in Munich. Nielsen walked into the job of moving the Consulate to new quarters, moving Americans out of the warring Reich to safety, assuming the burdens of the closed British and French consulates, and moving himself about in a blacked-out, rationed city. Even as Consul-General, Mr. Nielsen was stopped by German policemen and ordered not to drive his car outside the city limits —to save benzine for Hermann Göring's Stukas. His was not an easy mission. I was grateful for his presence, certain that I would have fared less comfortably after my arrest by the Gestapo for my investigation of the Bürgerbräu explosion, if the Nazi authorities had not remembered that an American C.G. was still very active only one block away from Gestapo Headquarters.

Mussolini's Consulate-General at the capital of Hitler's party was a vital part of the Axis. Consequently Il Duce installed a C.G. with ministerial rank and with a large staff of consuls and clerks to look after the interests of the many Italians in Bavaria. Minister Pitallis drove the largest car of any diplomat in Munich—a yellow Fiat longer even than Hitler's Mercedes. Wizened little Pitallis on several occasions was given a drubbing by rough-neck Storm Troopers, who mistook him for the arch enemy of the Axis, a member of the Semitic race, before he could produce his credentials.

The British, American, and Italian consuls in Munich got along with one another much better than they did with their Nazi hosts. Their relations were most cordial. Not only would they invite each other to a round of dinners and cocktail parties in their homes; together, a British and an Italian consul would go for a day's spin about the Bavarian countryside to indulge in the diplomats' favorite pastime: spotting the latest secret and underground landing fields being rushed to completion in the forests and innocent-looking fields of the peaceful south German landscape. It was not unusual for a Roman member of the Axis to impart to a democratic consul whatever information he knew would be appreciated by the British or American government. On the other hand, returning from some Nazi rally, oratory, or exhibition, I have heard members of the British and Italian consulates vying with each other in expressing their revulsion for Teutonic arrogance and Nazi tactlessness. It seemed very evident that although Italia was now legally married to Hitler, she still longed for her old boy friend, John Bull, whom she gave clandestine tokens of her affection whenever her severe lord and master wasn't looking.

The carefree life of consular diplomacy—interrupted by the Czech crisis in 1938—continued until after the Brown Derby races at Munich-Riem in July, 1939. On the day of the race for Hitler's Brown Ribbon, German army authorities clamped down on all filling stations in Munich. Many tourists were stranded as, one after another, the benzine pumps were locked up. Only with difficulty could they obtain enough fuel to drive out of the Reich. The Munich consuls and correspondents started laying in their own private supplies, purchasing old gas tanks, barrels, and other containers which they filled with benzine whenever they could buy an extra five liters at some obscure stations. My Italian press colleague, Dr. Enenkel, built up a reserve of two hundred liters in his back yard. Frankie Fulham did the same, preparing to make a dash in his car to Switzerland at the last moment.

With the Captain gone, Frankie and I carried on the tradition of cordial relations between the British press and His Majesty's Service in a series of farewell parties at home or in the Munich night clubs, for we both knew that the storm was about to break. We did not need to wait very long.

Toward the end of August, I dropped in to see him one morning at the Consulate. He was rushing about, directing the burning of documents. Smoke belched from the chimney in the Pranner Strasse as the furnace roared into the summer sky with countless records and secret files accumulated over a score of years in the Bavarian capital.

"Have you received your instructions to evacuate your citizens from Bavaria yet?" I asked Frankie.

"No, damn it, and things look blacker every minute," he answered dejectedly. He had been through the first war, and did not relish fighting the Germans again after acquiring a family and gray hairs.

"You will get them today, the *Daily Express* informs me from London," I assured him.

While we were talking, a Reichspost messenger delivered a coded telegram from the British Embassy in Berlin.

"Those are your instructions, I'm sure," I commented. But Frankie first had to decode the telegram. I left, returning to the Consulate several hours later. Fulham and another consul were still wrestling with the code book.

"We can't get the ruddy telegram to make sense," Frankie said disgustedly. He was forced to telephone to Berlin for a new coded message. The Reichspost had garbled the first, perhaps intentionally. It was not until evening that Frankie could officially warn British subjects in Bavaria to leave the country. I shook hands with him. "Best of luck, Old Man," said Frankie. That night, August 28th, I piled my roadster full of benzine cans and drove up the deserted *Autobahn* to Berlin to take over the *Daily Express* office, vacated by its Australian staff correspondent, Selkirk Panton, who had found temporary security in Copenhagen. A few days later, England and Germany were at war.

Frankie never made his dash to Switzerland. His beautifully furnished apartment and the new car which he had purchased that summer fell into German hands. Working around the clock, Fulham and his skeleton staff could not leave the sinking ship of His Majesty's Munich Consulate-General. One month after the British declaration of war, I received a letter from him through the American Embassy at Berlin.

"Life here is extremely dull," he wrote. "They are keeping us interned in the Hotel Bayerischer Hof. There is no beer on tap to be had. All we do is play chess. We are allowed a one-hour walk daily under supervision."

Frankie, the last member of the British diplomatic service in south Germany, and, I believe, in the entire Reich, to leave Germany, was detained over three months before Nazi authorities yielded to diplomatic usage and permitted him to go.

But the accuracy of the RAF bombings over the Reich may be an indication that men like Frankie and the Captain did not leave empty-headed. Nor did they indulge in a spot of social drinking and motoring with the "Axis" in vain.

***

"FRÄULEIN, GIVE ME LONDON..."

I have seen the leading actors in the Nazi tragedy, playing their parts on the Bavarian stage. Long before the climax—the outbreak of the war—I knew what the denouement in Hitler's theater would be.

Like a Greek tragedy, each act inevitably brought closer the final catastrophe. Sometimes the scene was Munich, sometimes Berchtesgaden, Nuremberg, Stuttgart, or Salzburg. Sometimes the spotlight shone on Chamberlain, sometimes on Viscount Halifax, the Duke and Duchess of Windsor, Benito Mussolini, Sudeten Leader Conrad Henlein, Colonel Beck, Joachim von Ribbentrop, Schuschnigg, or Danzig's League Commissioner Burkhardt, in an animated dialogue with the Führer. At other times a monologue by stage-struck Adolf would hold the attention of the international audience watching the spectacle in southern Germany.

In place of the Greek chorus, the Nazi slogans of shouting Storm Troopers formed a background to the brown drama. And there were many omens that pointed to the grim climax of the Third Reich's prewar scenes.

My major assignments as a Munich correspondent all covered direct or oblique factors that finally resolved themselves into the Second World War. Of course there were many good stories on other subjects, such as the death of Ludendorff, the *Merry Widow* episodes, international sporting events, and other happenings in Bavaria of interest to newspaper readers abroad. But my most important dispatches were connected with occurrences that led up to that fateful September in 1939.

It would be impossible to do justice to four years of telescoped and epochal history making by attempting to record chronologically all of the main events covered by a foreign correspondent assigned to the territory of the most powerful dictator of modern times, perhaps of all times. A few examples must suffice to illustrate the work of a Munich correspondent.

One of my jobs was to cover the annual conventions of the German "Foreign Organization" at Stuttgart in Swabia, a four hours' drive from Munich. Ten thousand Nazis from every corner of the globe came to Stuttgart, Hitler's official "City of Germans living Abroad," in August, 1937, as guests of the Reich. This rally of diplomatic, party, and commercial representatives of Germany in foreign countries was a startling revelation of the far-sighted and ruthless efficiency with which Hitler's regime was organizing its fifth columnists throughout the world, long before the Reich launched its blitzkrieg of conquest and occupation. The private conversations of fanatic Nazis from England, Canada, the United States, Norway, Holland, Belgium, and France, and the secret sessions of these Germans with Reich leaders belied the hypocritical protestations of good will voiced by Goebbels, Göring, Hess, and the English-born leader of the *Auslands Organisation* (Organization of Germans Abroad), Ernst Bohle, in the public speeches at Stuttgart. In retrospect, they help explain the success of the Quislings since the war began. Even between the lines of the public speeches, the outlines of the Nazi menace to the world were clearly perceptible.

In his opening address to his ten thousand guests, Herr Bohle, who was educated in England and who retained his British citizenship until he joined the Nazi party, declared:

"All Germans faithful to the Reich are National Socialists. They should be permitted to live their lives in foreign countries according to the principles which apply in Germany!"

The next day the Nazi leaders of German groups in foreign countries met with their chief behind closed doors. District leaders from England and other lands submitted confidential reports on their work during the year. I obtained a confession from a Dr. Urchs, who headed the delegation from India and Ceylon. He boasted to me: "Our success in these countries is a direct result of our most important work—namely, a systematic and, I should like to say, unmerciful training."

Every day during the eight-day rally, special groups of Germans residing abroad met at secret sessions with Bohle, Hess, Reich Justice Leader Dr. Hans Franck, and other Nazi chiefs, including the ubiquitous Gestapo boss, Heinrich Himmler. Here the foreign Nazis were given their instructions for espionage and propaganda for the coming year. One Canadian Nazi admitted this to me over the wine glasses, after I had led him to believe that I was a German from Wisconsin.

The work of the party's foreign organization was graphically shown by several exhibitions at Stuttgart. The displays included thirty-seven different party newspapers appearing in foreign countries, as well as other German publications in the various colonies. One hall was devoted to the training of Nazi "missionaries." It was revealed that seventy-two thousand packages of "educational material" were shipped abroad as early as 1936. This material included party literature, books approved by the Third Reich, and propagandist pamphlets against Jews and Catholics.

I was constantly bumping into "Americans" from New York, Chicago, St. Louis, and elsewhere. They would boast about "our successful fight in the States." One young man from Cleveland became very friendly, and confided in me about his work for the Bund. I listened politely in order to get his story. He was looking forward to the arrival of *Der Tag* in America. As he left for a private conference, he gave me the Hitler salute.

"Why you low-down, double-crossing bum!" I finally exploded. "And you call yourself an American!" After that, the American Nazi beat a hasty retreat whenever he saw me approaching.

Hermann Göring, coming directly from Hitler's villa at Berchtesgaden to address the foreign Germans for the first time in 1937, sounded an ominous note, that should have been studied more carefully at the time by democratic statesmen who were still laughing at the idea of a Nazi menace. These are some of his characteristic remarks to the ten thousand German "missionaries":

"There is a stream of power emanating from Central Europe. We are a great power, supported not only by the German Empire, but also by the Germans abroad."

"Never let foreigners penetrate into your unity abroad. The rest of the world forced us to be 'have-nots,' but you can be sure that I will achieve German independence in a very few years."

"The first duty of a German living abroad is to serve the Fatherland," he concluded.

Even athletics were used as a fifth-column tool by Nazi leaders at the rally of foreign Germans. The Reich Sport Leader, Herr von Tschammer und Osten, announced that he had signed a working agreement with the head of the Foreign Organization, Bohle.

Murdered Roehm's successor as Chief of Staff of Hitler's Storm Troopers, Victor Lutze, proclaimed that the future of sport in Germany would "serve the ends of toughening the body and rendering it capable of military service." He awarded the Storm Troops Sport Badge to political leaders of German groups abroad. This was the first time that the Storm Troop Chief had ever conferred the badge on German citizens residing in foreign countries.

"No physical training in Germany exists that is not permeated by the spirit of National Socialism," declared the Reich Sport Leader, "and this principle is just as valid for the sports clubs abroad that are composed of Germans. Today we have more than one hundred thousand gymnasts and sportsmen in foreign countries!"

After a solid week of secret sessions, Nazi pep talks, and flattering propaganda, the ten thousand Germans were taken to Nuremberg as special guests of the annual Party Congress. Here they were fed another eight-day diet of more speeches by Hitler, Goebbels, Göring, and the other Third Reich leaders, as well as impressive displays of Germany's armed might in sham battles and parades of the various *Wehrmacht* and party formations. Then they boarded their ships and trains to return to their outposts in the democracies.

Mussolini's first visit to the Third Reich in September, 1937, was another link in the chain of events that Hitler used to drag the world into war. It sealed the fate of Italy as an Axis partner. The Nazis prepared a welcome for Mussolini that rivaled the pomp of a Roman holiday. Days before Adolf was to shake hands with Benito in front of the Munich Railway Station, every German, from Nazi artist to Gestapo plainclothesman, was assigned his task to make the meeting of the two dictators a success.

The emblems of Fascism were hastily painted on countless banners taken from the storehouses of the decorations for the "Day of German Art." Munich again became a sea of flags. The main hall of the station was cleared of all newsstands, tobacco and flower shops, timetable bulletins, and kiosks. It was painted in bright Italian colors. A huge red carpet was laid from the platform where Il Duce's train was to arrive to the middle of the square in front of the station.

Ten thousand workmen were hired to hang draperies from the Munich houses. Sixty-foot triumphal arches bearing huge M's at the top were erected in the main thoroughfares. Hitler personally inspected the Prince Karl Palace, where he was to lodge his Italian guest. Venetian chandeliers, silk draperies, and glistening marble decorated the interior of the palace. Olive and laurel trees were uprooted from Munich's Botanical Garden and planted in the Duce's back yard. Hitler raided the city's art galleries to hang original paintings by the Old Masters in Benito's Munich headquarters. Overbeck's picture, "Germania and Italia," was given the most prominent place.

Mussolini's palace stood at one end of the Prinzregenten Strasse. At the other end was Hitler's apartment. Halfway between the dictators' headquarters stood a one hundred-foot column, ironically bearing the statue "Angel of Peace."

The Gestapo searched every house along the sixty-five-mile section of track from the Austrian border to Munich, to make sure that no irate Bavarian peasant would take a pot shot at Benito. In the party capital, they investigated every room facing the streets to be followed by the dictators. Some hotel guests were compelled to vacate because they were "politically unreliable."

Several hundred Munich residents were locked up in prisons and Dachau Concentration Camp for the duration of Il Duce's visit. The Gestapo ordered every householder along the route traveled by the Duce in Munich to surrender the keys, to their apartments and cellars, in order to make them accessible at all times of day and night. All the owners of apartments in these houses were compelled to sign a statement swearing that they would not admit any friends or relatives into their dwelling without notifying the police. Visitors staying in hotels along Mussolini's route were cleared out to make way for the guests of the Nazi party who had been invited to Munich from all over the Reich.

Even the Italian Fascists living in Munich, who paraded through the streets in the wake of their Duce, were searched for concealed weapons before they were permitted to march. A special detachment of thirty-five thousand Hitler Black Guards, quartered in forty Munich school buildings, was assigned to rope off the streets. Five thousand of Mussolini's own "OVRA" Italian secret service agents, dressed in the uniforms of Hitler's SS Bodyguards, were distributed through the cordons along the route followed by Benito. Every person arriving within the city limits by train or car was thoroughly searched before being allowed to proceed.

All in the name of Axis solidarity!

One incident during the Duce's triumphal reception spoiled the clocklike Nazi regimentation of the masses. It gave me an exclusive story. It also illustrated the workings of the Goebbels-controlled press and the totalitarian mentality of the Third Reich.

Hurrying back to my office to telephone an early description of Il Duce's arrival, I met a trusted "source." He informed me that he had just witnessed an accident, in which a van of SS Guards, speeding around a corner on two wheels to rush more men to cordon duty, had upset, throwing forty guards to the stone sidewalk. My source reported that ten SS men were killed and seventeen seriously injured. I flashed the news to Berlin Reuters office to be forwarded on their wire to London.

The story made front-page headlines in the British afternoon papers. But Berlin called me back, extremely distressed. They informed me that Goebbels' Propaganda Ministry definitely had denied the occurrence of any such accident, and had branded my report a "lie."

"Don't let yourself be intimidated," I reassured my Berlin colleagues. "That story is true. But I'll check on the accident and give you further facts."

I immediately called Munich police headquarters.

"Could you tell me please on what street the SS van upset?" I asked.

"On the Belgrad Strasse," came the prompt reply. Knowing the location, I at once called the nearest hospital, the Schwabinger Krankenhaus.

"Are the injured SS Guards in your hospital?" I inquired, without introducing myself.

"Yes!" answered an unsuspecting nurse.

I hopped into my car and drove out to the Schwabinger Krankenhaus, requesting to see the head surgeon.

"May I see the list of injured SS men that the ambulances brought here?" Grudgingly a secretary brought me the list. Twenty-one SS Guards, with injuries ranging from broken legs to fractured legs and spines, had been delivered to the hospital! The head surgeon appeared.

"Are you from Reuters?" he asked.

"Yes, I came to inquire about the Black Guards hurt in the accident."

"Oh yes, of course. Herr Pope, I just received a call from the Propaganda Ministry in Berlin, and I can assure you that the accident is not nearly as serious as you imagine. There are only a few minor injuries!" said the head surgeon, himself in charge of the victims.

It was not necessary for me to explore any gruesome morgues in SS barracks for the missing dead guards. For by denying the entire accident, Goebbels had put his clubbed foot in it. Dead men tell no tales, but the list of injured was sufficient proof to make further confirmation superfluous. There must be no hitches in the smooth functioning of Third Reich machinery!

Nineteen hundred thirty-eight was a year of mounting tension. Rumors were rampant. The Czech crisis was gaining momentum. Like a spider in his web, Hitler was asking more and more flies to walk into his Berchtesgaden chamber. Hurry calls from Berlin and London sent me racing down the *Autobahn* to the Obersalzberg at all hours, as the news broke that this or that statesman was on his way to the Berghof. Often I saw some dignitary off on the train at the Munich station, then drove to Berchtesgaden in time to watch his arrival at the foot of Hitler's mountain.

I had already observed the tall, thin figure of Viscount Halifax the previous winter, alighting from a special coach at the Berchtesgaden railway station and being driven up the Obersalzberg in Hitler's special six-wheel winter car. A very small crowd of natives had cheered as the British lord, umbrella in hand, descended from the mountain again late that afternoon to return to England in a snowstorm after a chilly conference with Hitler.

The Berghof became increasingly inaccessible. The gateway to Hitler's villa was closed to all except one or two favored foreign correspondents. In 1938, Ward Price of the London *Daily Mail* was the rare exception permitted to accompany the Führer's visitors. At that time Price was an appeaser, who had stressed the few favorable arguments for Hitler's annexation of Austria in his stories. He had also written flattering passages about Unity Mitford in a recent book. The rest of us could get only as far as Adolf's gate, and this only by hiring a special taxi driven by a trusted Nazi resident of Berchtesgaden.

The normal procedure for a Berchtesgaden story was as follows:

I would drive to the Grand Hotel on the hill facing Hitler's Obersalzberg. I would register there, knowing that the Führer's guests were always put up at this hotel. Then I would either await their arrival at the station, or hang about the lobby to see who was accompanying them, and who from the Obersalzberg would escort the guests to the Berghof. For a while, a sizeable tip to the staff members of the Grand Hotel would secure most of the information to be obtained from the Berchtesgaden visit. Even these sources dried up in 1939, when the hotel was taken over by the Gestapo manager of the Deutscher Hof in Nuremberg.

At the hotel, or by telephone to the Berghof, I would squeeze further information out of Reich Press Chief Dr. Dietrich or his assistant, Herr Lorenz. To this I added whatever I could worm out of the Gestapo who, in the leather shorts of Alpine peasants, patroled the railway station and the two roads leading to the Berghof—or Haus Wachenfeld, as Hitler's villa is sometimes called. These roads were two miles apart at the base of the Obersalzberg, so that a Hitler party might slip away via one exit while I watched at the other. A police guardhouse at the bottom of the Berchtesgaden approach to the Obersalzberg checked every vehicle and hiker attempting the steep ascent to the top of the Obersalzberg. This road leads past the entrance of the Berghof to the Platterhof, an inn from which approved visitors can look down to the guest house near Hitler's own villa. It also leads to Göring's mansion, which the Field Marshal had the audacity to build at a higher level than his Führer's own mountain home. On the way up to the Berghof gate, one passes several other sentinel posts, concealed machine-gun nests and the high-voltage fences that make the Berghof impregnable. It is not a comfortable feeling to approach the gateway to Hitler's estate. And you must pay the Nazi taxi chauffeur six dollars for the ten-minute ride up the steep Obersalzberg. Since the summer of 1939 no amount of money would open Hitler's road to the foreign correspondent.

Finally, after Adolf's company had left the Nazi Mecca, I could secure some more material from the hotel staff or the burly chief of Hitler's Berghof Bodyguard, who consumed Nikolashkas by the dozen in the Grand Hotel Bar, and was usually willing to answer a few questions and even volunteer a bit of harmless but colorful information about his chief's guests.

As the Czechoslovak cauldron began to bubble, despite the cooling efforts of Lord Runciman's Sudeten commission, I again motored to the Grand Hotel to keep an eye on Hitler's visitors. A sleek, black Mercedes drove up to the hotel one day. It bore Czech license plates, above which flew two large Swastika flags. From it stepped Conrad Henlein, the implacable leader of the Sudeten Germans and the greatest menace to the Czech Republic.

The Nazi press had been violent in its screaming accusations of Czech "persecutions." Yet this "villainous" regime had permitted Henlein to leave the country to see its worst potential enemy, Hitler, in a car given him by the Nazis and flying the emblem of the man who was plotting to carve up the country that issued Henlein's license plates!

I spoke to Conrad Henlein just before he saw Hitler. I was the only foreign correspondent in Berchtesgaden. The Sudeten Leader was obviously nervous. He paced up and down on the terrace of the Grand Hotel. He ordered his adjutant to bring him another glass of Vermouth. Then, after committing himself far enough to state "I shall try to persuade the Führer to help the cause of my oppressed Sudeten followers," he was driven up the Obersalzberg. He came back smiling, but refused to tell me any more about his conversation with Hitler. Then he scampered back to Sudetenland in his Mercedes.

I motored back to Munich, and soon thereafter to Julius Streicher's Franconian capital for the last Party Congress before the war, the "Party Day of Greater Germany," thus named by Hitler to celebrate the Anschluss of Austria. (A few months later the Führer proclaimed that the 1939 *Parteitag* would be called the "Party Day of Peace." On the day scheduled for its celebration, Hitler invaded Poland.)

The eight-day Nazi convention in the first half of September, 1938, was another milepost on the road to war. It began with jubilation at the year's Austrian addition to the Reich's territory. It ended with the Führer's concluding vehement speech, in which he shouted that he could no longer tolerate the situation in Czechoslovakia. In between were sandwiched mass demonstrations of the strength of the party formations and the bare-chested men from the Labor Service Camps—and above all the "Day of the *Wehrmacht*," which glorified Hitler's army with very realistic sham battles, mock attacks by dive-bombing Stukas, clashes between tank troops, and all the other branches of the armed forces that were to invade Poland on the day fixed for the *Parteitag* of Peace.

The Nuremberg rallies are an ordeal both for the Nazis and the foreign correspondents. The Nazi leaders exhaust themselves in a series of lengthy, lung-bursting harangues. Their followers work themselves into an eight-day frenzy of incessant marching, "Heiling" and maneuvering in the huge stadiums and winding streets of the city. They keep up the mad pace by spending their few free hours drinking rather than sleeping. The journalists tire themselves out by rushing from one event to the next, trying frantically to get long-distance connections on the jammed telephone wires, finishing their stories after midnight, being driven out to uncomfortable beds in sleeping cars side-tracked in a freight yard several miles away from the press headquarters, and arising at six o'clock the next morning for another day's grind.

Only Hitler and the Nuremberg prostitutes get a chance to sleep peacefully during the Party Congresses. The rest of the town is awake all night. A cordon of regular policemen encircles the Führer's hotel, the Deutscher Hof, for a radius of several blocks to prevent pedestrians and cars from approaching the hotel and disturbing his dictatorial slumbers with the noise of their boots or motors. I attempted one night to walk past the Deutscher Hof, but was turned back by the police and told to proceed on the other side of the ancient Nuremberg moat and town wall. I picked my way through the narrow street a few blocks until I was almost opposite Hitler's hotel again on the other side of the wall. Here I was turned back once more—this time by SS Bodyguards detailed to block off the city's red-light district for the duration of the Rally.

After a week of this bedlam, reporting inflammatory speeches, covering theatrical Teutonic ceremonies and mock warfare that revealed some of the Reich's latest war machines, reporting new Nazi exhibitions, attempting to ferret out Nazi policies being formed behind the scenes, discovering Henlein and other carefully guarded guests of the Führer, struggling with Nazi mobs, Black Guards, miserable telephone service, and irate Nazi officials, and finally hearing Adolf beat the war drums over the Czech situation in his violent concluding address to all of the members of his government and party—I was glad to return to Munich for a rest, leaving Hitler to climb his mountain to plot the rape of his eastern neighbor.

I was just crawling into my first warm bath in ten days when my telephone rang. London calling.

"Listen, Pope old boy, get down to Berchtesgaden as fast as you can. Reserve several rooms, if possible at the Grand Hotel. 'Phone us the moment you get there. Chamberlain is flying from Croydon tomorrow morning to see Hitler!"

I hurriedly made arrangements for my assistant to cover the Prime Minister's arrival at Munich, threw on some clothes, and hopped into my little roadster. No chance for a bath or meal until I had prepared the ground in Berchtesgaden. "Chamberlain is flying to see Hitler!" droned around in my head as my car chewed away at the monotonous, straight kilometers of Hitler's Munich-Salzburg highway. "The British Mountain coming to the Nazi Mohammed! What next?"

Journalistic reinforcements from all parts of Europe began flocking into the little mountain village. Star reporters from the big London dailies even had chartered a special 'plane to follow the Prime Minister's glistening craft. Our Reuters team consisted of four men, one of whom arrived after the conference was over. I was compelled to bulletin Chamberlain's arrival single-handed. That was what I was paid for: to be first on the Bavarian scene, before competition was able to invade the territory.

What a strange contrast between this peaceful Bavarian mountain resort and the turbulent world that one of its residents had pushed to the brink of chaos! It was hard to believe that the Prime Minister of the world's greatest empire and the Supreme Commander of the world's strongest army were about to stand face to face for the first time in their lives in this little village: to decide the fate of all Europe. Hard to imagine that thousands of newspaper editors all over the globe were waiting breathlessly for the feeble electric vibrations of a few thin wires emanating from the local telephone exchange. Yet, in Berlin, Goebbels was pumping stories of "Czech Outrages" into the vast distributing system of his propaganda

185

machine. A hundred miles from this idyllic Alpine retreat, arrogant Sudeten Germans and sullen Czechs were at swords' points, burning each others' farms or committing actual physical violence; embassies and state departments of all civilized nations were beehives of activity, buzzing with the latest speculations and reports about the Berchtesgaden meeting. Conrad Henlein had just fled into Germany, and from the safety of his powerful big brother had issued a proclamation demanding the annexation by Germany of the Sudeten territory in Czechoslovakia.

How ironical that one of America's newest airplanes upon which Great Britain was to base her hopes for defeating Hitler a year later, was the machine in which England's Prime Minister placed his trust to enable him as soon as possible to shake hands with the Führer of the Third Reich. It was a twin-motored Lockheed Electra, recently purchased from America by the British Airways, that flew Neville Chamberlain to Munich on Thursday morning, September 15, 1938. The 'plane arrived at the birthplace of National Socialism at 12:30 P.M. Swastikas and Union Jacks decorated the Oberwiesenfeld Airport. Reich Foreign Minister von Ribbentrop received Chamberlain, and whisked him to Hitler's waiting, bomb-proof train. Had the band not blared so loudly at the airport, Chamberlain could have heard the roar of hundreds of airplane motors at a nearby factory, being tested before their installation in the Nazi bombers that were being made ready to Coventrize England.

In Berchtesgaden, my first view of the famous, tragic appeaser was against a somber, portentous background. Six black-uniformed, steel-helmeted giants with fixed bayonets clicked to attention as Chamberlain alighted from his car and entered the hotel. A soulless guard of honor with six bayonets—to watch over one gaunt, trusting old man with an old black umbrella.

The British Ambassador to Berlin, Sir Nevile Henderson, Chamberlain's two flying companions—William Strang of the British Foreign Office and Sir Horace Wilson, chief industrial adviser to the British Government—and the Munich Consul occupied the English quarters of the Grand Hotel. Twenty minutes after he had entered the hotel, the British Prime Minister and his Anglo-German entourage were driven to Hitler's villa.

"How swiftly the car climbs!" Chamberlain remarked to von Ribbentrop as they sped up the steep, winding trail to the Berghof. (How swiftly Ribbentrop climbed over his own precipitous, winding agreements!)

Hitler was waiting for his distinguished guest on the steps of his mountain home. The forty-nine-year-old dictator was wearing black trousers, a double-breasted brown jacket, a white shirt with stiff collar and brown four-in-hand tie as he came down the steps to salute the sixty-nine-year-old democratic leader at five o'clock that afternoon.

Tea was served in the spacious hall of Hitler's villa. For twenty-five minutes the British and Nazi delegations conversed together. Then Hitler conducted Chamberlain to his study on the second floor. Here, closeted alone with Dr. Paul Schmidt, the Reich's official interpreter for the Foreign Office, the two statesmen laid their cards on the table. The historic interview lasted two hours and thirty-five minutes. At 8:15 P.M., tired but smiling, Neville Chamberlain returned to the Grand Hotel. His collar was wilted, his mustache disheveled. He looked like a ruffled, but unscathed Daniel emerging from the Lion's den. About thirty of us correspondents stood at a respectable distance in the lobby. The Prime Minister lingered a moment. Press photographers' bulbs flashed. Then Chamberlain retired to his suite.

Outside, the drenching rain came steadily down. The mountains were cloaked in misty Alpine clouds. A true Shakespearean motif! Nature fitting the mood of the drama. We knew that mountain peaks were there. We knew that Chamberlain had risen to new heights in his talk with Hitler. But the outline of the conversation was hidden from us as impenetrably by official silence as the Berchtesgaden mountains enveloped in the heavy fog.

At nine o'clock, Sir Nevile Henderson came down to the lobby. He gave us the text of the official communique issued after the

Berchtesgaden meeting. The total fruits of the three-hour dramatic visit handed to the press were the following three sentences:

"The Führer and Reich Chancellor had a discussion today with the British Prime Minister at Obersalzberg in which a full and frank exchange of views on the situation took place.

"The British Prime Minister will return to England tomorrow to consult the British Cabinet. A new conversation will take place in a few days!"

Even this terse communique was wolfed by the foreign correspondents, and disappeared in a flash down the long gullet of international press wires, to be digested by ravenous editors and statesmen all over the world. Where would the dictator and the democratic leader meet again? Berlin? Munich? Frankfort? The Führer had told Chamberlain that he would meet him halfway. At last it leaked out that Godesberg on the Rhine would be the scene of the next epochal conference.

When I had sent my last message through the bottleneck of the Berchtesgaden telephone exchange, I returned to the lobby of the Grand to join my colleagues' post-mortem of the unprecedented day's events. Neville Chamberlain, worn out by his long and unaccustomed flight, and the strain of arguing with Adolf Hitler, was fast asleep upstairs. Nevile Henderson was not asleep. But he might just as well have been. For the scene I witnessed through the glass doors of the private dining room left an uncomfortable impression on my mind, which became justified a year later.

The British Ambassador to Berlin, dapper as any English gentleman could be, a red carnation in his buttonhole, was sitting among his German associates of the Nazi Foreign Office. Champagne flowed. Laughter was frequent and protracted.

Everything seemed very jolly. But I could not help feeling that the laughter of Ribbentrop's henchmen was at the expense of this slim, boyish-looking diplomat. As I saw Henderson chatting with the heavy-set, scar-faced veteran of several German regimes, State Secretary Dr. Otto Meissner, I thought instinctively of a cat playing with a mouse. Just a week ago, Meissner had kicked an SS

Bodyguard all the way down the stairs of the Deutscher Hof in Nuremberg because the Guard had not stepped out of his way quickly enough. If a member of the Nazi Foreign Office could be so brutal and ruthless to one of his own men, what lay in store for a member of the British Foreign Service the moment he should attempt to hold back the juggernaut of Third Reich policy?

When I arose early the next morning, the sun was trying desperately to break through the clouds. I had breakfast with a few colleagues. Ralph Barnes, one of the most conscientious journalists I have ever met, was busy with many sheets of paper, reviewing the story he had sent to the New York *Herald Tribune*, checking and rechecking it, incorporating new material for the coming day, and rewriting sentences painstakingly to perfect them with a more descriptive adjective, a different preposition, or a better verb. Little did I suspect at that time that he was destined to become the first American victim of thwarted appeasement. Ralph, as a war correspondent in the Balkans two years later, crashed to his death in a British bomber.

The Bavarian Alps seemed so peaceful that morning.

From Munich, Chamberlain flew back to London, stopping at Cologne on the way. I hummed along the *Autobahn* back to my apartment, and at last had my bath.

My orders were to stay in Munich, ready for any eventuality. Consequently I was spared the grind and ordeal of covering the Godesberg conference, which ended in a stalemate between Hitler and Chamberlain. The October Festival, the combination state fair, carnival, amusement park, and circus that spread over more than one hundred acres of the Theresienwiese meadow below the city's Exhibition Park, was in full swing. This annual event, starting the middle of September and lasting one month, is as much a part of the true Bavarian's life as Christmas, the Winter Carnival or Easter Holidays. My Munich friends and I went there almost every day. It helped us forget the Czech crisis. The lusty Bavarian bands, the shouts of young people whizzing down the roller coasters, the shrieks of girls clutching at their skirts as they walked across hidden wind jets on the floors of the side-show booths, drowned out the rumblings of the black war clouds gathering on the horizon. Until one evening: September 26, 1938....

Suddenly the roller coasters stopped. The barkers' voices were cut short. The brass bands in the beer halls were silenced. The merry-go-rounds ceased whirling. The October Festival froze in its tracks. Across the Theresienwiese blared the maniacal voice of Adolf Hitler. In a few minutes, two hundred thousand merrymakers were transformed into dejected groups of apprehensive listeners. The Führer was raging against Czechoslovakia and [Czechoslovakian President Edvard] Beneš in the Sportspalast at Berlin. Nazi law compelled every German to listen to his broadcast war whoops. Even outdoors at the October Festival. As Hitler raged on for one hour and thirteen minutes, an ever-increasing number of women and girls burst into tears, some of which saltened the beer mugs that had been lubricating their laughter a few minutes ago, before Festival officials turned on the loudspeakers. "This means war, dammit," cursed their male companions. Never have I seen such a large crowd of people change from elation to gloom so instantaneously. A thunderstorm could not have spoiled the evening any more thoroughly for the Munichers than did Adolf's tirade against the Czech government.

The next few days were a nightmare. Hitler issued an ultimatum to Prague. The Nazi press ran riot with screaming headlines about "Czech atrocities against our Sudeten brothers." Munich stations were packed with soldiers from the Seventh Army Corps of Bavaria, herded into freight cars and rushed to the frontiers. The telephones at the British and American consulates rang incessantly, as anxious Anglo-Saxons asked frantically for advice. The consuls could only reply that their embassies at Berlin had issued no orders to evacuate their nationals from the Reich. Most tourists did not wait; they left the country in crowded trains and cars. At midnight, September 27-28, Great Britain mobilized her fleet. The next morning, British correspondents deserted Berlin for safety in adjoining countries: Denmark, Holland, Belgium, and France. My Munich colleagues made a hasty flight to Zurich in Switzerland.

On the afternoon of September 28, the Reuter Parliamentary Staff in London secured the historic announcement that Chamberlain, Daladier, Hitler, and Mussolini were to meet in Munich! I was able to send an exclusive description of the preparations for the next day's Munich Conference, while all the other British correspondents were scrambling to get back to the Reich at all costs.

But that was not all. I was able to spare the remainder of the British and American colonies in Bavaria, including the staff of His Majesty's Consulate-General, hours of mental anguish. News travels much faster over press wires than through diplomatic channels. The British consuls in Munich were pushed to the limit, hastily selecting and burning documents and records to keep them from falling into the hands of the potential enemy, answering telephone and personal inquiries every few seconds as best they could, and desperately cabling and telephoning their embassy in Berlin for instructions. The American Consulate likewise had no orders to pass on to uneasy American citizens.

The moment I hung up London after hearing the news of the impending conference, I called the consuls-general of Great Britain and the United States. They were tremendously relieved. Now they could tell their countrymen that Mars had sheathed his sword. Not until several hours later did they receive their first notification of the Munich appeasement meeting from their diplomatic superiors at Berlin.

On the eve of the conference I watched Nazi workers and artisans feverishly dusting off the Prince Karl Palace to make it ready once more for Benito Mussolini. I learned and reported that Daladier was to be given his headquarters in a suite of the Gestapo-controlled Vier Jahreszeiten Hotel, Chamberlain in the Regina Palast Hotel. The lights were blazing into the night from the usually vacant Führer Haus, as it was hastily groomed for the most famous event ever associated in history with the name "Munich." After dispatching messages to my London chiefs on the pre-conference Munich scenes, I organized an emergency crew to help handle the situation and hold the journalistic fort until reinforcements could arrive the next afternoon. My staff included a British-born artist working in Munich, my English Fascist tipster Phillip Spranklin, and the most intelligent American student I could find at Munich University. I coached them in their parts most of the night, gave them advance payments for expenses and typed out press credentials for them on Reuters stationery.

The morning of September 29, 1938, was bright and sunny. Munich was a happy playground of exultant, rejoicing, childish Germans, who had just seen the terrifying goblin of war dispelled by the valiant knight who was flying to them from a strange land, to bring a happy ending to the Czechoslovakian story with the aid of other magical characters: Daladier, Mussolini, and their Führer. Adolf Wagner had issued a proclamation, calling all Munich citizens into the streets, telling them to decorate their houses and to cheer the great statesmen coming to the Bavarian capital.

Regiments of SS Black Guards again were rushed to cordon duty. Bands blared forth the anthem of the Sudeten Germans. The Tricolor and the Union Jack flew proudly between Swastikas at Oberwiesenfeld Airport. They hung over one of the two main entrances to the Führer Haus, with the Fascist and Nazi flags over the other. No mere Hitler or Mussolini visit ever had released such jubilation in Munich. Chamberlain was the real hero of the day.

At 9:15 o'clock that morning, Hitler met Il Duce's train at Kiefersfelden-Kufstein. During the following one-hour ride to Munich, Benito clinched his arguments to make Adolf see reason and adopt a tractable attitude toward the democracies. The two dictators left the Munich station together amid mad shouts of "Duce!" "Duce!" Two of my men covered their triumphal arrival.

With my other assistant I was at the airport, keeping a wire open to Berlin. Twenty-five minutes after the Axis partners' appearance, the French 'plane taxied up the runway at Oberwiesenfeld. Daladier and his staff descended, and were met by Foreign Minister von Ribbentrop. The band of Hitler's SS Bodyguards struck up the "Marseillaise." That was the last time the anthem of the French Republic was to be played at the birthplace of National Socialism. How strange it sounded! After reviewing a guard of honor, Daladier was escorted by Ribbentrop to his hotel. Tremendous crowds lined each side of the four-mile route from the airport to the Vier Jahreszeiten.

The Nazi Foreign Minister returned just in time to welcome the British Prime Minister after another twenty-five minutes had passed. The same band that was soon to play "We are sailing against England" struck up "God Save the King."

Last of the four statesmen to arrive at Munich, Neville Chamberlain was the first to enter the conference building, being driven directly to the Führer Haus. Then came Hitler, escorted by his adjutant, Fritz Wiedemann, whom the Führer later sent to California as his Consul-General. Field Marshal Göring, whose air force was mainly responsible for bringing France to her knees, accompanied Daladier through the democratic entrance to the Führer Haus. Finally Mussolini, smiling broadly, entered with the Führer's Deputy, Rudolf Hess. Sandwiches and Moselle wine were served to the appeasers and the appeased. At 12:45 P.M., they sat down under the stern gaze of a painted Bismarck for the first two-hour session of the historic twelve-hour conference.

After dispatching bulletins to Berlin and London over the congested wires from the airport, to cover the arrivals, I went to the Regina Palast and flashed the beginning of the conference. My first reinforcement had just arrived. He was Clarke, head of the Rome Reuters Bureau, who had taken the Italian journalists' train which trailed behind Mussolini's special across the Alps to Bavaria. Two hours after the beginning of the Munich meeting, Bettany, head of our Berlin office, arrived tired and in not the pleasantest of moods from his Amsterdam refuge. He had hoped never to see the Third Reich again. The bedlam of the Nuremberg Congress—his first experience with these eight-day binges—had soured him for any more reporting on the Nazi front. Late that evening, Cornelius Murphy, head man in the Paris Reuters Bureau, turned up at the Regina.

In a tempest of wild rumors and speculations, fighting for long-distance connections and telegraph wires, we fed London the news of the Four Power Conference. Access to the interior of the Führer Haus was denied all foreign correspondents. The sessions lasted from 12:45 P.M. to 2:45 P.M., 4:45 P.M. to 8:20 P.M., 10 P.M. to 12:35 A.M. Chamberlain's hotel was nearest to the conference hall. Between sessions, the statesmen would retire to their headquarters for a respite and for private discussions of the proposals. Each time they rode through the streets of Munich, they were wildly cheered by the grateful Munichers.

We munched sandwiches and swallowed hot coffee during trunk calls and after sallies to the Führer Haus and the quarters of the other statesmen. At last, after one o'clock the next morning, we received the text of the Munich agreement. This most important document had to be squeezed through the overloaded trunk lines to London. To assure fastest coverage, we also relayed the dispatches via Berlin with "blitz" calls at $10 for every three minutes. The Reich made enough money on the Day of Appeasement from the telephone tolls of the international press to finance the construction of a squadron of Stuka bombers.

Mussolini left for the Brenner and Italy almost immediately after the signing of the Four Power Pact. The remaining signatories spent the night in Munich. At four A.M., our work was done, for a few hours.

The next morning, Chamberlain and Hitler met and signed the short-lived Peace Pact between Great Britain and the Reich. People crowded around the Regina Palast, clamoring to see the Prime Minister who had brought them freedom from the specter of war. Women threw flowers at him or pressed bouquets into the hands of the British delegation. Neville Chamberlain was deeply touched. It was only too evident that the German people had wanted appeasement, that they were thanking the Englishman for sparing them from the consequences of their Führer's insanity.

The gaunt old Britisher was the most popular idol in Munich in the autumn of 1938. After his visit, all Munich swarmed happily to the October Festival on the Theresienwiese. The beer that was consumed in toasts to Prime Minister Neville Chamberlain could have floated a score of Nazi submarines.

On the blizzardly winter afternoon of March 14, 1939, Selkirk Panton of the Berlin *Daily Express* Bureau came through on my trunk line:

"Popey old boy, get down to Vienna as fast as you can. We think Hitler is going to march into Czechoslovakia tonight. I'll cover the Prague angle; you cover the Brno-Bratislava side of the invasion. It looks like a big story!"

It certainly did. After the lull following the Munich Conference and the return to the Reich of Sudetenland, Hitler had aroused Mars prematurely from his winter hibernation; the god of war was stirring restlessly in his Central European bed. For the preceding few days I had been busy reporting the unofficial mobilization of Bavarian troops. I had described how private cars and contractors' trucks had suddenly been requisitioned by *Wehrmacht* authorities, and had set off in columns down the Führer's *Autobahn* to Salzburg and points east, how soldiers were being crowded into box cars on the freight sidings of the Munich *Ostbahnhof* at night, to be shipped to other sections of the Czech border. Only the preceding night I had secured a beat for Reuters and the British Broadcasting Corporation on the calling to the colors of the class of '13, young Germans taken suddenly from their jobs—including male extras from the cast of the *Merry Widow*.

The snow kept falling and drifting so heavily that it seemed unwise to risk getting stuck at midnight somewhere on the 350-mile stretch between Munich and Vienna in my light open roadster. All commercial 'planes were grounded. Nothing was left except the night train, which did not arrive in the Austrian capital until eight o'clock the next morning. My "string" correspondent, a German, met me at Vienna's Grand Hotel.

"The army has been on the move all night," he informed me. "They have already crossed the Czech frontier toward Brno, but have met no resistance so far, as nearly as I can discover."

Together we tried every military authority remaining in Vienna, in a vain attempt to secure permission for me to accompany the *Wehrmacht* forces in their occupation of Bohemia and Moravia.

"But you permitted, and even welcomed, foreign journalists to report your occupation of Sudetenland last fall," I pleaded, "so why not allow me to follow your troops into another part of Czechoslovakia?"

"That is out of the question! The German Armed Forces will positively not grant permission to any correspondent to accompany their troops, let alone provide them with transportation. Heil Hitler!"

There I was, stuck in Vienna. It looked like a wild chase after Hitler's goose-stepping legions.

Finally, toward noon, I secured a rickety old Viennese cab, twice as old as anything that moved on wheels in the motorized Swastika. The heavy glass windows rattled in their frames; the wind whistled through the cracks in the ancient tonneau. Fine snow formed little drifts on the floor. Leaving my string man within call of the Grand Hotel's telephones, I set off with my bewhiskered Austrian chauffeur, who had never seen as large a tip as the advance payment I gave him to start us off on the wind-swept country road to Nickolsburg, sixty-five miles north of Vienna, in the wake of the invading army.

The archaic vehicle swayed from side to side on the icy road as terrific gusts of the broadside winter wind hit its top-heavy side. By some miracle, however, we neither upset nor skidded into a ditch, although we came close to it countless times.

We caught up with the stragglers of the army after an hour's drive. First came Hitler's motorcyclists. Cowering behind trees, their ears frostbitten, they waited helplessly for the wind to abate, their two-wheeled steeds useless on the slippery highway. One forlorn *Feldgrau Soldat* to each tree.

Then the trucks, hundreds of them, jutting out of the ditch on each side of the road. Army trucks with a wheel snapped off. Munich beer trucks peering disconsolately at the Austrian sky, miles from their accustomed routes through the Bavarian capital. Officers' sleek Mercedes, skidding helplessly backward on uphill grades, wheels spinning while privates cursed as they tried to push them in the direction of new conquest.

Perhaps out of spite for the new regime, my old Viennese *Fiacker* made every hill, even if I did have to get out and push while the driver gingerly encouraged his senile engine. Twice we threaded our way past columns of forty to sixty ambulances: If this was a "peaceful invasion," Hitler certainly was taking no chances, after having forced M. Hacha, the Czech Prime Minister, to sign his country up for Adolf's "protection" at Berlin the previous night.

The derelicts got thicker as we went on. We had to pick and wind our way through the *Wehrmacht's* trucks and gun carriages that dotted the roadside at all angles. At the bottom of a steep hill, we skidded to a stop in front of a beautiful traffic jam. A heavy army lorry, carrying a fifteen-ton tank, had smashed into a huge supply truck, upsetting both. A dozen soldiers shivered around the wreckage.

Four of them crowded around my cab. "May we ride with you, please?" their spokesman begged. "We must report to our commander."

"Sure, hop in, boys," I mumbled in my best Bavarian. Here were four men to help push in case I got stuck. But more important, here were four sources for a story. They piled into the cab with their heavy boots. One of them even threw two sacks totaling fifty loaves of army bread on the creaking roof.

Poetic justice. *Noblesse oblige.* Returning good for evil. The southern part of Hitler's army curtly had refused to take me with them. So here I was, transporting part of the southern army! And a British newspaper was paying the cost of moving Hitler's troops toward their next victim!

Fortunately the field-gray boys did not come from my section of the Reich. By dint of little talking, much listening, and gruff mumbling through my scarf, I managed to pass myself off as a Bavarian journalist. My frozen companions soon warmed up, and told me from where they had come (Graz), when they had received their orders, and other interesting details which contributed to my knowledge of the Führer's latest coup.

Near Nickolsburg, after averaging ten miles per hour from Vienna, my "army transport" caught up with the soldiers' officer. They clambered out of my hack, leaving puddles of snowy water on the floor, and unloaded their bread. We had already passed the old pre-Munich Czech frontier, where Nazi soldiers had jubilantly demolished the wooden gates of the customhouse like football fans tearing down the goal posts of the defeated opponent. I proceeded through Nickolsburg to the new Czech frontier. Here military sentinels absolutely refused to let me proceed to Brno, now in the process of being forcibly occupied by Hitler's army without the formality of an appeasement conference. That was my thanks for taking aboard some of their stranded soldiers!

But I was really glad that I could not continue my queer taxicab expedition. It was already getting dark, I had my story, and still had the most essential task ahead of me: to telephone it to London. Moreover, I was chilled to the bone, starving, and beginning to long for a warm bed.

Turning back to Nickolsburg, I finally succeeded in reaching my man at Vienna, and with many interruptions at last gave him a story to relay to London. I shivered at the prospect of the perilous one-hundred-kilometer stretch back to the Grand Hotel. My chauffeur was none too happy either.

"My benzine tank is just about empty," he informed me. "How are we going to get back?" The Nazi army, of course, had drained every filling station dry along the route. I had a sudden, albeit expensive, inspiration.

"Go to every drugstore in town," I told the driver. "Buy up all the medicinal benzine you need for the trip back."

That was our salvation. Our return trip was made on pure surgical gasoline, three times the price of the commercial product. But it worked, with minor adjustments of the carburetor.

While the driver was making the rounds of the pharmacies, I had phoned my story, bought some bread and sausage and a bottle of Schnapps. Then we started back. Huddled in a corner of the tonneau, munching my bread while the icy blasts rocked the old chassis, I wondered whether we would ever see civilization again.

More skidding up and down hills. The headlights lit up the debris of the *Wehrmacht*. We passed many limping army trucks being towed back to Vienna. The route taken by Hitler's forces from Vienna to Brno via Nickolsburg looked more like a modernized version of Emperor Napoleon's retreat from Moscow across the barren winter fields of Russia than like the Nazi newspapers' glowing descriptions of Hitler's "triumphal entry" into Prague.

After an interminable ride, we arrived in front of the bright lights of the Grand Hotel. That day my staunch cabbie pocketed forty dollars. But he confessed that he would not make another trip like that for any money. I telephoned a complete story of the southern end of Hitler's invasion to the *Daily Express,* then slept until noon of the next day.

The general reaction I obtained from the Viennese to the latest Swastika conquest was simply: "It serves the Czechs right. The only people we Austrians dislike as much as the Prussians are the Czechs. Why should they be any better off than we are? Let them feel what Hitlerism is like too!"

Between reporting Munich conferences, Berchtesgaden meetings, and the movements of the *Wehrmacht,* were sandwiched more pleasant interludes of nonpolitical journalism. Among these I enjoyed covering international sporting events. The horse races at Riem were one of them. Another was the international winter sports week at Garmisch-Partenkirchen.

A different kind of event which brought various nations together was the convention of the Lilienthal Society for Aeronautical Research in the German Museum at Munich in October, 1937. One of the highlights of this meeting was a scientific discussion of the Hindenburg disaster, in which the pride of the German Zeppelin fleet had met and distributed death at Lakehurst, New Jersey. No reference was made to the possibility of sabotage, as claimed by radical Nazi leaders.

At the Lilienthal convention, papers were read by a professor from the Massachusetts Institute of Technology, by a representative from an American airplane propeller factory, and by four British scientists, including a member of the Air Ministry and an executive of the British Broadcasting Corporation. Aviator Ernst Udet and General Mikh, head of Göring's *Luftwaffe,* were two of the principal speakers to address the international gathering.

It was at this convention that I first met Colonel Lindbergh. I met him again a year later at the Hotel Vier Jahreszeiten, just after he had completed a survey of the Nazis' colossal *Luftwaffe* factories. Colonel Lindbergh did not speak at the convention. He was a very interested observer. With Mrs. Lindbergh, he had flown his black and orange monoplane to Munich from England. After the Lilienthal meeting, he flew it back again. Half a year earlier, the American aviator had piloted his 'plane from Zagreb, the capital of Yugoslavia, to Munich. Publicity-shy, he then had staged a make-believe hop-off for London, ringing the Oberwiesenfeld airport to wheel out his 'plane, jumping into a taxi—and then spending the day looking at the exhibits in the German Museum. My conversation with the famous flyer in the Hotel Vier Jahreszeiten left me convinced that he was no Nazi sympathizer.[7] It left me equally convinced that he was impressed with the stupendous air-expansion program that the Third Reich was carrying on while European politicians were still making fun of the Brown Shirts rather than holding them up as a serious menace to the world.

[7]*Charles A. Lindbergh (1902–1974), first to solo the Atlantic in an airplane in 1928, was accused by some of being, if not a Nazi sympathizer, an admirer. He later participated in* America First, *an isolationist movement in the U.S. Once the U.S. was involved in the war, Lindbergh lent his considerable talents to the war effort and even flew some missions in the south Pacific.*

After the rape of Czechoslovakia, events began to move with ever-increasing rapidity toward the finale of Hitler's Dance of Death. Diplomat after diplomat roared up the Obersalzberg road, to be roared at by the Tyrant of Berchtesgaden. The Bavarian scene showed ominous signs of the impending war. I was convinced that Mars would not wait much longer. But, as a correspondent for the British press in Munich, I could not deliberately say so and still keep my job. The best I could do was to hint.

The value of having competent observers in Bavaria, far from the artificiality of Berlin officialdom, is best illustrated by the poll of its European correspondents which the *Daily Express* took and published on *August 7, 1939—less* than one month before Great Britain declared war on Germany to make good her guarantee to invaded Poland. The results of this poll were splashed on the front page of Lord Beaverbrook's paper. They are a startling revelation of how badly the British public was informed regarding the proximity of the impending calamity. Here is a reprint of the chief features of this amazing story:

Daily Express Holds Canvass of its Reporters in Europe.

And Ten out of Twelve Say—

NO WAR THIS YEAR

Berlin Emphatic: Hitler Is Not Ready

Daily Express reporters in Europe believe that there will be no war this year.

That is the result of a canvass conducted in the principal capitals of the Continent last week. Our reporters were asked to give their views on the prospects of peace or war in 1939, and this is how they voted:

	Peace	War
BERLIN (three men)	3	
PARIS (two men)	2	
ROME	1	
MUNICH		doubtful
VIENNA	1	
BUDAPEST		doubtful
WARSAW	1	
GENEVA	1	
ANKARA	1	

It is significant that the three reporters in Berlin are the most confident of peace. None of these men believe that Hitler is ready to wage a major campaign.

Selkirk Pant an, chief reporter in Germany, says: "Hitler, despite all his mysticism, is a hard-headed, hard-boiled politician, and is prepared to wait his time. His time may come next week, next month, or next year. But he is not going to risk everything on some hasty action.

"Hitler does not run his head against a brick wall. He climbs over it or goes around it. And if he cannot do either, he sits down and waits for time to crumble it.

"BIT-BY-BIT"

"So it is with the Polish problem, of which Danzig is only a part. He will not use his 'smash-and-grab' policy of the Czech adventure unless he knows he can make a clean get-away.

"Instead he will more likely use his 'bit-by-bit' program, whittling away at his opponents until they find they have suddenly lost—without bloodshed — what they were prepared to fight for until the last man.

"The only danger I can see for peace is if Hitler should make a misjudgment in the speed of his 'bit-by-bit' plan."

Laurence Vaughan Jones, another Berlin reporter, holds the view that Danzig is not a problem which Hitler is concerned about overmuch.

"There appears to be not the slightest chance of any conflict over the Free City," he writes. "To incorporate Danzig involves enormous risk for a small gain. As Danzig is already 97 per cent Nazi, Hitler can afford to wait until the general situation is more favourable for him.

"The genuine Nazi ambitions point southeastwards, where Hitler wants to be boss right up to Turkey. The aim of the Nazi Reich is to weaken all these southeast European states internally and subject them to Nazi hegemony.

"This will be an evolutionary process from within rather than a military conquest from outside, and it is unlikely that there will be any specific incident to allow British and French military forces to intervene.

"Germany, in my view, plans to confine herself east of the Maginot Line. The last idea in Hitler's mind is to risk a clash with a Great Power because in a few months he might lose everything that he has built up since 1933."

Edward G. de Pury, the third of the Daily Express Berlin reporters, says categorically that Hitler does not believe there will be a war this year.

"Hitler," he reports, "worked out a formula in Berchtesgaden last month for incorporating Danzig into the Reich without a war. He is convinced that his process of peaceful 'infiltration' into Danzig will not provide the Polish generals with an opportunity of asking Britain to join in a war against Germany.

"Hitler's disbelief in war this year is shared by the German people—a well-drilled machine which will only catch the war fever when told to. The German people are at present mobilized for the harvest, Goring's four-year plan, and the building of the fortifications."

E. R. Pope, Daily Express Munich correspondent, is the most reserved of the reporters in Germany. He writes: "Barring accidents, I do not believe that there will be a European war this year, but I would not bet more than a week's salary to back up my belief.

"In the past half-year the chances for peace have fluctuated between 51 per cent and 60 per cent in my opinion, and now stand at 55 per cent.

"Last week I gave peace a 59 per cent rating, but since then large numbers of reservists have been called up in Bavaria for manoeuvres, and the Reichswehr have requisitioned most of the petrol and three-quarters of the tank lorries supplying Bavarian motorists.

"This is the first time since the Czech crisis last March that civilians have been unable to buy petrol, and yet there is officially no crisis in Bavaria.

"Germany has reached the peak of her war power, while her potential opponents continue to gain daily. Astrologists, in whom Hitler places great faith, say that his lucky star is now declining rapidly, so he may decide to act before fate turns against him."

The day after the *Express* had published its "No War" story, I was sent to Salzburg to cover two events. One was the tour through southern Germany of the "Link" organization: Britishers on a goodwill trip through the Third Reich, fraternizing with Nazis, naming their local groups in the various English towns after German cities, while the German counterpart of the "Link" reciprocated in kind. The other event, amazing as it seems, was a week-long sports rally in which *British motorcyclists competed over Bavarian highways with their two-wheeled friends of Hitler's motorized Wehrmacht!*

The outward signs of Mars' awakening in Bavaria were alarming. Work on the new Munich subway and other civilian projects was stopped as contractors, their equipment, and laborers were requisitioned and sent off to the west, frantically to hurry the completion of Hitler's Siegfried Line. Train after train was taken off the normal time tables as military transport crowded out civilian travel. My young Munich friends were called away to "maneuvers," yet sadly said farewell, realizing that we would never see each other again. Filling stations ran dry, as the *Wehrmacht* requisitioned all available supplies of benzine. Private cars and trucks again were drafted into Adolf's motorized columns. Soap, coffee, tinned foods, and other supplies disappeared from the grocery stores. And huge cranes began hoisting antiaircraft guns to the roofs of the larger buildings in Munich. Bavaria held its first practice air-raid alarms and blackouts. "No War!" English newspapers might as well have announced that Hitler was going to shave off his mustache!

My last major story for the British press from south Germany was the coverage of the Ciano-Ribbentrop meetings to seal the military fate of the Axis, which took place at Salzburg during the second week end in August.

After this final prewar huddle of the Axis, I was left stranded in the city of Mozart without fuel. Only with the signed permission of the *Kommandant* of *Wehrmacht* Headquarters at Salzburg could the driver of a private car now obtain benzine. I appealed to the local Gestapo chief (the only Nazi on duty Sunday), who by telephone arranged with the Commander for fifteen liters, enough to get me back to Munich. I immediately drove to army headquarters. The Austrian private on guard duty ushered me into a hall, and asked me to wait while he fetched the Commander.

"What do you want?" barked the Prussian general.

"I refer you to the telephone call from Gestapo headquarters at 1:15 P.M. today, in which I was assured that you would give me written permission to purchase fifteen liters of benzine."

"You get no benzine! We need it for more important things!"

"But I am a foreign correspondent, and need the fuel in the performance of my duties. Furthermore I was promised the permit," I remonstrated.

"You get no benzine. Go away and don't bother me!"

I became so angry at this Prussian insolence that I didn't care a whoop who the Commander of the Salzburg Army Corps was.

"Look here, Herr Officer," I exploded. "Where is your German honor about which I hear so much? You promised that I would get the benzine. If you don't immediately give me the permit, I shall use my news agency to tell the British Empire, France, and North and South America that you, a General of the Führer's supposedly impeccable *Wehrmacht,* have lied to and insulted an American citizen and the special representative of the world's greatest news agency!"

"Oh! Ahem! Pardon me! What did you say your name was?"

"I told you once, and you also have it on my card. The permit, please!"

"Excuse me. I shall write it for you at once." Red as the proverbial beet, the general stepped into his office. While he was gone, the guard grinned at me.

"That's right," he chortled, "just show these Prussian bastards your fist! Wish I could too!"

The general returned with the permit. The Austrian guard clicked his heels to attention and saluted. I enjoyed my drive back to Munich on my hard-earned benzine that day more than any previous trip I had taken on Hitler's *Autobahn.*

On August 19th, the British Ambassador to Berlin made a hasty trip to Berchtesgaden to appeal to the Führer's reason. Evidently Count Ciano had taken the last vestige of Adolf's common sense back to Rome, for Hitler gave Sir Nevile a cruel, stony reception which sent the British Ambassador scuttling back to Berlin to issue orders to prepare for closing up His Majesty's Embassy.

During the lull before the storm, a German friend of mine dropped in on me on his way back to Berlin from Italy. He was a young chap, bright enough at the age of thirty to occupy the position of first assistant to the editor-in-chief of Germany's leading illustrated sports weekly, the *Reichssportblatt.* During the Olympics, we had spent many pleasant hours discussing his hero Buffalo Bill, Daniel Boone, Harley Davidson motorcycles, and his favorite character from Karl Mey's books for German schoolboys: "Old Shatterhand."

"Pope, *mein Junge,* I have had my last vacation," Frantz told me with a sigh. "Thank God I managed to get myself a three-weeks' trip through Switzerland and Italy. I had a swell time and spent all my money. My last fling! We'll be at war in a few weeks, and then it's curtains for Frantz as far as enjoying life goes. I'll be seeing you in the blitzkrieg!"

He did, almost sooner than either of us expected. A week before the war started, I dropped everything in Munich to take over the Berlin office of the *Daily Express* for Panton, who had established emergency headquarters in Denmark.

After I had closed the Berlin office of the *Express,* and was assisting Bill Shirer[8] in his broadcasts for CBS and Sigrid Schultz in her Berlin bureau of the Chicago *Tribune,* I looked up my sporting friend, Frantz. We spent many pleasant evenings in the "Taverne," where journalists gathered after hours in the blackout to forget the war. But Frantz could not forget. When last I saw him, three months after the fighting had begun, he told me grimly:

[8]*William L. Shirer (1904–1993), later author of the hugely successful* The Rise and Fall of the Third Reich, *still in print, read, and cited after more than fifty years.*

"I am going to enlist as a rear gunner in the *Luftwaffe!* I would much rather hunt scalping Indians with you and a 45 Colt. But I can't. I hate civilian life in this wartime capital. Sports? Bah! There is no such thing as sport left now. We have gone mad. And so have I. I don't want to live any more. I can't ride my BMW motorcycle any more. I can't travel abroad. I have lost my English friends. I can't have any more fun. So one last thrill, zooming in a heaven of bursting shells and whirring propellers—then I hope I get shot!"

This is the spirit of despair which has driven many members of Hitler's *Wehrmacht* to defy death in his blitzkriegs.

They knew and loved life before the Third Reich. Now they do not care to live. They prefer an honorable death at the hands of an RAF machine-gun bullet to a lifeless existence in warring Nazi Germany, or death from Adolf Hitler's merciless firing squads.

***

NAZI NIGHT LIFE

Next to the *Wehrmacht,* the beer hall is the most important single institution in the life of the National Socialist party. Hitler never would have become the Führer of the Third Reich without the help of Munich's huge mass-production, mass-consumption guzzling establishments. Nor would he have been able to retain his power as the dictator of an oppressed nation if he had attempted to check the Niagara-like flow of *Dunkles* and *Helles* in the innumerable taverns so dear to the German heart. Hitler's regime has set fire to synagogues, dynamited churches, plundered art galleries, abolished confessional schools, torn down entire blocks of apartment houses, removed statues, changed traditional landmarks, and wiped out historic monuments—but it has taken great pains not to tamper with the beer halls.

National Socialism was born in the back room of the Sternäcker tavern on Munich's shabby Tal Strasse, where six Nazis gave Hitler Party Number Seven and organized the movement. It was suckled in the Hofbrau Haus a few blocks away, where Hitler proclaimed the twenty-five points of his party program. Nazi intrigue has been fomented amidst the fumes of fermenting brown mash in breweries all over the Reich. National Socialism first attempted to strike out for itself in the Bargerbrau Keller across the Isar River on the road to Berchtesgaden when Adolf organized the 1923 Putsch among a rowdy group of beer-soaked Storm Troopers. It celebrates Christmas Eve with the Old Guard Nazis in the enormous halls of the Lowenbrau Brewery near Adolf's Brown House.

The *Bierkeller* has taken the place of the church in Nazi Germany. Instead of absorbing sermons from pulpits, Hitler's followers receive spiritual guidance listening to Brown-Shirted orators—including the Führer—barking Third Reich doctrines from the tops of wooden drinking tables. Instead of centering their social activities around church suppers, Sunday-school meetings, Christian Endeavor gatherings, and choir practice, they meet at the *Stamnmtisch* to congratulate each other on the latest raids of the *Luftwaffe,* to sing marching and fighting songs, and to curse the pluto-democracies. And instead of slipping quietly into a pew to fmd spiritual solace in prayer, they slip into the nearest beer hall to drown their sorrows while listening to the deafening crashes of a Bavarian brass band. This is the backbone of German morale. Without beer halls, the German people could not endure Hitler's regime.

War has always brought with it an increase in night life, drinking, dancing, looser morals, and the other by-products of the attitude, "Eat, drink, and be merry, for tomorrow you die." The fact that Germany has actually been at war ever since the Nazis came to power explains the excessive whoopee that I saw rampant in the party capital. Every crisis released greater quantities of alcohol. And, when the German guns opened fire on Poland in September, 1939, German waiters opened reserve stocks of firewater to vanquish the blues of a nation that suddenly found itself plunged into war against its will by its fanatic, teetotaling Führer.

The Third Reich's myriad beer spigots have been used by, clever Nazi propagandists as an effective sprinkling system! to prevent the spontaneous combustion of smoldering German discontent. Further to control the pent-up feelings of a regimented, totalitarian populace, the Nazis have permitted the use of safety valves in the German powerhouse: entertainers who provide an outlet for the unhappy public.

In Munich, the comedian, Weiss Ferdl, is the main Nazi safety valve. From all over the Reich, Germans come to see him in person, after laughing at his antics on the screen. His reputation in Naziland as a comedian compares with the fame of Laurel and Hardy, W.C. Fields, and the Marx Brothers in America.

Weiss Ferdl and his troupe of Bavarian buffoons put on a show every evening on the rustic stage of the Platzl, a beer emporium opposite the famous Munich Hofbrau Haus. The comedians are known as the "Dachauer." Not only do they come from the countryside around grim Dachau Concentration Camp—several of them have actually been inside its somber walls for a short disciplinary spell after overstepping the poetic license granted them by Nazi authority as Hitler's safety valves.

Chubby Weiss Ferdl himself suffered a forced absence from his Platzl stage for making the following wisecrack:

"I saw the strangest sight the other day," he had told his audience. "Imagine: A great big twelve-cylinder supercharged Mercedes driving through our Munich streets, without a single Nazi in it!"

This blunt reference to party graft and the poverty of Germans who have not climbed the Nazi bandwagon brought down the house. But it also brought the rage of the Munich Gestapo down on Ferdl's rosy bald head. When he returned to the stage from Dachau, there was not even standing room in the Platzl, so eager were his fans to welcome him back. As the opening curtain went up, Weiss Ferdl stepped forward to the footlights amid resounding applause. For several minutes he stood there, motionless and silent. Then he spoke, his first public words since his fateful gag several months previously:

"You know," he whispered, his round face solemn as a monk's, "I made a mistake. There *was* a Nazi in that car after all!"

The quantities of beer and potato salad consumed in the Platzl at each performance would take care of a regiment. After the tenth stein and Weiss Ferdl's sixth joke, plus buxom Katie Tellheim's yodeling and a few peasant skits revolving around the favorite themes of the farmer's daughter, the drunken preacher, and the miserly old father on his deathbed, the patrons are willing to forgive and forget Hitler for compelling them to work overtime at no extra pay, making them march, and forbidding them to marry non-Aryans. "The simple pleasures are the best" is Goebbels' formula for making Germans contented with their lot.

The number of jokes attributed to Weiss Ferdl is legion in Bavaria. Most of them have a political tinge, some even dealing with the dreaded concentration camps. The following two are typical:

"I don't understand why Dachau Concentration Camp is guarded so carefully," the Bavarian comedian once declared. "It has barbed-wire and high-voltage fences, a moat, machine-gun nests, and very high walls. Yet if I wanted to, I could get inside Dachau without the slightest effort!"

"I met my friend Heinz the other day on the street. I hadn't seen him for two years. 'Where have you been all this time?' I asked.

'In Dachau!'

'*Donnerwetter!* How was it?'

'Wonderful.'

'What, really? Tell me about it.'

'Well, the SS Guards were most courteous to me. We all played tennis, swam, saw movies, had the most excellent food and wine, the finest beds; in fact the life there was glorious.'

"I looked at his face. 'But tell me,' I remarked, 'I see you have a broken nose, a cauliflower ear, a black eye, and a big welt across your cheek. How come?'

'Oh, you mustn't believe these things. They are just the evil lies of the yellow, foreign, pluto-democratic press!'"

Germans know that a released Dachau inmate will be sent right back to concentration camp if he describes its horrors to his friends.

Since the war, Weiss Ferdl has been compelled to exercise extreme caution in playing the dangerous role of a Third Reich safety valve. Yet his stage presence is so funny, and his reputation as Hitler's jester so firmly established, that his bow to the public immediately evokes roars of laughter, even before he has a chance to open his mouth. Now he specializes in this kind of political satire:

Ferdl appears on the stage and walks up to the footlights wearing a crown and the colors of extinct Bavarian royalty. The spectators go wild. When the applause finally dies down, he merely says, "I know what my public wants...." and walks off into the wings.

Or, in an ordinary business suit, Ferdl makes his usual bow, greeted by the unfailing cheers of his fans. The ovation is followed by minutes of silence, during which Weiss Ferdl just stands and gazes at the crowd. At last he speaks:

"*Meine Damen and Herren;* this concludes the political part of tonight's entertainment!"

A silent, yet very telling satire on Nazi censorship!

Number Two Safety Valve in Munich is a comedian of a different type: Karl Valentin. While roly-poly Weiss Ferdl looks and acts like a stunted walrus, and twists his bushy eyebrows, beetle eyes, and padded rubber face into an expressive series of contortions, Valentin is a gaunt, scarecrow type of dead-pan artist. His points are driven home with a semblance of utter, hick-Bavarian stupidity. Yet his wit is far more subtle, and consequently is appreciated by a smaller group of Germans. Add to this his consistent refusal to be a party member, and you will understand why he and his equally funny partner, Lizzie Karstadt, know more about the inside of Dachau than Weiss Ferdl. The following Valentin gag is one reason:

Karl Valentin meets his stooge Lizzie on the street. She greets him with a "Heil Hitler."

Valentin pulls two photographs from his pocket and shows them to her.

"Notice anything peculiar?" he asks.

"Naw, I don't," replies Karstadt.

Valentin scratches his head a while.

"You sure you don't see nothing strange?" he asks.

"Darned if I do."

"Well, what are them two pictures, anyway?" questions Karl.

"Why, one's a picture of you, and the other of our beloved Führer."

"Don't you really see sumpthin remarkable about them two photos?" Valentin continues.

"Nope."

"Do we look like each other?"

"Not a bit," states Lizzie emphatically.

"Hmmmm," mumbles the puzzled yokel, deep in thought. Finally he bursts out: "Well, then I'll be danged if I can understand why everybody says 'Heil Hitler' to me!"

211

The daring comedians like Weiss Ferdl and Karl Valentin have been forced to yield more and more to the typical Nazi master of ceremonies. These Swastika M.C.'s, although they appear in tuxedos without party pins in their buttonholes, in reality are propagandists for Third Reich policies. In the night clubs and cabarets, they sandwich in their gags and stories between floor shows, musical numbers, magicians, beauty dancers, and slapstick clowns. Their jokes are decidedly on the off-color side of humor, illustrating the pleasures of unexpected incidents in Reich Labor Leader Robert Ley's "Strength-through-Joy" excursions for men and women of the working classes, the amorous adventures of Nazi soldiers, or the eccentric encounters between Bacchus and Venus. Or they attempt to squeeze humor out of the collection-box street begging of Hitler Youths, Nazi Winter Help, state taxes, rationing, and the other schemes employed by the Reich to strengthen Hitler's war machine.

Herr Gondrell, whose "Bonboniere" night club is nearest to the Gestapo-managed Vier Jahreszeiten Hotel in Munich, is an exponent of this type of patter. His audience is composed of thoroughly Nazified German youth and the brown-shirted tribe of "Old Fighters" whose microscopic intelligence and strong-arm services to the party sufficed to get them a small-time sinecure and the leadership of a handful of Storm-Troop roughnecks. The guffaws that burst out from the well-lubricated throats of this crowd at the slightest reference to human anatomy make the Nazi M.C.'s job an easy one.

Joseph Goebbels' call for more "healthy eroticism" brought an immediate response from the night clubs as well as the theaters. Munich has a total population of eight hundred thousand, most of which is too poor to seek entertainment in anything except the movies and beer halls. Yet dancers with completely bare torsos can be seen blitz-teasing their thirsty public in almost a dozen amusement centers every night. Since the war, the night clubs have been crowded with young German soldiers on leave, who, after seeing their first action in battle, now thrill to the delights of seeing their first public nudes. The Bonboniere, Benz, Malkasten, Annast, Odeon Casino, Central Palast, and Serenissimus are a few of these

Munich hot spots in which I have watched the exponents of healthy eroticism serving the German public. In the less expensive of these cabarets, like the Malkasten and Serenissimus, the dancers also serve as hostesses.

Benz, a few blocks from my home in Munich-Schwabing, was my favorite night club, because I never tired of seeing Karl Valentin perform there. It is also the regular hangout of one-armed, stocky little Reich Director Max Amann, who grafted himself into the position of czar of Germany's great publishing house, the Franz Eher Verlag in Munich. Amann and his bankroll never tired of the hostesses in Benz. He always sat in a special nook of the night club with two blondes and a brunette, paying little attention to Valentin and the rest of the show—except when the dancers appeared. His average nightly consumption, according to my count, was ten bottles of imported French champagne at sixteen dollars per bottle.

The Gestapo cannot arrest an active army officer. They can only report his questionable acts or utterances to the *Wehrmacht* authorities, who will court-martial the offender if they wish. But the German army despises the Gestapo, and sticks up for its own men, even if they are tinged with Bavarian royalism. Many of the members of the *Wehrmacht* appreciate and make use of this privilege.

During the Yuletide blackout in 1939, I dropped into Benz around midnight with "G," a Bavarian flight-lieutenant who had been shot down and imprisoned by the Russians in the Spanish Civil War. He was a career army aviator. His salary as a German "volunteer" interventionist was six hundred dollars per month. When he returned to Germany, my friend bought himself a car—an English MG. We became very chummy. His best friend, whom he had seen as recently as that summer, was an English officer in the RAF. G was a loyal Bavarian Catholic who cordially disliked Nazi upstarts.

As we sat in a corner near the bar, some German soldiers stomped in. One very drunken private, with his arm in a sling, wore his coat. Military etiquette forbids soldiers to enter night clubs with their army coats on. As he passed our table, G said, "Take your coat off, soldier." Before G could move, the drunken soldier sailed into him

213

with both hands, screaming: "I'm a *Kriegsverwundeter* (war-wounded) from the Polish campaign. How dare you insult one of Adolf Hitler's soldiers?!"

G, on leave from training 350 aviators in blind flying and bombing, was in mufti. He was pounced upon by the drunk's companions until the waiters finally restored order. But my wiry friend managed to get in a few stiff punches first. Then he pulled out his first lieutenant's credentials. The sling-armed drunk was ordered by his comrades to apologize to G, and left Benz in disgrace. If G had wished, he could have disciplined the drunken "hero" of Hitler's Polish blitzkrieg. But he let him go.

The fight had centered the attention of Benz's guests on our table. A Storm Trooper in brown uniform left the bar and accosted me.

"I can tell you are a foreigner," he growled. "What are you doing here?"

"What's it to you?" I replied somewhat heatedly at the intrusion.

"We don't want any foreigners in Germany, understand! We hate everything foreign. What's your nationality?"

"I take the liberty to be an American."

(The German expression, *"Ich bin so frei,"* means: "I take the liberty" or "permit me" or "with pleasure." This phrase has an added significance when you tell a regimented Nazi that you are so free as to be an American. I used it often in Munich, and "with pleasure.")

"If you hate everything foreign, Storm Troop Man, why in hell d'you drink the most expensive licker in the house—your enemy's Johnny Walker whisky?"

The Brown Shirt muttered a threat, retreated to the bar, paid, and quickly left.

Then G and I went to the bar ourselves. G paid for a round of drinks. The bartender gave him the change.

"Keep the 'silver,' just give me the copper," said G, loud enough for everyone to hear. "I want to forge the copper into a nice big pineapple that will go 'boom.' It might have better luck next time!"

The Munich bomb explosion which missed Hitler was still vivid in our memories. Some of the patrons stifled a grin, others laughed outright.

After a few more drinks, the German aviator, loudly addressing nobody in particular, said, "For Christmas I want the head of Herr Huber hanging from my tree!"

Everyone in Germany knows that the pseudonym, "Herr Huber," stands for Adolf.

Just before the war, G had made an agreement with his buddy in the RAF.

"If I fly over England, I'll bring a case of beer with me; and you'll slip a bottle of Scotch to me in the internment camp."

"Righto," said the Englishman. "And if I fly over Munich, I'll bring a load of Scotch along, provided you'll have me interned in the Hofbrau Haus."

Now one of the two aviators has perhaps unknowingly shot the other. It is difficult to pick out your friends when you are approaching each other at six hundred miles per hour.

My last evenings in Munich with G were a welcome relief from drinking with the Brown Shirts. Although I have studied Munich night life with both foreign and German anti-Nazis, I frequently sat at beer tables with ardent disciples of the Swastika. A foreign correspondent must hear and see all sides of his assigned territory.

Drinking beer with a Storm Trooper is monotonous business. It is a duty rather than a pleasure, to be performed in the hope that after about the eighth mug, the loud-mouthed Trooper may blurt out some information useful to the correspondent. The average Storm Trooper is one of a million little Hitlers all cast in the same mold, repeating the same chant that he has heard countless times from the loudspeakers installed in every beer hall.

The first stein of beer can be depended upon to start off the evening litany with praises of constructive National Socialism, such as "Don't you think Hitler's highways are wonderful? I bet you don't have anything like that in America!" Or, "Have you seen the classic beauty, the proud, simple lines of our Führer's House of German Art?"

The second round brings up "The Treaty of Versailles, its injustices, the starvation of the German people, the negro occupation of the Ruhr," and, by the time the stein is empty, "the heroic vision of Adolf Hitler in destroying the Treaty."

If you do not care to count the beers, you can look at your watch to compare your companion's performance with the average standard of your previous Storm Troop talkers. Three minutes from now it will be the Jews, you can predict to yourself with reasonable accuracy. That will take five minutes. Then it will be the Church in its "sabotaging" of the Nazi program. Four minutes of this, then ten minutes explaining that the Führer knows what he's doing, whether he fights the Soviets or allies himself with them. You know that a few more beers will bring encirclement, pluto-democracy, and finally, unless he has passed out already, the glorious and invincible *Wehrmacht* which will place Deutschland über Alles.

Beer is just as likely to make the simple-minded Brown Shirt insulting. I took an American girl out one evening to see the Nazis carousing in their taverns. We sat down at a wooden table, facing half a dozen young Storm Troopers. A zither orchestra played Bavarian songs, so we all joined in the choruses. During the intermissions, we refilled our glasses. One of the Brown Shirts struck up a conversation, which I interpreted periodically to the American girl. The talking itinerary outlined in the previous paragraph was followed for a while. Then the poetical-minded Storm Trooper borrowed some paper and a pencil to make up a rhyme about the *"Amerikänisches Madchen."* After scribbling a few minutes, he handed me his opus, highly pleased with himself. I read it. The Brown-Shirt bard had written that my companion's fingernails and make-up reminded him of "the oldest profession in the world."

"That's not funny," I told him, tearing up the "poem." "What do you mean by insulting my companion?"

He seemed surprised. Groping for words and forcing a smile, he finally blurted, "You Americans don't understand our sense of humor."

"That dirty poem of yours has nothing to do with humor, understand!" I snapped. "I demand an apology."

"Heil Hitler!" came the truculent answer.

"Nix with your Heil Hitler. Apologize, you boor."

"Heil Hitler," repeated the stubborn idiot.

"I'll give you one minute to apologize," I warned him.

"Heil Hitler," he yapped, then strutted off, bringing his boots down on the floor with extra vigor as he retreated.

When Nazis can think of no argument or excuse for their misdeeds, they seek refuge in the only exorcism they know. They raise their right hands and shout "Heil Hitler."

The golden youth of Munich, the students and children of prominent families, with an unsatisfied yearning for good old international recreation, crowd the dance floors of the Regina Palace Hotel, the Cherubin Ballroom of the Hotel Vier Jahreszeiten, and the House of German Art Bar. Although swing music, the Lambeth Walk, Boomps-a-Daisy, and other manifestations of "democratic decadence" are officially prohibited in the Third Reich, business is still business to the proprietors and the German jazz bands. There is little difference between an evening in the Regina Ballroom and in one of the popular New York spots as far as the music, the girls' dresses, and the style of dancing are concerned. The only noticeable contrast is that some of the young male partners do their swinging in German army uniforms. Three Munich cafes have regular "Cocktail Hours," which are always crowded with young Munichers doing their best to imitate their foreign friends and movies in spite of Hitler, ersatz coffee, and highballs at one dollar each.

The elderly, bourgeois Munichers flock to the Café Luitpold, around the corner from the offices of the American Express Company. They sip a beer or a Rhine wine all evening as they listen to waltz music by the Hungarian violinist, Barnabas von Gezy, or some other orchestra leader imported from a country friendly to the Axis.

The few remaining intellectuals in Munich attempt to bask in the last rays of liberal entertainment, hiding its light in the small back room of Germany's oldest cabaret, Simplicissimus, where Ringelnatz and other famous German humorists of pre-first-war days recited their poems to brilliant students at the turn of the century. "Simpl" has been raided frequently by the Gestapo as a speakeasy in which thirsting Germans can still find bootlegged human spirits prohibited by the Third Reich. It has been padlocked for staging parodies on Third Reich institutions, and has been permitted to reopen only because so few people can hear the skits in its ten-by-sixteen foot cabaret.

The outspoken young Nazi artists, career party members, and Gestapo agents naturally spend their nights in the bars and drinking rooms of Hitler's Artists' House. This building can accommodate a thousand Nordics intent on Nazi intrigue, love-making, and intoxication. Since the war, many couples have found the Artists' House most convenient, for it saves them the trouble of going home in the blackout.

Some of the regular addicts of the Künstler Haus are glamorized prostitutes, employed by the Gestapo to report the conversations of drunken Nazi leaders, many of whom are turncoats: former Communists, Social Democrats, or even Bavarian Royalists.

Over the beer tables, wine glasses, and Schnapps bottles, Munichers take advantage of the music and other distractions to whisper the latest jokes about the Third Reich to each other. Here are a few samples:

A peasant went to a cattle dealer to replenish his stock. "I want to buy a National-Socialist cow," he told the dealer.

"A Nazi cow? Don't know whether I have one. What is such a cow like?"

"Well," said the peasant, "in the first place, a National-Socialist cow is brown, like the official color of the party. Secondly, it is as fat as Göring. It has a head like Hitler's and a mouth like Goebbels'. And finally, it must allow itself to be milked dry like the German people."

The Gestapo raided a Jewish home. They confiscated all valuables, then examined the victim's papers. They picked up a suspicious-looking notebook. Turning to the first page, they read:

"God preserve Adolf Hitler!"

Astonished, one of the Gestapo said, "What a strange Jew! So patriotic, despite all persecution."

He turned the page. On it was written in large letters:

"God preserve Joseph Goebbels!"

"This Jew must be okay," exclaimed the Gestapo.

They looked at page 3, which said:

"God preserve Heinrich Himmler!"

"Too bad this loyal German is a Jew," the amazed Black-guards remarked.

Page 4 bore the inscription:

"God preserve Hermann Göring!"

"We must make this fellow an Honorary Aryan," the Gestapo burst out in unison. Then they turned to page 5. On it was written:

"God preserve Ernst Roehm."

Below this was the penciled note:

"Preserved—June 30, 1934."

When Il Duce called on Adolf at the Führer Haus in Munich, to arrange the armistice terms for defeated France, Hitler's SS Bodyguards were lined up at attention in the luxurious hall where the two dictators conferred.

"Everyone of these men is willing to die for me at a moment's notice," Der Führer boasted to his partner.

"I don't believe it," chided Mussolini.

Incensed, Hitler asked the first Bodyguard whether he was prepared to die immediately.

Yawohl, Heil mein Führer!" replied Guard No. 1, clicked his heels, dove out of the window, and was smashed to pieces on the street below.

"That man must have been crazy; bet you can't do it again," exclaimed Il Duce, somewhat taken aback. So Hitler popped the same question to the next Bodyguard.

"Of course I am ready to die, *mein Führer,"* snapped the second SS Guard, running to the window. But, before he could take the plunge, Mussolini caught him.

"My God, man, are you insane! Were you really going to follow your comrade to death, just like that?"

"Certainly. Heil! Eviva!" replied Bodyguard No. 2.

"But how in the name of the Axis could you perform such a rash act?" queried the astonished Duce. "How could you nerve yourself for such a horrible death?"

"Well, what the hell do I get out of this —life anyway?!" yelled Hitler's Bodyguard, tearing himself loose and hurling himself out of the window.

Such jokes have often been whispered to plainclothed SS Guards. Heinrich Himmler's toughies laugh raucously, then repeat them to their comrades if they are new and funny. If the Gestapo boys have already heard them they snarl, then arrest the unfortunate raconteur.

***

NAZI MORALS

Munich, the home of the National Socialist revolution, proved to be an excellent observation post from which to study the revolution in German morals that was encouraged deliberately by Hitler's totalitarian regime.

A city with a population of eight hundred thousand, in which industry, commerce, education, art, and agriculture were combined, Munich represents a typical cross-section of life in the Third Reich. Here I saw how the old German traditions of family life, the concepts of love, home, and sexual morality were being broken down by the Nazi party to achieve the Führer's goal of absolute fidelity to the Fatherland—to a Reich whose entire energies were being harnessed to Hitler's paranoiac schemes of power politics.

At first the Nazi movement courted hesitant Germans by appearing puritan, and even spartan. There were vigorous campaigns against the "immoral" attitude of liberal politicians. "Nordic purity" was held up to the disillusioned people as one goal of Hitler's regime. A revivalist wave of "moral renaissance" swept the country that was just recovering from the conscience-bitten hangover of the First World War. Fashionable clothes were banned as indecent, and books burned as immoral. Red-light districts were purged and street walkers arrested. Polished fingernails were castigated as a "Jewish outrage." "A German girl does not smoke" was a slogan that incited Storm Troopers to knock cigarettes from the lips of independent-minded women in the Reich. (Now it is no longer a slogan on moral grounds. On November 7, 1938, Julius Streicher told a group of 1,000 medical officers at Nuremberg: "Women who smoke cannot have so many or such healthy children as those who don't. Yet I prefer a graceful woman smoker to a hobnailed feminist." Four years previously, he would not have dared make such a statement in the face of the puritanical Nazi tide, which reached its high during the 1936 Olympic season, and then began to ebb, leaving an ever-increasing stench on the uncovered beach of the Third Reich.) The regime cracked down hard on everything that could be called vicious, decadent, or weak. "The re-establishment of a happy family life" was declared a Nazi objective.

Ruthless, hypocritical, or ignorant Nazi leaders flooded schools and newspapers with crackpot, pseudoscientific laws of biology, to advance their own political purposes under the guise of "social progress."

Instead of fostering family life, Naziism began destroying it. It ordered men, boys, and girls into camps and herded them into nightly exercises and meetings so that there was no time for home life. It turned children into informers against their parents. Several cases came to my attention in Munich in which fathers were arrested by the Gestapo and sent to concentration camp as the result of tip-offs by their own, fanatically Nazi sons. One fifteen-year-old Hitler Youth in Munich telephoned Gestapo Headquarters to report that his seventy-year-old grandfather, an ex-officer of Wilhelm II's imperial army, had toasted the Kaiser with his old cronies. In twenty minutes the Gestapo were at the door to take the old man away.

Naziism called to the boys and girls, "Come into our Hitler organizations; we are the new German youth, and we have no respect or tolerance for old-fashioned restrictions." To workers it said, "Come to 'Strength-through-Joy' meetings. There and on our travels you will find all the joys you are looking for."* Suggestion of a "new freedom" was made continually by articles in Gestapo Chief Himmler's SS paper, *Das Schwarze Korps,* more often by word of mouth, but most effectively of all by the examples of leaders and their uniformed disciples. Next to politics, love and sex—with emphasis on the latter—became the principal topics of discussion in meetings of Nazi organizations.

They do, crowding together like cattle in farmhouses rented by the Reich Labor Front for the night. The only difference is that animals don't get drunk (footnote in original).

The Hitler Youths, for instance, had before their eyes the example of their leader, Baldur von Schirach. His numerous affairs were an exciting theme. Schirach, after a while, was married by order of Hitler to the daughter of Heinrich Hoffmann, the party photographer. But that did not change his way of life.

Robert Ley, leader of the Labor Front, went on several "Strength-through-Joy" voyages, and openly carried on affairs with working girls aboard. To give fullest publicity to this "spirit of Aryan freedom," Ley's office sent to all German newspapers a series of pictures showing him against a Norwegian landscape with various blondes on his lap. Ley crowded his "Strength-through-Joy" ships so full of young workers of both sexes that intercourse on the high seas inevitably became the logical Nazi deck sport. In the farmhouses of the scenic Bavarian lake and mountain regions, Ley crowded the same kind of groups together in much the same manner that a peasant does when he hopes to increase his livestock. An ironical touch to the debauched character of Ley is the official title Hitler has conferred on his labor chief: "My Greatest Idealist!"

Numerous other party leaders set similar examples. Goebbels is particularly notorious for his affairs with actresses. He is dictator of stage and screen, and has no scruples about thus using his power to make women's careers and then break them when he tires of their company. Every movie and stage extra in Germany 'knows his nickname: "The Stallion of Babelsberg." Babelsberg is Berlin's Hollywood. Frau Goebbels several times appealed to Hitler for a divorce from her errant husband. In 1939, according to my sources, she finally obtained a secret divorce, but not until she had promised Hitler to appear with the Propaganda Minister at all public functions. The Führer has blandly accepted Goebbels' excuse for his many affairs with women: "I am tubercular, and cannot live without extra stimulation."

The crippled dwarf who dictates the fate of German actresses once paid a visit to the Bavaria Film Studios near Munich. As he was being escorted through a set where some scenes were being filmed, none of the electricians or cameramen saluted him. Instead, they ignored him. The actresses and extras likewise gave the Berlin magnate a cold shoulder. Not because they objected to him on moral grounds. For they themselves had plenty of affairs with their own Bavarian directors. Simply from a sense of physical revulsion and their inherent Bavarian dislike of Prussian domination. Fuming because he failed to make any headway with the Bavarian girls,

Joseph Goebbels stormed back to Berlin, ordered the two pictures being made at Bavaria Studios canceled, and to be produced back in his own pasture at Babelsberg. The Nazi film czar thereby threw several hundred Bavarian movie people out of work for three months, merely because his libido had been frustrated in southern Germany.

From the highest leaders down through the lesser officials to the rank and file, the party has been tearing down old sexual standards. It has consciously encouraged immorality. There is satanic method in this madness.

The dictatorship has erected patroled walls around every thought and normal feeling. It has chaperoned the German political mind. Yet it is clever enough to realize that the people must have some outlet, some area in which they are not under restraint, some avenue of emotional release beside "Heiling" Hitler. An unhampered sex life is the outlet least dangerous to the regime, and one of the most completely distracting. It is also the cheapest luxury, requiring no imported raw materials. To an enslaved people, this has seemed one chance to escape restraint, one way to a kind of happiness. For the same reason, the Reich has encouraged drinking; Bacchus is the slave of Venus, and Venus the mistress of Mars in the Third Reich.

This governmental effort to distract the German mind with sex is obvious on all sides. Every observant visitor who knew the old Germany and the Germany of early Hitler days has been startled by the change. On June 30, 1934, Hitler executed his Storm Troop leader Ernst Roehm "for homosexuality." In order to seize power, Hitler had previously encouraged this perversion[9] as an instrument for the "esprit de corps" of his followers. Once enthroned, with a remilitarized Reich under his command, Hitler fought the same instrument, since it now stood in the way of his population policy for a Greater Germany. He first attended long, heavy performances of Wagnerian opera, to dream his expansionist dreams and to find poetical justification for murder, theft, incest, and adultery. After the Austrian Anschluss in 1938, a marked change came over the Führer. He himself relaxed, intoxicating himself with the champagne of comic operas, the seductive melodies and nude actresses at the Munich performances of the *Merry Widow*. This turn in Adolf Hitler's conduct was the signal for government-approved, nation-wide debauchery.

[9]*Pope's unfortunate use of this term is typical of the time of publication.*

"Appeal strongly. Use sex appeal," became Goebbels' order. So the magazines were filled with sexy pictures, mostly of blond nudes, and sexy stories, where "blitz" love triumphs. The German moving pictures have erotic scenes; nakedness that would never pass the Hays censors, double beds, illicit love, smiling illegitimate children of happy parents, "healthy" farmhouse intrigues are the main themes. Before Goebbels could launch the mass production of German erotic films, he imported the sexiest films his agents could buy in Paris, synchronizing them for the Germans.

The new Reich is ringing with erotic songs—pretending to be folks songs, they are actually synthetic propaganda products. Most of them deal with consummated love at first sight, not romantic love. Cabarets specializing in these songs have sprung up like mushrooms in many blacked-out German towns. Here these songs are sung to the young soldiers and civilians who have brought their girls to the cabarets, paying cheap "Strength-through-Joy" prices, and here nude dancers flit past the crowded tables, filling the young couples' minds with but one thought before they walk out into the darkened parks.

Hitler has made purse snatching a capital crime in the Reich. Yet on December 13, 1938, he pardoned a twenty-one-year-old Austrian girl who was sentenced to death in Nuremberg for shooting and robbing a taxi driver, when he learned that she was pregnant. Her accomplice, the father, was decapitated. His work was done, and there were many who could take his place. Babies at any price is the first law of present-day Nazi morality.

Professor Ziegler, President of the German Chamber of Art, announced "Artists must give German men the incentive to have many children. They must depict beautiful nudes." Ziegler's contributions to the annual Exhibition of German Art at Munich for the past four years have been nudes every time; his models were his secretaries, and his paintings resembled cheap colored photographs. These pictures are exhibited for several months for Hitler boys and girls to see, then bought and hung in the private homes of prominent Nazis.

I have read countless unabashed advertisements in the Bavarian press by men and women frankly seeking assignations. Before Hitler, such advertisements were common enough, but veiled. A gentleman was hoping to meet a lady "interested in music," for instance. In the Nazi newspapers, they are worded like the following: "Educated gentlewoman with her own apartment wishes she had gentleman friend to dispel the loneliness of the holidays." "Gentleman wants cultured traveling companion-secretary. Must be lady. Reply, with photograph, full length." In addition to advertisements for future husbands and wives, the back page of the *South German Sunday Post* is filled with small announcements like this one: "Two comrades home on leave from the battle front seek the companionship of two friendly, sportloving blondes, not over 5 ft. 4 in., for skiing holidays." The popular magazines run many stories about amorous adventures on such holidays.

And at the lowest point of depravity are the articles in the two million weekly copies of *Der Stürmer,* which by government order is compulsory reading in all groups of the Hitler Youth. Copies are also posted on street corners near the schools. Under the guise of crusading against "Jewish sex crimes," *Der Stürmer* fills its pages with filthy stories, invariably accompanied by lurid illustrations glorifying the Nordic female body. The Propaganda Ministry also turns out salacious and pornographic stories about Jews, priests, and nuns, last of whom are dubbed "population saboteurs," "parasites who do not contribute children to the Reich."

Hitler's population policies help explain the Nazi persecution of the Church in recent years, especially the Catholic church. Celibacy, the sanctity of home and marriage ties, the preservation of human souls even in unfortunate bodies, premarital chastity, and the sublimation of the sex instinct make the Church the declared enemy of the Third Reich. Souls and bodies must be dedicated and produced for the armies of the Fatherland; they must not serve another master.

At the lavish banquets and festivals arranged by Nazi leaders like Goebbels, Reich Press Chief Dietrich, and the Gauleiters to entertain their guests, sex was used to promote Nazi propaganda. The government actually has a corps of girls to entertain important visitors. This "Beauty Guard" was an idea of von Ribbentrop's, quickly adopted by other Brown-Shirt bosses. Whenever the chiefs wish to entertain celebrities, the girls are summoned, being flown to Munich, Salzburg, Vienna, or wherever the delegation is to be received. Benito Mussolini was loaned some of the best young Nordic stock on his first visit to Munich to encourage his enthusiasm for the Axis idea.

All this propaganda to stimulate sexual indulgence has borne a harvest of unhappiness, and worse. A number of scientific and professional journals have held their own against the rigid control of the Nazi press. Through them, one may get glimpses behind the scenes of the Nazi sex show.

The *Medical World,* a yearbook as authoritative as its title indicates, still is published. In the 1939 volume, Dr. Freisler, Secretary of the Ministry of Justice, reported that Special Youth Courts "have been very active during the last years. Nearly half of the cases were acts of immorality involving boys and girls under eighteen. Also numerous have been the verdicts for inducing youths to homosexual acts."

Franz Elmer, reporting in the *Monthly Magazine for Criminalistic Biology,* stated that general criminality had decreased since the Nazi regime, but "exceptions are murder and sex crimes of all kinds." In Number 30 of the *Criminalistic Reports,* 1937, Alfred Eber reported an "increase of incest in south Germany."

I could not help noticing the increasing number of rape cases reported in Munich and provincial Bavarian newspapers, often accompanied by murder. My German colleagues told me the details of several crimes committed along the banks of the Isar near the city. The descriptions were so terrible that they could not be printed even in the Nazi press, which revels in gory details. These acts of lustful violence are the result of the forces unleashed by the Nazi erotic drive, whenever they encounter an occasional obstacle. The results for the women who do not yield to this drive are dire.

In 1939, with the war fever mounting and finally boiling over, I observed the disgusting frequency with which young German women were accosted in public. On many occasions I have seen the conductors of crowded streetcars merely shrug their shoulders in a gesture of futility when women passengers complained that men were taking advantage of their forced proximity to impose their attentions on the women.

The situation has got out of control of the overburdened German police, who cannot catch up on the trail of numerous perverts and mass murderers of girls and young boys, since they are too busy tracking down "political criminals."

The German homes likewise have lost control of their children. Here is part of a letter written by a sixteen-year-old BDM girl to her Munich parents:

"There are forty-eight girls in our labor camp. Near us is a boys' camp. We see the boys very often, and mend their clothing as well as spend the evenings with them. A funny thing: of these forty-eight girls, thirty-five are pregnant. And still funnier, I'm one of the thirty-five...."

The letter-writer's horrified mother rushed to the camp to investigate and discipline her daughter. The young girl replied hotly that if her mother did not go home and leave her alone, she would report her to her camp leader, who in turn would report the mother to the Gestapo, who would then take action against her for "sabotaging German motherhood."

Typical of the spirit being fostered among German girls in the Nazi youth organizations is the scene I witnessed one day when I paid a visit to Munich's North Cemetery.

A Guard of Honor of young BDM girls was standing at attention in front of one of the plate-glass windows in one wing of the cemetery

228

building, where visitors could take a last look at the departed before the lid was clamped down on the coffin.

Behind the plate-glass window of this bier hall, reclining in an open coffin surrounded by Swastikas and flowers, lay a fifteen-year-old member of this BDM group. In each of her arms reposed a stillborn twin baby. The Guard of Honor was holding aloft a banner with the inscription:

"She died as a brave German mother."

Another case in point is the young Nazi woman—married this time—whose newborn child died in a Munich maternity hospital. Instead of weeping over the loss of her own flesh and blood, the mother blamed the nurse for carelessness, and instituted legal proceedings against her "for losing a child for Adolf Hitler." German doctors have encountered innumerable cases of pregnancy in fourteen-year-old girls who only remembered the father's first name and the color of his uniform.

There are two estimates of abortions in the 1939 *Medical World.* Dr. Pfaundler states without comment that in Germany, thirty per cent of all children conceived are aborted. A second estimate is forty per cent. Births in Germany were put at 1,300,000 for the year, abortions 820,000, In pre-Hitler days, abortions were estimated in various medical journals as between 400,000 and 600,000. This reflects in part the strict regulations against the sale or use of contraceptives. By an order of November 5, 1937, a German physician who gives contraceptive information to a patient must face exclusion from his profession, frequently followed by a term in concentration camp. In pre-Hitler Germany, the sale of contraceptives was under no limitation; a well-known contraceptive was advertised even in the streetcars. In 1935, the last advertisement disappeared: a stork with bound wings. Hitler permits only one effective contraceptive to be sold today, and this only as a concession to the war against venereal diseases. Other, ineffective products are still sold, in order deliberately to deceive the young women who refuse to bear children. They soon discover their mistake in buying these Nazi "contraceptives."

Yet the above figures on abortion are now once more on the decline, for the law against it has been implemented even more severely than the laws against birth control. There is one exception: The Nazis permit, indeed encourage, abortions for Jewish women. What may mean death, concentration camp, or heavy fines for Aryan women and physicians in Germany is heartily favored for Jewesses, as is sterilization. But, even to save a human life, a private German doctor does not dare examine a suffering female Aryan patient, lest he be accused by the Gestapo of an illegal operation, and thus lose his position and his already-restricted freedom. The overburdened doctors of the old school in Germany now stand with one foot in the grave, and the other in a concentration camp.

Only a committee of several SS (Himmler-Gestapo) physicians in a state hospital is permitted to decide the fate of an unborn child. Unless the expectant mother has a transmittable disease or is physically unable to bear children, she is forced by Third Reich laws to have the baby. Once the authorities learn—from gossiping housewives or "friends"—that a married or single woman is pregnant, she is shadowed by the Gestapo until after her confinement. The result of this vigilance has been a sharp rise in the birthrate of babies, with an equally sharp rise in the deathrate of young women, whose fear of the law and dread of Nazi childbirth (German mothers have been told to welcome pain in the childbed as soldiers do in battle, and must obtain special permission to bear their child in a hospital instead of at home) lead them to commit suicide or take the most desperate measures. Here is a case on which I have authentic information as an example.

A young, unmarried Bavarian girl was permitted by the SS doctors to have an abortion performed in the municipal hospital at Munich because she had an advanced case of tuberculosis. Scarcely had she left the hospital, when she was ordered to report to Gestapo Headquarters at regular intervals for a check-up on her activities and physical condition. Despite her experience and supervision, the girl again conceived. Fearing the Gestapo, she attempted a clumsy experiment which brought about her death. Such cases came to my ear from various sources with alarming frequency in Munich.

On the other hand, the drugstores were flooded with all kinds of aphrodisiacs. The open advertisement and sale of sex-stimulators for both men and women has kept pace with Goebbels' propagandistic peddling of eroticism. *"Titus Pearls," "Okasa," "Misteltropfen"* are just a few of the commercial brands known to the average man and woman over thirty in the Third Reich. Physicians and clinics are encouraged to prescribe even the more potent of the fecund wares of Aphrodite. There is hardly any magazine or newspaper in Germany that does not blatantly advertise books and medicines dedicated to the great Nazi god Eros.

The mainspring of Nazi sex policy is, of course, the drive for an increased population. As one German doctor put it, "A nation with a declining birthrate is losing its hitting power. A nation which likes to bear many children will always know how to secure new living space for its citizens."

Extensive legal and propagandistic measures have been taken to serve this "populating" policy. The bachelor tax for men and women is the highest in the world in Germany. On the other hand, the state lends one thousand marks or four hundred dollars to each family that has had its fourth child. Women with ten children get a gold medal from Goebbels, their husbands a "Strength-through-Joy" trip from Ley. Hitler has officially adopted hundreds of children born after the first ten in a family. In the towns with housing problems (and there were many of these in the Reich even before the advent of British bombers), only families with children are permitted to rent an apartment. Childless couples must take single rooms, or less. Nazi organizations distribute thousands of baby carriages annually as gifts, after they have been sent to Hitler as his most popular birthday present from his wealthier subjects. Certain articles of baby clothing are exempted from the wartime clothes-ration card.

Houses of prostitution are prohibited in the Reich (except by special decree, as in Julius Streicher's city of Nuremberg), while the female peripatetic profession is dying a natural death at the hands of amateur competition. Blitz love has taken its place. An unmarried woman, call her *Fraulein* Schmidt, may officially assume the name *Frau* Schmidt when her baby is born. Since 1939, an unmarried couple can call on their local party authorities and announce their intention to have a child. Provided their health and Aryan certificates are in order, and the woman has not yet conceived, the party will assume the hospital and first-year expenses of the issue for the unmarried mother.

It is characteristic of the Third Reich that the word "illegitimate" child does not exist. Instead, it is called an "un-wedlocked" child. The word "bastard" is restricted by the Nazis to describing a child whose parents, although married, are of two different races. "Scientific" Nazi journals as well as Goebbels' own noisy propaganda mill have openly asserted that "The United States of America is composed principally of bastards."

Heinrich Hirnmler's million and more SS men are Hitler's racial shock troops on the unwedded front. Stalwart Nordics, with perfect physiques, they are the real fathers of the Third Reich. Their leader exhorts them in his speeches and in their journal, *Das Schwarze Korps* to spread the gospel of single—but not childless—blessedness. In the populous SS barracks of Munich, the Black Guards pool their funds. The older an SS man without offspring is, the more he must contribute per month on the SS sliding scale to the pool. The proceeds are used to pay for the support of the Black Guards' "un-wedlocked" children.

Himmler has taken even more drastic steps to insure a maximum postwar generation in Germany. Before I left Germany, several months after the war had begun, I learned from three separate and unimpeachable sources that Heinrich Himmler had issued a secret order to his men, telling them to obtain the names and addresses of women whose husbands were fighting as soldiers in the *Wehrmacht*.

"Persuade these German women," the Gestapo chief's secret instructions read, "that as it is their husband's highest duty to the Fatherland to die in battle, so it is their own loftiest task to bear children for the Reich... Since their husbands are not in a position to become fathers, offer the women your services in the name of Germany's future."

In *Das Schwarze Korps,* SS Guards announce the birth of their children in this manner: "I am proud to announce the birth today of my first daughter, HELGA. May she always be a brave fighter for Adolf Hitler."

Marriage laws have undergone a complete revision under the Swastika. The marriage regulations "make impossible any marriage planned without children." Every person desiring to marry in Germany can do so only after securing from the local Health Office an "Attest of Marriage Ability"—which means ability to reproduce. Divorce is granted automatically on the grounds of sterility of one party. Incompatibility is another of the related grounds. Both marriage and divorce have been made easy for childless couples. The waiting rooms at the Registrar's offices in Munich were filled with pamphlets and posters giving "Advice to Mothers." After the wedding, the German bride and groom were given two gifts from the state official who performed the Nazi ceremony. One was a copy of *Mein Kampf.* The other a fancy geneology book with blank spaces to record the births of nine children.

Before the war, bearing children out of wedlock found a friendly toleration, which developed into encouragement as a national duty. In September, 1939, SS Boss Himmler published an order in the *Schwarze Korps* declaring it the highest duty of every German boy and girl to see that the German race should not be diminished through war. This order promised full protection for all children, whether legitimate or illegitimate, whose father should die in battle. Goebbels made a similar declaration. Yet no really constructive measures were taken to secure the social position of illegitimate children. The only official measure was an order allowing marriage by proxy. The soldier at the front who learns that some girl is expecting a child by him can be married without returning home. You hear, by short-wave from Berlin, a message like this one, broadcast on August 29, 1940, to "Capt. Lieut. Ernst Gunther Kray, at present a prisoner of war in Canada: Your desired marriage by proxy took place July 20 in Engerau on the Danube. Mrs. Kray and your parents-in-law send you many hearty greetings."

Yet despite all the incitement, encouragement, subsidy, and propaganda, the population policy of the Nazis so far has failed. In German cities of fifteen thousand or more population, accounting for half of the people in Germany, children average five for every three married couples. This is fewer than the "two-child system" which the Nazis denounced so furiously as a defect of the previous Reich and as inadequate for Germany's needs.

After Germany's young manhood already had begun to be decimated by the defensive fire of allied guns, a prominent German obstetrician confessed to me that "last year's crop of babies was the worst quality I have ever seen." Nazi food rationing, overworked German mothers, medical malpractice by stupid party doctors and nurses applying the unscientific teachings of Third Reich doctrines, plus the fact that the better classes in Germany prefer to renounce sex life under present conditions, were blamed by this doctor for the poor German baby harvest.

Although homosexuality is severely punished, Nazi authorities as yet have failed to legislate against the friendships of women. Consequently, many German girls, dreading the results of intercourse with their male friends, yet caught in the millrace of the Third Reich's erotic flood, have diverted their libido to their own, safe sex, thus throwing another wrench into Goebbels' populating machinery.

I have recorded the observations in this chapter after spending six years within the confines of the Reich. The picture is sordid, discouraging to civilization. In justice to truth and objective reporting, however, I must add that there are still many decent young men and women in Germany struggling against the brown flood of Nazi morality. But their number is fast decreasing. They would be branded as "die-hards," "reactionaries," or "internationalistic milk sops" by Hitler's radical chieftains, whose one aim is to secure the greatest amount of "Nordic human material" for the Third Reich's postwar generation. For their Führer needs this material in his plans to dominate the world.

***

HITLER BREAKS HIS TOYS

"Before we let National Socialism come to power, we had no rights. Now it serves us right!"

This indictment of Hitlerism was coined in Bavaria, where opposition to the Nazi system is stronger than in other sections of the Third Reich. Born in Munich, National Socialism emigrated to Berlin to come of age. When it returned to the scene of its cradle days, its character had changed. It had become a Prussian system. The Bavarians have always disliked the Prussians. When they discovered its Prussian nature, their dislike of National Socialism grew stronger. By then it was too late to trade in the Third Reich for a Fourth. But, when the time comes, the Bavarians will be the first to cheer the demise of Hitler, who converted the sovereign lands of their Catholic kings into the backyard playground of rough-shod, pagan Nazis.

Hitler betrayed the Bavarians. They tolerantly permitted him to get his start in their capital. They trustfully believed his promises, for was he not a south German like themselves? When he revealed himself as a turncoat to Prussianism, their impotent wrath against the Reichsführer became greater than their instinctive dislike of the north Germans. By 1939, Adolf had so alienated himself from the hearts of the Bavarians that he knew it was hopeless for him to attempt to win them back by peaceful methods, to prevent their rage from boiling over in spite of all odds. The only solution to his predicament was to plunge the Reich into war. With an outside enemy pounding at its walls, even the incensed south Germans were obliged to realize that they must support the Führer's military machine or else suffer the revenge of the common enemy. In the summer of 1939, I estimated that more than 80% of the German people in my territory were definitely against the Nazi regime. Yet so long as Germany has external enemies, they must swallow their domestic troubles and support the government, no matter how much they have hated Hitler.

"Volksgemeinschaft" is a Nazi slogan shouted repeatedly by Hitler in his claims that the German people were united for the first time under the Third Reich.

"We are no longer Prussians, Bavarians, Austrians, or Saxons," boasts the Führer. "We are all National Socialist Germans, one great *Volksgemeinschaft* (united community of people) under the Swastika banner!"

If Adolf rode in Munich streetcars, instead of in his bullet-proof Mercedes surrounded by sycophantic SS Bodyguards, he would hesitate to make such an unwarranted assertion.

The Munich trams, painted in the cheery blue and white colors of the defunct Bavarian monarchy, are a public institution that reflects the spirit of Bavaria at least as faithfully as the beer-table seminars of its staunchest citizens. They are the chosen vehicle for airing private opinions in public. The following incident, which occurred shortly before the war, is an eloquent testimonial to the solidarity— or *Volksgemein-schaft*—of the Munichers.

A portly gentleman of the old school boarded a tram on one of the main lines. One seat on the two parallel rows of benches was still vacant. To one side sat a black-uniformed SS Guard; on the other an elderly lady.

"Permit me, Madam?" the gentleman asked politely before sitting down next to her.

"You must say 'National Comrade' *(Volksgenossin)!*" barked the SS Guard. "The word 'Madam' no longer exists in the Third Reich!"

"Neither does 'Butter'!" growled a passenger.

"Who said that?" snapped the SS Guard. "Do you know?" he demanded of the nearest passenger.

"Nope."

"Do you?" the angry Black Uniform asked the next one.

But all his cross-examinations proved futile. None of the passengers would give away the man who had dared to ridicule the SS Guard. Red in the face, with a fuming "Heil Hitler," the Guard jumped off at the next stop. When he had left the car, a bearded Bavarian in leather shorts and green *Loden Frey* hunting jacket stood up and addressed his fellow passengers.

"I thank you for your loyal *Volksgemeinschaft!* God be with you," he chuckled, dropping off at his destination.

God and Hitler are fighting it out in Bavaria. The Lord has made a strategic retreat from Prussia, where glaring signs in public buildings proclaim: "Here the only recognized German Greeting is 'Heil Hitler!'" God has given up Prussia as a bad job. He would not like His name taken in vain in the Wilhelmstrasse any more than in Inferno, where the denizens of the underworld are doubtless compelled to say "Heil Satan." But there is still hope for the southern territory of the Third Reich.

For centuries the Bavarians have been greeting each other with their beloved *"Grüss' Gott"* (God greet you). A few years of Hitlerism cannot make them change their habits. To be sure, Bavarians in public office are required to say "Heil Hitler" or lose their jobs. But they quickly add a *"Grüss' Gott"* to neutralize it and take the bad taste out of their mouths. Adolf has not dared to outlaw God officially from the German stronghold of Catholicism.

Many stories mock Hitler's mania for tearing down old buildings and erecting Nazi party projects on their foundations. The following true incident soon was going the rounds among the leather-trousered natives of the beer-hall city.

Opposite Munich University on the Ludwig Strasse stood a little institution of the greatest convenience to generations of Munichers staggering back to their suburban homes from the Hofbrau Haus. One Municher returned to his city in 1938 for the first time after an absence of three years. Naturally he headed straight for the HB Haus. While he had been away, Hitler's architects had razed the comfort station and erected a large new party building on the site it had occupied for many years. On his way home from the beer hall the returned Municher, ignorant of this change, stood baffled in front of the strange edifice.

"What in hell is this building?" he complained to a passing pedestrian.

"That's Hitler's new House of German Justice," he was told.

"*Himmelherrgottsakramentdalekstmi!!*" swore the frustrated Bavarian, "for all the justice we've got in the Third Reich, the old building would have been good enough!"

Opposition to Nazi regimentation is not confined to poking fun at Hitler and his regime. There are few more rugged individualists than the Bavarian peasants. Reich Minister of Agriculture Walther Darré has attempted without uniform success to hitch the German farmer's plow to the Nazi blitzkrieg machine. He has made farm products state property. He has confiscated grain, pork, and other agricultural materials for the Reich, permitting the farmer to retain only the minimum required to feed himself, his family, and his farm hands.

"If I can't make any profit, why should I work for anyone except myself?" one Bavarian peasant told me. Forced labor has contributed a certain amount to the Reich's food supply since the war. But in Bavaria and Austria, many grim peasants are still succeeding in sabotaging Darré's regimentation, refusing to grow any more crops than they need for themselves, or can bootleg to their city friends for hard cash. Even ruthless Nazi officialdom finds it difficult to make any headway against this stubborn resistance.

In one village near Munich, the peasants were holding their May Day celebration. This festivity centered around a tall Maypole striped with the blue and white colors of Wittelsbach royalty. The local party commissars received orders to remove the pole, which expressed allegiance to Bavarian monarchy instead of to the Swastika. When the Storm Troopers and SS Guards attempted to chop down the Maypole, the irate farmers jumped on them and beat them so severely that two of the Nazis had to be hospitalized.

Storm Troopers employed in the night shift of the Bavarian Motor Works were ordered by their captains to take part in the window-smashing during the November 1938 Pogrom. The factory was compelled to pay their wages despite their absence from their lathes and benches. After the pillaging was over, nonparty workers at the factory called in a group at the manager's office.

"We want you to know that *we* had no part in this anti-Semitic violence," they declared. Henceforth, in the factory's canteens, they refused to sit at the same table with any Storm Trooper who had joined in the Pogrom.

Not only the "little people" are anti-Nazi at heart. Many prominent members of the party and *Wehrmacht* are biding their time, paying lip-service to Hitler as they wait for an appropriate moment to turn the Third Reich inside out. The peasant, the worker, the shopkeeper, the doctor, lawyer, and other civilians yearning for the return of a Christian monarchy in Bavaria have been deprived of all arms. A popular uprising is impossible. Telephones are tapped, and even local mails censored by Gestapo officials transferred to southern Germany from Prussia. Organized opposition by ordinary German citizens is out of the question. Revolution can come from the top alone. A military putsch similar to the method used by Batista to seize power overnight in Cuba, while not probable during the continuation of present hostilities, is a definite possibility for the overthrow of the Nazi regime either if Germany should win the war, or be dangerously near defeat. I know of two German officers serving actively on Hitler's General Staff (it would be unwise to name them) who are sworn enemies of his regime. They are ready, under favorable conditions, to oust Himmler, his SS legions, Goebbels, Ribbentrop, and Hitler from the control of Germany's destiny.

A "Nazi" lawyer in Munich is compiling dockets of the activities of Berlin ministers for future reference, listing their nefarious activities for the day of reckoning. Among this lawyer's records is a photostatic copy of a check for five thousand Reichsmarks made out to a Munich film starlet by Joseph Goebbels as hush money. This young actress had been called to Berlin by the Propaganda Minister with the promise of a star part in a Babelsberg—Ufa film. When she arrived, arrangements were made for a Goebbels chauffeur to drive her to his home for an interview about the film. No sooner were they alone, than Pal Joey ordered her to undress. When she refused, he raped her.

"Now, my child," Goebbels calmly concluded, "beat it back to Munich, and don't let me see you again. Here's a check for your trouble. I trust it will help you forget this unfortunate incident. My driver will take you to *Anhalter Bahnhof.*"

In Munich, the actress's first steps were to the lawyer. Here she signed a sworn statement. After the check was photographed, she mailed it back to Goebbels.

A persistent thorn in the Propaganda Minister's hide has been the "German Freedom Station," which came on the air with elusive regularity every evening to blast at Hitler's regime and the lies of the Goebbels-controlled Reich radio stations. Actually, the Freedom Station consisted of several separate transmitters, operating alternately in various parts of Germany. One of these, I discovered, was operated by *German Alpine army officers* in the Wendelstein Mountain region, only fifty miles from Hitler's Berchtesgaden home.

If so many of the Bavarian soldiers and officers are opposed to Hitlerism, why have they proved so effective in fighting Hitler's wars? It was Bavarian and Austrian Alpine troops who climbed the Norwegian mountains to master the passes and drive out the British. The same soldiers gained a fatal supremacy over the Allies in the rocky heights of Greece. On the face of it, this does not look like anti-Naziism.

Bavarians are some of the Führer's best soldiers for several reasons. Most of them come from peasant stock. They spent their youth felling trees, climbing up and down the precipitous Alpine meadows with heavy loads, wrestling each other on holidays around the village taverns, or fighting their neighbors from the next hamlet because one of its youths had dared to invade their own parish to woo one of their own girls. The Bavarian youth is the toughest physical specimen in Germany. He is not nasty-tempered like the Prussian; he does not walk around with a chip on his shoulder. But once aroused, he puts all he has into the fight and likes it. A Prussian soldier fights for the glory of the *Vaterland,* for medals and promotion. A Bavarian doesn't care what he is fighting for. Give him some hand grenades, a gun, and a bayonet, point out his enemy, and he will joyfully go to work on him for the primitive pleasure of the struggle.

It does not matter whether the mountains are near Garmisch, Athens, or Oslo—the young Bavarian will climb them with a machine gun on his back with the same eagerness as if it were a *Rucksack* on a skiing holiday, but, although they like an occasional fight, the Bavarians are not fond of extended army life. They want to tussle with the enemy and get it over, so that they can shed their uniforms and climb back into their well-worn, comfortable chamois shorts once more.

The Bavarian soldier would be just as glad, and perhaps more so, to fight the Prussians. In fact many of them are wholeheartedly belligerent with but one thought in mind: to bring Hitler's war to a conclusion as soon as possible, so that they can then "put the Führer and the Prussians in their place."

When the German army was fighting in Poland, Hitler paid a visit to a Bavarian regiment. Nazi propaganda pictures showed the Führer "rubbing elbows with his boys in gray." Nevertheless, the commanding officer disarmed his men completely, including their side arms, before they were sent to be photographed around the field kitchen with Adolf in their midst.

The king-loving, religious south Germans are bitterly disappointed at the British failure to crush Hitler during the first year of the war. Many disillusioned Munichers, who have seen Adolf break all of the promises he made to them while he was stumping the party capital's beer halls, said to me repeatedly before the war:

"When is England going to help us? Why didn't she declare war when Hitler marched his troops into the Rhineland? Why doesn't she attack Germany right away? We can't get rid of Hitler by ourselves. He has disarmed us and surrounded us with the Gestapo. The only way we can throw off the yoke of National Socialism is to have the British knock out the Supreme Commander of the *Wehrmacht* quickly and give us back our south German sovereignty before a protracted war inflames nation-wide hatred of Germany's exterior enemies and makes our people forget that their real enemy is Hitler, not the British. The only way we can ever get a square deal in Central Europe is to crush Prussianism. Since Hitler became Chancellor, he has depleted our resources for the benefit of northern Germany, and has placed Prussians in key positions in the military, economic, and political life of Austria and Bavaria."

The Bavarians' list of grievances against the Hitler regime is long. Dachau Concentration Camp, a few miles from Munich, is a constant reminder of missing friends and relatives who could not check their individualistic tongues under the new dictatorship. The monotonous marble party buildings all over the city are chronic eyesores to the tradition-minded Munichers. The padlocked fraternities of the various student religious associations look reproachfully at the uniform "Comradeship Houses" of the National Socialist Students' League. Rationed, ersatz food gnaws at the insides of the bonvivant Bavarians. The blackout darkens the mood of the lovers of light and gaiety.

The women of Munich and other South German cities cannot forgive Berlin authority for sending their young men to other parts of the Reich, and to fight on foreign soil while Prussian SS Guards invade their sacred Bavaria, forcing their attentions and strange, harsh dialect upon them. The devout churchgoers wince every time that Berlin's Goebbels, Rosenberg, and Himmler blaspheme Christianity and torture their priests. The artists suffer untold spiritual agonies at being forced to draw, paint, write, compose, or act to suit the fancies of Hitler and the *Kulturkammer* (Chamber of Culture).

Munichers still find ways of circumventing Hitler's will. Behind locked doors they gather with their friends to listen to foreign broadcasts. They bicycle into the country with knapsacks and their hoarded cash, returning with fresh food that Adolf would like to requisition for his Prussian soldiers. Despite wholesale arrests, they crowd into the churches, knowing that here they will find a spirit of solidarity which the Führer himself cannot command. They smuggle some of their substance to their life-long Jewish friends, whom he would like to see starved to death. They are constantly devising private codes to baffle the Gestapo on the telephone, as they innocently talk about the "weather," "cumulus clouds," "the wheat crop," and the "health of their friend, Herr Humdinger." They make private deals for a square meal with restaurant proprietors, and establish secret clearinghouses for ration cards, so that a woman who can't eat meat can buy a spring coat while a man who likes lamb chops disposes of his well-stocked wardrobe. They whisper birth-control information to their uninformed friends, who wish at all costs to cheat the Third Reich out of future cannon fodder. They lend each other books banned by the Reich, which they have carefully secreted in hidden libraries. They get tough with Nazi officials whenever there is a fair chance of risking it.

Thus a farmer friend of mine, tired of slaving for the Reich, managed to go on a two-months' spree to Italy early in the spring of 1940. He applied at the local Nazi authority for permission to go South for a rest cure. The Brown Shirt refused. The wily farmer gave all the local doctors fat hams and home-cured sausages. They certified him as "tubercular."

Armed with this document, he again approached Nazi officialdom.

"I am the backbone of the *Wehrmacht,*" he declared. "The Führer said so himself at the last Thanksgiving-Day rally. I have proved myself to be a capable farmer. I can grow crops as well as, if not better than anyone around here. If I die from TB, I will weaken the Reich's war effort. You must let me go to sunny Italy to recuperate in preparation for the strenuous agricultural season."

The local dictator could not find any counter-argument. Grudgingly he gave the young peasant permission to take a trip to Italy. When I saw him in Sicily, he was enjoying himself at a pace that would invite tubercular bacilli into the bodies of less rugged individuals.

Two weeks before Hitler smashed his *Wehrmacht* into Poland, while the Nazi newspapers were screaming atrocity stories that promised no good for the Bavarians' love of their *Gemütlichkeit* and their hedonistic *Weltanschauung,* I overheard the following conversation in a Munich bakery:

A *Hausfrau* asked for a quarter loaf of bread.

Pulling out her foot-long, saw-toothed breadknife, the saleswoman viciously sliced off the required amount of the loaf.

"I wish to Christ this was Hitler's throat!" she exclaimed to the eight customers in her shop.

Such a comment would have been impossible in Berlin, where the few dissenters are afraid to open their mouths. In Munich it was the daily spice of the Bavarians' regimented life.

After Hitler annexed Austria, Nazi mobs and Nazi newspapers shouted: "We thank our Führer."

In the bleak, cold days of the winter stalemate that followed the Polish campaign, I was discussing German casualties with my corner tobacconist.

"We thank our Führer," he mimicked.

Then he made a noise. In America it is known as a Bronx Cheer.

Munichers have dubbed it "The Hitler Salute."

When I came back to Munich from Berlin, two months of war already had changed Hitler's playground considerably. The city is still Adolf's recreation center. But he has been forced to alter it to suit his new enterprise, the blitzkrieg. He broke a few of his toys, poured water in his playmates' beer, turned the lights out on them, and wrecked their playhouse, the Bürgerbräu Keller, where his gang had met ever since they banded together in November, 1923, under his leadership to beat up every other gang in the country.

Munichers resent the wartime blackout. They grumble over their diluted beer, even if Hitler has not dared to impose a war tax on it higher than 2/3 of the beer tax he charges the Prussians. They curse when they stumble into the open air-raid trenches in their beloved parks and squares. They blame Hitler for starting his fantastic Third Reich building projects —a new opera house, railway station, and subway—and then leaving this work incompleted to spoil the face of their beautiful Bavarian captial. And they hate Hitler for permitting Goebbels to order Himmler to blow up one of their most cherished beer halls and kill seven of their citizens for the propaganda effect of trying to make them hate the British. Der Führer's war has made the Bavarians realize even more than in the "peacetime" Nazi Reich what the Swastika has done to disrupt their traditional way of life.

Hitler and his Nazi henchmen still play in Bavaria. They attend the Munich theaters. They have their private parties in the Artists' House. They celebrate the Day of German Art, even if they dispense with the bright lights and some of the decorations. But the Bavarian people can hardly wait until the war is over, so that they once more can sit in brightly illuminated beer gardens, stroll through the streets without seeing the same gaping holes—made not by RAF bombers, but by Hitler's architects—sit in the parks listening to open-air concerts, and finally so that they can return to their peacetime jobs instead of working themselves to death in the sweatshops of Adolf's war factories.

Three months after hostilities had begun, a Bavarian gleefully recited the following poem to me, which was on its clandestine rounds through Munich:

> Oh Lord, I pray, send the Führer to England;
> Please hear my most fervent "Te Deum."
> Send him soon, nicely stuffed, for I want my king-land
> And they want him for their British Museum!

While I was listening to this poem, shells from antiaircraft batteries were bursting overhead. An enemy 'plane had been picked up by the sound detectors. But it dropped no bombs. In it, perhaps, was the RAF friend of my *Fliegerleutnant* G, who knew that the Bavarians in their hearts were on his side, not Hitler's. It was not until months later that any bombs were dropped from above Munich, and then sparingly and strictly on military objectives. Whereas Hitler destroyed the sovereignty of Bavaria, turned it into his playground, and then ran off to fight without cleaning up his toys or mending his broken promises.

My last weeks in Munich, before I finally turned my back on the Swastika after six years under its shadow, were devoted to the slow process of winding up my affairs. It took me over a month to sell my car. There were plenty of prospective customers, Munichers who had been through the first war and the subsequent inflation. Even if they were no longer permitted to drive, they thought it much better to invest in some tangible, material object than to save their money and perhaps find it worthless later on. But, when they went to the bank after promising to buy my car, Hitler's Berlin authorities would not allow them to withdraw their funds. Adolf had clamped down even on the private savings of his "little people," for whom he had vowed to create his Third Reich. At last I succeeded in selling my car to a dealer who had permission to purchase vehicles for the *Wehrmacht*. After closing the deal, he invited me to a beer.

"This war is a terrible thing," he confided. "In the last one, I flew over London several times in the Zeppelin. Now both my sons are in the *Luftwaffe*. I may never see them again. I was lucky enough to get out of the Kaiser's war alive. But I'm afraid my sons won't be so fortunate in Hitler's damned blitzkrieg!"

A toothache held up my departure some more. Finally my dentist informed me that he could save the molar by careful treatment, but that the job would require four weeks.

"Pull it out!" I told him. "I would rather lose a tooth than stay here one month longer." It pained me almost as much to see my dejected Munich friends suffering under the war which they hated and never wanted.

"You lucky fellow," they kept repeating at our farewell parties, "You can get out of this mess. We can't. We hate to see you go after so many years. But you had better leave while the going is good."

I bought a trunk, the only decent trunk left in rationed Munich. It cost sixty dollars. In the United States, I could have purchased the same type for one fourth as much. When I had finished packing it, my friends prevailed upon me to stay over Christmas and New Year's Eve. New Year's Eve we listened to a vicious radio address by Goebbels. When the clock struck midnight, heralding the coming

246

year, my friends burst into tears. I did not feel too happy myself. Then they repeated the story about the Shepherd of the Bavarian Forest:

One hundred and fifty years ago, there lived a soothsayer in the Bavarian Forest, a shepherd known far and wide for the remarkable accuracy of his predictions. (I have verified the truth of the legend that this shepherd really existed.)

One and a half centuries ago, the Shepherd of the Bavarian Forest had made the following prophecies:

1.   He predicted the defeat of Napoleon.

2.   He predicted the year and the place where the first "iron horse" would run in Germany.

3.   He predicted the First World War and Germany's defeat.

4.   He predicted the subsequent Third Reich, with the "Crooked Cross" as its symbol.

5.   "Then," the Shepherd had foretold, "will, come the Reds. But they won't be the red uniforms of the French soldiers. They will be strange Reds from the East." In other words he foresaw the Berlin-Moscow pact and the partitioning of Poland. Perhaps he foresaw even more about Russia.

6.   "Then," the Shepherd had continued, "it will be time to take to the woods, if you can, for then will come the time of the Universal Killing. If you meet a friend in the woods, you will say: 'What! Are you still alive?' But after the Universal Killing, it will not yet be time to leave the woods again, for then will come the Universal Dying. Starvation and pestilence. If you see a cow or a loaf of bread, it will be worth its weight in gold.

"Finally, after the Universal Killing and the Universal Dying, it will be safe to leave the woods again. For then will come the Great White King, and there will be peace on earth once more."

Countless south Germans believe in the Shepherd of the Bavarian Forest, and pray for the "Great White King." Their modern soothsayer, the "Holy Therese of Konnersreuth," died under mysterious circumstances in 1939 after predicting the death of Hitler. The Bavarians know that the Shepherd's predictions from No. 1 to No. 5 have come true. They have seen the beginning of No. 6 running true to the prophecy. No wonder my friends wept when the New Year was rung in!

***

CONCLUSION

"One People, One Reich, One Führer" is the slogan which Hitler has tried to impose on his entire domain. Bavaria is no exception. To a certain degree, like Austria, it has succumbed to the dictates of the Third Reich. The party capital of the Nazi movement is geographically in the heart of Bavaria. But the heart of Bavaria is not in the Nazi movement. It is in the snow-capped Alps, in the true art of Munich—not in Adolf's House of German Art—in the old buildings that Hitler has not yet torn down, in the waters of the "green Isar" and the Bavarian lakes, in the Vatican—not in Walhalla—in the colors blue and white—not brown—in the tombs of the Bavarian monarchs—not in the coffins of the sixteen Putschist Nazis next to the Brown House on the Königlicher Platz.

"Munich is the capital of the movement," proclaims Hitler. But National Socialism does not mean the same thing to the natives as the word "Munich." When the Municher hears the name of his Bavarian capital, he thinks of the *Greek* Monopteros temple, where lovers do their wooing in the *English* Garden after strolling there from the outdoor restaurant at the *Chinese* Tower.

Der Führer has not dared to change these names that symbolize the anti-Axis forces right in the cradle of National Socialism. What is more, every large city in Germany *except Munich* under the Third Reich has been compelled to rename one of its prominent squares "Adolf Hitler Platz." The only risk Adolf has taken in tampering with Bavarian tradition is to change the Konigs Platz (King's Square) into the Königlicher Platz or "Royal Square," for around it he placed his new party buildings, which Hitler may consider regal. But he knows that he could never pose as a king in Bavaria.

The Bavarians are fighting, not to save Hitlerism, but their own necks, which Adolf succeeded in sticking out too far for them. They wear their brown shirts and their field gray uniforms to keep themselves and their families from starvation, concentration camps, and firing squads. But they don't feel comfortable in them. Like a new suit or a pair of shoes that looked attractive in the show window, they acquired National Socialism only to discover that they did not fit in it—when it was too late to return the outfit to the clever, dishonest salesman.

The south Germans are part of the crew of Adolf's ship of state. Once signed up as able-bodied seamen, they must obey orders without being permitted to chart the course. They realize that Captain Adolf has steered them into such a terrible storm that mutiny would be as disastrous to them as to their Führer. But if the "S.S. (Black Guard) Third Reich" should ever get back into calm water, the Bavarians will try either to mutiny or to jump ship. If it should sink, they will kick the Captain and his officers off the lifeboats and clamber in themselves.

Munich is Hitler's playground, war or no war. A playground always belongs to the strongest bully. When he comes on the scene, the weaker, prior owners of the grounds must yield their playthings to him and play his games. But they secretly hope that a stronger neighbor will beat the bully eventually...and will not only remember who started the fight, but also who was compelled to take his side under duress.

Adolf Hitler's Nazi motto is "Kampf"—Struggle, Fight. The motto of the Bavarians is "Gemütlichkeit"—Hedonistic, cheery, peaceful enjoyment of life. It is epitomized in the classic Song of Munich:

> As long as St. Peter's Chapel
> Stands on our Peter's Hill;
> As long as the green Isar River,
> Its Munich bed can fill;
> As long as there on the Platzl,
> The Hofbrau House still stands,
> So long will our Gemütlichkeit
> Never die in Munich's hands.

Does that sound like "Deutschland über Alles" or the "Horst Wessel Lied"?

No! Hitler's national Nazi anthem was written in Berlin. In Prussia, Hitler is the Nazi Führer, Reich Chancellor, and Supreme Commander of the Wehrmacht.

In Bavaria, he is the world's most extravagant, egotistic playboy.

THE END

Made in the USA
San Bernardino, CA
19 December 2016